BLACK & DECKER®

THE COMPLETE GUIDE TO
CREATIVE LANDSCAPES

Designing, Building and Decorating Your Outdoor Home

CREATIVE
PUBLISHING
international

CHANHASSEN, MINNESOTA

www.creativepub.com

Contents

THE COMPLETE GUIDE TO CREATIVE LANDSCAPES
Created by: The Editors of Creative
Publishing international, Inc. in
cooperation with Black & Decker.
Black & Decker® is a trademark of the
Black & Decker Corporation and
is used under license.

Library of Congress Cataloging-in-Publication Data

On file.

Cover photo courtesy of Idaho Wood

Copyright © 2000
Creative Publishing international, Inc.
18705 Lake Drive East
Chanhassen, Minnesota 55317
1-800-328-3895
www.creativepub.com
All rights reserved

Printed on American Paper by:
R.R. Donnelley
10 9 8 7 6 5 4 3 2 1

President/CEO: Michael Eleftheriou
Vice President/Publisher: Linda Ball
Vice President/Retail Sales & Marketing: Kevin Haas

Executive Editor: Bryan Trandem
Editorial Director: Jerri Farris
Creative Director: Tim Himsel
Managing Editors: Jennifer Caliandro,
   Michelle Skudlarek

Authors: Jerri Farris, Tim Himsel,
   Bryan Trandem
Additional Writers & Editors:
   Christian Paschke, Daniel London,
   D.R. Martin, Phil Schmidt
Art Directors: Kari Johnston,
   Gina Seeling
Photo Researcher: Angie Hartwell
Mac Designers: Patricia Goar,
   Jonathan Hinz, Kari Johnston,
   Jon Simpson, Brad Webster

Assisting Project Manager: Julie Caruso
Illustrators: Jan-Willem Boer,
   Bret Meredith
Copy Editors: Janice Cauley, Alice O'Hara
Indexer: Jennifer Caliandro
Technical Artists: Mike Perry,
   Jon Simpson, Rich Stromwall
Technical Photo Editors:
   Scott Christensen, Tom Heck,
   Joel Schmarje, Phil Schmidt,
   Keith Thompson
Technical Photo Stylists: Sean Doyle,
   Christopher Kennedy
Photo Stylist: Gina Seeling
Technical Consultant: James Wagner
Studio Services Manager:
   Marcia Chambers

Photo Services Coordinator: Carol Osterhus
Photographers: Tate Carlson,
   Jamey Mauk, Chuck Nields,
   Andrea Rugg, Rebecca Schmidt,
   Joel Schnell, Paul Weber
Photographer Assistant: Greg Wallace,
   Kevin Timian
Scene Shop Carpenters: Troy Johnson,
   Greg Wallace, Dan Widerski
Director of Production Services: Kim Gerber
Production Manager: Stasia Dorn

DESIGNING YOUR OUTDOOR HOME

The ideas that grew into Part 1 of this book were born out of my experiences as a volunteer Master Gardener in my home city, Minneapolis. While working answer booths at garden centers, answering phone calls on the Master Gardener hotline, and talking with friends, neighbors and coworkers, I was often asked to explain the art of landscape design. Now, Master Gardeners generally offer help in horticultural problems rather than landscape aesthetics, but since the subject has always interested me, I began to gather and assemble notes and ideas I could share with others. Some of what I learned came from talking to dozens of professionals: landscape designers, nursery owners, and university professors. Other great ideas came from many conversations with other Master Gardeners and talented amateur landscapers. Gradually, I began to organize these ideas into a coherent landscape design process, which you'll find in Part 1 of this book. A word of warning: our process is a bit different than that found in other landscaping books.

First, we're going to encourage you to design your yard as an "outdoor home," so it meets your day-to-day needs rather than some set of abstract design standards. Traditional landscapes created by professionals may be very artistic, but they aren't always practical. We feel that a well-planned outdoor home should first and foremost be a landscape that satisfies your lifestyle. Second, we want you to trust your own instincts when it comes to visual style. We'll introduce some easy, common-sense design concepts; however, the goal isn't to change your tastes, but rather to help you clarify your opinions and develop your own personal style.

Mostly though, we want you to enjoy yourself while designing your landscape. Most folks who have followed this process find it to be great fun, and we're delighted to now bring it to you in this innovative book.

Bryan Trandem

4

Design Basics

It's time to throw away your old landscape ideas and begin thinking of your yard as an *outdoor home*—an integrated living space with various "rooms" that serve different activities. If you can cultivate this outlook, planning your new landscape will be entertaining, exhilarating, and just plain fun. The planning process might be challenging at times, but neither the experience nor your landscape will be boring.

In this section, you'll find important background information that will help you plan a new landscape. You'll learn the advantages of turning a standard "front yard, backyard" landscape into a lively outdoor home with four or more distinctly different living spaces.

Then, we'll look more closely at the elements that make up the rooms of your outdoor home: the floors, walls, ceilings, utilities, furnishings, and decorations. Adopting the same language and concepts used for indoor remodeling, we'll show you how to think about landscaping in a refreshing new way.

Finally, we'll review the wide choice of materials and plants you can use to construct your outdoor home, discussing the pros and cons of each. You'll learn how to evaluate cost, durability, aesthetics, and ease of do-it-yourself installation when choosing materials for your landscape.

IN THIS SECTION

Rooms

To transform an ordinary yard into an outdoor home, you'll need to begin seeing your landscape as a series of outdoor "rooms," each serving a different function for you and the members of your family. Adopting this viewpoint may stretch your imagination more than you think. For many people, a landscape is still little more than a decorative front yard with a large expanse of open grass, and a utilitarian backyard where most outdoor activities take place.

We're suggesting a much different landscape philosophy: an outdoor home based entirely on practical needs and personal tastes rather than traditional expectations. For some people, this might mean doing away with a formal front yard altogether—a concept that would have shocked suburban neighborhoods just a few years ago. Today, you might choose to use this space instead as a hobby den for pursuing favorite pastimes, a sports and exer-cise studio, or an expansive recreation space where friends and family can socialize.

Of course, you don't have to be a complete revolutionary when designing your outdoor home. A great, innovative landscape can also retain traditional themes. If you enjoy the look of a decorative front room carpeted with grass and decorated with familiar foundation shrubs, by all means include that in your design. But plan the space in a way that is practical for you. Instead of a huge formal front yard, for example, you might think about reducing its scale to make space for other rooms as well. In today's landscape, almost anything goes, so long as the design satisfies your needs and tastes.

The design method you'll learn on the following pages is applicable to a yard of any size. If yours is a big suburban property, the landscape can include as many as eight different rooms. But even in a small urban yard, it's usually possible to include three or four distinct spaces. The smaller your yard, in fact, the more important it is to use every square foot of it wisely.

On the following pages, you'll see some examples of outdoor rooms dedicated to specific uses, and explore how the floors, walls, ceilings, and furnishings contribute to the function and ambience of the space. As you read, take mental notes about the types of outdoor rooms that appeal to you. A clear understanding of your own needs and preferences is the foundation on which you'll plan your great new outdoor home.

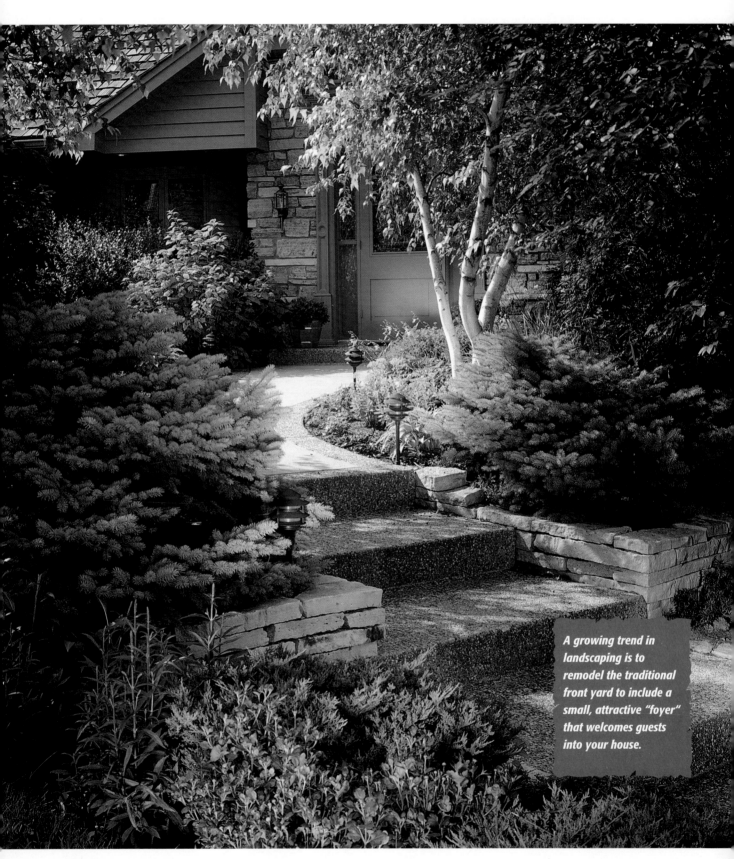

A growing trend in landscaping is to remodel the traditional front yard to include a small, attractive "foyer" that welcomes guests into your house.

Front Rooms

In many houses, the architectural design includes some type of foyer or entryway where you greet guests joined to a formal living room or parlor where you can entertain guests in style. A growing trend in landscaping is to include an outdoor front room that serves the same function: welcoming guests into your home. The front room plays a prominent role in your landscape, and it deserves careful consideration as you plan.

Floors in a large front room often consist of lawn grass or another living ground cover. Smaller front rooms are sometimes paved with durable natural stone or brick. And in some instances, the entire floor is paved to create a patio courtyard. In other landscapes, planting areas are integrated into the front room.

Walls usually enclose one or two boundaries of a front room, but the space shouldn't be completely enclosed. A front room that's completely walled off is forbidding and makes people feel claustrophobic. Walls may be solid, consisting of living hedges, garden wall, or wood screen; or they may be formed with low planting areas or beds of shrubs. The goal is to create a sense of cozy intimacy, while still providing "windows" to the surrounding landscape and neighborhood. The primary wall in a front room often includes a formal gate or archway that marks the entry to the space.

Ceilings for a front room most often consist of open sky to provide good light, but a ceiling of shade trees or wood screening can also be appropriate, especially in warm climates.

Utilities in a front room should include good lighting. Entry lighting at the door to your home can improve safety and discourage intruders. Low-voltage landscape lighting can be used to mark walkways and highlight attractive landscape features. A hose spigot or underground sprinkler system is helpful if your front room includes lawn space or planting areas that need regular watering.

Furnishings for a front room often include a simple bench or a small patio table set. A few pieces of top-quality outdoor furniture are a good investment for this room of your outdoor home.

Decorations may include ornamental shrubs and trees, and flower garden beds. One or two accent pieces, such as a fountain, statue, or birdbath, can provide focal points in a front room.

A paved courtyard is a common front room in some landscapes, such as the Mediterranean-style outdoor home.

A traditional lawn can be part of the front room in your landscape. The front lawn in today's outdoor home is often smaller than it once was, with less grass to mow and more ornamental planting areas for visual appeal.

A fire pit or brick barbecue provides a place to cook meals and snacks, but it can also lend a cozy atmosphere ideal for evening socializing.

Dining Areas

A welcome addition to any home is a patio or deck that extends the cooking and dining areas into the outdoors. In an outdoor dining room, even a simple meal becomes an occasion, maybe even a chance for family and friends to linger and talk.

If possible, locate the outdoor dining space adjacent to the indoor kitchen or dining room, which allows for convenient, easy movement between the spaces. If possible, link the indoor and outdoor areas with sliding patio doors or double French doors.

An outdoor cooking and dining area needs to provide about 25 square feet of area per person, and a minimum of 100 square feet. If you plan to entertain guests, plan on at least 150 square feet total. If your landscape will include a fruit or vegetable garden, you may want to position it near the outdoor kitchen.

Floors for dining areas are often carpeted with grass if informal picnicking is the norm; but wood decking, natural stone, or paver bricks are usually better choices, since these materials are durable and easy to clean. Wherever possible, choose outdoor flooring materials similar in texture or color to those used in the corresponding indoor space. Paving your patio with tiles similar to those used in the adjacent kitchen unifies the indoor and outdoor spaces, making both seem larger.

Walls should provide shelter from strong wind and direct sun, which can quickly spoil a peaceful outdoor meal. Wood screening or trellises trained with climbing plants are good choices, offering privacy, shelter, and a sound buffer.

Ceilings are common in dining areas. They can range from simple, portable umbrellas to shingled roofs. A retractable canvas awning can be a good choice, especially if you have a small yard where a permanent roof structure isn't practical.

Utilities for dining areas should include a gas or charcoal barbecue, or a brick fireplace. Include at least one electrical outlet to operate plug-in appliances. Low-voltage lighting lets you extend your dining into the evening hours. An outdoor sink makes food preparation and cleanup easier.

Furnishings should include comfortable seats and one or more dining tables. If space is limited, think about using portable fold-up furniture. A dining and food prep area also benefits from a storage space for utensils, dishes, and linens. Decorations often include planters or potted plants. Ornamental furniture made from wrought iron or teak can be used both for its function and its visual appeal.

Redwood deck photo courtesy of California Redwood Assn.

Built-in plumbing fixtures and food preparation appliances make it more convenient to dine outdoors. Several manufacturers offer sinks, cooktops, and refrigerators designed for outdoor use.

Masonry is a classic choice for dining areas. This dining area includes a stone fireplace that is both practical and decorative.

Elaborate play houses are now available in kit form designed for do-it-yourself construction. Once the kids have outgrown this structure, it can become a storage shed, artist's studio, or private getaway for adults.

Spaces for Kids

If you have active, growing kids, devote some space to their needs and activities. Not only will the kids be happier, but you'll be more content, as well: the other rooms in your outdoor home will survive much better if one area catches the brunt of your children's exuberance. A good location for an outdoor play area is adjacent to an indoor play room. This lets kids move in and out without disrupting the rest of the home.

Safety is an important concern, especially for small children. Try to position play areas so they're visible from the areas used by adults. And keep the safety of your kids in mind when choosing construction materials and furnishings.

Kids grow up, so think about how play spaces can be converted in the future. For example, a play structure can lose its swings and be used to hang plants and a porch swing. A large sandbox can be easily converted to a fire pit when the kids reach the teenage years, or perhaps a raised planting bed for everyone to enjoy.

Floors should be durable, but forgiving when children trip or fall. A large bed of sand or smooth pea gravel works well. Wood chips are often used, but they're not the best flooring material for these spaces, because bare feet and knees may easily pick up tiny slivers. Grass is pleasant to walk on, but it won't hold up well in areas where foot traffic is heavy.

Walls in play areas should provide security, where necessary, to keep small children in and to keep strangers and neighborhood animals out of the yard. Solid wood or chain-link fences with locking gates will make the yard secure and give you peace of mind.

Ceilings for play areas are often nothing more than a shade tree canopy that protects kids from harsh sun. Canvas awnings and wood roofs are sometimes included on timber play structures. Open sky is best for open areas where lawn games are played.

Utilities aren't essential for a play area, although lighting is a good idea if kids play outside after dark. A drinking fountain can also be a welcome addition.

Furnishings often include a general-purpose play structure and storage. A chair or a bench will let you relax while supervising the kids. For older kids, you might want to include a basketball hoop, or a backstop for practicing tennis skills.

Wood timber play structures in kit form are now widely available for do-it-yourself installation. Modular styles can be upgraded with new features as your budget allows.

A sandbox is one of the least expensive play features, but it's very popular with almost all kids. A sandbox is also easy to convert to another use once children outgrow it.

Lawn grass flowing like a river through your landscape can serve as a passageway from one space to the next. It also lends unity to the landscape.

Passageways

Your outdoor rooms should have passageways connecting the various living spaces. These sidewalks, driveways, stairs, and walkways tend to receive little attention when a landscape is designed, possibly because their function doesn't seem very glamorous. In many homes, durable poured concrete is used for all passageways.

But as you design your new outdoor home, think carefully about the visual appeal of passageways and look for ways to make traditional, utilitarian sidewalks more attractive. Paver bricks or flagstones, for instance, are almost as durable as concrete, and are much nicer to look at. Ordinary concrete can be colored, and finished with a pleasing texture that resembles cobblestone.

A passageway often begins or ends with a gate, which can serve either practical or aesthetic purposes. A sturdy wood or chain-link gate provides security, while a decorative archway creates a visual invitation for visitors to explore your landscape.

Some passageways are designed primarily to serve the eye rather than the feet. The value of a stepping-stone pathway lies more in its artistic appeal than in its practical use. Passageways can also be used to create visual unity in a landscape, linking the various outdoor rooms. A river of lawn grass or a loose-fill path running in sweeping curves through your landscape serves this function.

Floors for outdoor passageways can be made of almost any building material. In a more formal landscape, poured concrete, paver bricks, or mortared natural stone is a good choice. Informal landscapes can use stepping-stones or loose-fill materials.

Walls for outdoor passageways are usually symbolic rather than structural. A basic concrete sidewalk can be edged with paver bricks or low plants, for example, to define its boundaries.

Ceilings usually aren't a big concern for outdoor passageways, though you can achieve a striking effect by enclosing a garden pathway with a tunnel-like pergola that creates both walls and a ceiling.

Utilities may include low-voltage landscape lights that improve safety and provide decoration.

Furnishings and decorations aren't essential, but a well-chosen accent—a bench or small ornamental statue, for instance—can provide an interesting focal point in a passageway.

An ideal passageway is both attractive and practical. This walkway of paver bricks arranged in a herringbone pattern is interesting to the eye, but also provides a wide, comfortable route between the garage, rear entrance, and garden.

A stepping-stone path is a good way to introduce the texture and color of natural stone into your landscape. A pathway extending out of view creates mystery and invites exploration.

17

A swimming pool is a great place to exercise and relax. Although a pool still represents a major investment, new materials make pools more affordable than ever. Do-it-yourself kits for in-ground swimming pools are now available for as little as $5,000.

Sports & Fitness

If physical exercise is an important part of your life, your outdoor home should be designed to serve this need. A space devoted to physical exercise can range from a patch of secluded lawn for practicing calisthenics or yoga, to an in-ground swimming pool. The types of sports you enjoy will determine the building materials and other elements you use.

Remember that many outdoor sports require a large, open space with a relatively flat ground surface. On a sloped yard, you may need to move a lot of earth to create the necessary space. The chart below gives typical space requirements for common outdoor sports.

GAME	MIN. OPEN SPACE NEEDED
• Badminton	17 ft. × 44 ft.
• Croquet	37 ft. × 85 ft.
• Tennis (singles)	50 ft. × 100 ft.
• Handball	20 ft. × 40 ft.
• Volleyball	29 ft. 6" × 59 ft.

The exact location of your exercise area will vary, depending on the activity. A swimming pool, for example, is best situated away from trees that shed leaves, in a spot where afternoon sun can warm the water. An area for croquet or badminton, on the other hand, can benefit from some afternoon shade.

Floors should be durable, especially for sports that involve lots of running, such as tennis and basketball. For sports of this type, asphalt and concrete floors are best. Lawn sports, such as boccie ball, badminton, and croquet, require a flat, well-tended lawn surface, but the spaces around a swimming pool should feature a floor of concrete, brick, or wood decking. For volleyball, a bed of sand or smooth gravel is ideal.

Walls are essential for some sports. Your local Building Code probably requires a tall protective fence if you have a swimming pool. For a tennis or basketball court, a tall chain-link fence will help keep balls in play. A wood fence can provide privacy for any sports area.

Utilities may include plumbing lines for an outdoor shower or drinking fountain, and electrical service for nighttime lighting.

Furnishings can include storage accessories, and benches or seats. Decorative accents usually aren't an important part of active sports areas.

A versatile sports court can be included if your yard has room for a large, paved area. A concrete or asphalt court can accommodate tennis, basketball, handball, shuffleboard, and other outdoor games. A variety of surface treatments are available to make a paved sports court less slippery and more durable.

A portable basketball unit can be an ideal solution where space is at a premium. These adjustable standards can be stored in the garage and rolled out onto a driveway whenever they're needed. Some models have adjustable heights.

Butterflies and other wildlife can be drawn to your yard by the right mixture of flowers. Good plants for a butterfly garden include zinnias, asters, foxglove, marigold, lupine, butterfly weed, purple coneflower, and violets.

Hobby Spaces

If you have a favorite pastime, you probably want to dedicate a portion of the landscape to the enjoyment of that hobby. Some hobbyists—especially gardeners—devote the entire yard to their pastime. The layout of the space and your choice of features will be dictated by the nature of your hobby.

Gardening. If gardening is your hobby, you'll probably want to designate a large section of the landscape for growing plants. Areas that enjoy good soil and lots of sunlight are ideal spots. If your passion is for decorative flowers, plan your outdoor home so the ornamental garden is clearly visible from inside the house. Raised planting beds make it easier to tend plants, which is an important consideration for older gardeners or those with physical limitations. One or more storage sheds or cabinets are useful if you own many tools and supplies.

You'll almost certainly want to include water service, either in the form of an underground sprinkler system or a simple hose spigot for filling a watering can. Landscape lighting lets you enjoy the garden during the evening hours.

Wildlife study. As an animal lover, you'll want to create an outdoor home that welcomes birds, butterflies, squirrels, and other animals. Animals have much the same physical needs as humans: shelter, food, and water. Make sure to include the features that satisfy these needs—trees, shrubs, birdhouses for shelter; feeders or edible plants for food; and a pond, birdbath, or fountain for water. If possible, include seating areas where you can sit quietly and watch visiting wildlife up close.

Choose plants that appeal to your favorite animals. Butterflies and hummingbirds are drawn to bright flowers, especially red and violet annuals. Birds will be attracted by sunflowers and other flowers that produce lots of seed. Ducks and geese favor landscapes with large ponds. Squirrels and other small mammals are drawn to trees that produce nuts.

Visual arts. If you're a painter, photographer, or wood carver, your landscape should be designed with visual interest in mind. If you plan to designate yard space as a studio, make sure this outdoor room receives the soft, warm light of morning and early evening. Decorate your studio space for visual appeal, with striking plants, garden statuary, and other ornaments that can provide subject matter for your craft. If areas beyond your property are especially

This outdoor passageway doubles as a showplace for a wonderfully odd and interesting assortment of collectibles.

The owners of this landscape are true animal lovers; they keep bee skeps in the garden. Bees pollinate plants and can also provide honey.

attractive, design your landscape so it includes "windows" that allow open views.

Equip your space with the furnishings and props necessary for practicing your hobby. A photographer may require electrical service to power lighting equipment, while a painter might need a classic garden bench on which models can pose. Privacy is important to many arts, which is why high garden walls or hedges are often included. You might find a small, secure shed with windows useful, both for storing equipment and materials and for providing shelter when the weather turns bad.

Recreation areas are designed with social activities in mind. Comfortable furnishings are essential to these spaces.

Recreation Areas

For many families, a recreation space devoted to social fun is the largest and most important of all the outdoor rooms. A spacious deck or patio often forms the centerpiece of this area, which may include a dining area.

Floors should be durable enough to withstand heavy foot traffic. Brick, wood, stone, and concrete are the best flooring materials. In a large outdoor recreation room, a patio or deck may open onto an expanse of open lawn where you can play croquet and other games.

Walls in recreation spaces are usually designed with privacy in mind—to preserve your own privacy as well as that of your neighbors. A living hedge or structure covered with climbing plants helps muffle noise as well as block the view. In areas where insects are a problem, a screened porch or gazebo allows you to extend your recreation time well into the night.

Ceilings for recreation areas should be chosen with your climate and lifestyle in mind.

In warm southern regions, shelter from the sun—provided either by overhead trees or artificial screens—is almost essential, while in cooler northern areas, the open sky can be a welcome ceiling year-round. In a wet climate, recreation spaces may need protective awnings or a gazebo to provide quick shelter when needed.

A large recreation space may have several different ceilings. For some activities, an open sky is the best ceiling. A poolside patio, for example, is best placed in the open rather than beneath a tree canopy. But for dining or social entertaining, a lattice screen ceiling can diffuse the sun, greatly improving your enjoyment of the space.

Utilities usually include lighting, and sometimes plumbing lines. A fire pit can be a delightful, cozy touch in climates where the evenings are cool. In a large recreation space, plumbing and electrical service may be necessary for a hot tub or swimming pool. A weatherproof sound system fed from an indoor stereo is a relatively inexpensive and easy-to-install amenity for your outdoor recreation space.

Furnishings and accents should stand up to heavy use, since recreation areas see lots of activity. Chairs, benches, and tables should be made from sturdy wood or iron. Ornamental lanterns and planters are good decorative touches for recreation areas.

A hot tub is ideal for family relaxation and small, informal social gatherings. Privacy screens can make a hot tub seem more intimate and less exposed.

A large recreation space can include unusual features, such as a putting green. Several manufacturers offer supplies and directions for installing do-it-yourself putting greens.

Peace, quiet, and privacy are the hallmarks of an outdoor room dedicated to reflection and relaxation. In the space shown here, the elements are designed to appeal to all the senses.

Private Retreats

Socializing is a big part of our lives, and a well-planned outdoor home needs to provide space for these activities. From time to time, however, most of us need to get away from social activities and spend time alone.

If quiet relaxation and reflection appeal to you, then make sure your outdoor home includes a private retreat where you can nurture your soul. Even a small landscape can include this important space, since it's generally used by only one or two people at a time. A retreat can be as simple as a hammock strung between two trees or as elaborate as a gazebo.

Perhaps the most important feature of an outdoor retreat is privacy. In a large yard, it might be possible to literally hide your retreat from sight, but even in a smaller yard you can strive for the illusion of privacy by careful use of walls and screening plants. Privacy lends an air of mystery that encourages relaxation and meditation.

Walls for private retreats can include hedges, vine-covered trellises, wooden screens and fences, and stone garden walls. Because privacy is the goal, the walls for a private retreat are often quite tall. Softscape walls—a shrub hedge or climbing vines— are popular because they dampen sound.

Floors should be appealing, both to the eyes and to the feet. Grass or another living ground cover, natural stone, and brick are all popular choices. A decorative pathway of stone or loose-fill material can lead the way into your private retreat.

Ceilings often use a canopy of vines or trees, which provide shade and an air of mystery. Shade is an important element of most retreats, although a sun lover may opt for an open view of the sky.

Utilities may include water lines for a pond or fountain, and landscape lighting. If you prefer a more rustic atmosphere, include a fire pit in your retreat.

Furnishings should include comfortable benches or chairs, and possibly a small garden table. Also consider accessories that draw birds, butterflies, and other creatures to your landscape. Decorations should appeal to all the senses—scent and sound, as well as sight. Wind chimes, a garden statue, fragrant flowers, or a small fountain can help create a perfect personal escape. A pond with fish is particularly soothing. Oriental themes often are considered calming, which makes them a good choice for accent pieces.

A gazebo makes a good private retreat, especially on a large site where it can be truly isolated.

A unique garden bench can be the focal point for a private retreat. This custom-built bench encircles a shade tree on which flowering vines grow.

A garden shed is a practical feature, but it can also be a design element or even a symbol of romance. Husband-and-wife gardeners designed this delightful shed as a mutual anniversary gift to one another.

Utility Spaces

Most utility rooms aren't as ornamental and "romantic" as other rooms in the outdoor home, but they're just as essential to a well-balanced landscape. Just as your house has closets, a washroom, and perhaps a workshop, your landscape should have some spaces dedicated to storage and other utility functions. And with a little imagination, utility spaces can be as attractive as any other room.

By providing a space to work on essential maintenance tasks and to store tools and materials out of sight, a well-planned utility space can actually improve the look and function of your entire landscape. Some utility features, such as a garden shed or potting bench, can also serve a decorative function if they are designed to be attractive.

In many homes, a garage or basement is expected to serve all the utility needs, but it's much better if you can also designate some actual yard space to this purpose. If possible, plan outdoor utility rooms in spots that are convenient, but slightly separated from the rest of the landscape.

The space between your house and your neighbor's yard can be an ideal utility space. This area may already serve as home to a central air-conditioning unit or electrical meter and can also be used to store garbage cans, recycling containers, or a compost heap. A well-designed utility space keeps these features organized and hidden from view.

Pet spaces. Family pets—especially dogs—can have a dramatic impact on the outdoor home. Animal wastes can ruin grass and ornamental plants, and make children's play areas unhealthy and unusable. An exuberant dog can dig up expensive ornamental plants or gnaw wooden structures to pieces.

The answer to this problem is to dedicate an area of the landscape to your dog's needs. When the family is outdoors, a dog can be allowed to romp with the kids. But it's a good idea to have an area where pets can be confined and sheltered when necessary.

A standard kennel with a fence, concrete or brick floor, and a shelter is perhaps the best choice for a dog, because it is easy to clean and protects the rest of the landscape from damage. For most dogs, you can get by with an 8-ft. × 8-ft. kennel with 6-ft.-high chain-link walls, though the size of the dog obviously affects this decision.

Another alternative is to reserve a segment of your lawn for the pet. If you choose this option, it's best to fence in this area to simplify weekly cleanup chores.

This full-featured gardening center takes up little space, yet includes storage shelving, a potting bench, and compost bin. Decorative fencing hides the utility room, and gravel provides a durable, easy-to-maintain floor.

A good dog kennel has a concrete floor that's easy to clean, and chain-link walls that allow your dog an open view of the yard and provide for good air circulation.

Elements

By now, you're beginning to think about your landscape as a connected group of outdoor rooms. Now it's time to look at the individual elements that make up those rooms.

The principles used for designing and remodeling interior rooms and outdoor living spaces are remarkably similar, even though the construction materials used can be much different. Outdoor living spaces have the same elements as indoor rooms: floors, walls, ceilings, plumbing lines, furnishings, and decorations. Anyone who has remodeled an indoor room can also successfully convert a tired landscape into a full-featured outdoor home.

In a well-planned landscape, the floors, walls, and other elements are constructed with materials that are well suited to the use of the space. One of the keys to good landscape design is choosing construction materials that are attractive as well as practical. This simple, commonsense principle is overlooked surprisingly often.

A wall of thorny shrub roses looks great—unless those walls form the boundary for a play area for small children. Here, you'd be better off with a sturdy chain-link fence planted with climbing vines—a combination that provides privacy, muffles noise, and creates a pleasant backdrop for other landscape features, such as planting beds.

A driveway made from expensive flagstone loses its appeal once heavy vehicles break the stone slabs into rubble. The more practical option might be a sturdy concrete driveway built with colored cement or finished with an attractive patterned surface.

A huge lawn punctuated with large beds of fine perennial flowers isn't very appealing if you don't have the time or interest to do yard work. In that case, a landscape with large areas carpeted with low-maintenance ground covers would suit your lifestyle better.

As you read the following pages, pay attention to how practical function and visual appeal affect your choice of elements for the outdoor home.

Floors

The floor of an outdoor room is one of the most prominent visual elements of a landscape, and it must also be one of the most durable. An outdoor floor is expected to tolerate heavy use—by people, pets, bicycles, or even automobiles. The choice of

A single outdoor room may use several different flooring materials to provide aesthetic variety. This setting includes stepping-stones, bark mulch, concrete, and lawn grass.

flooring is a crucial decision, so don't automatically opt for a carpet of traditional turf grass and plain concrete paving.

In reality, you have dozens of materials to choose from when planning the floors for your outdoor living spaces. Your choices will depend on many factors—cost and installation difficulty, for example. But above all else, the flooring material must be appropriate for the intended use of the space, and it should provide a neutral or complementary backdrop for the other elements of the landscape.

Lawn areas. The grass lawn has been with us for centuries, though it's now groomed by machines rather than by grazing cattle and sheep. Standard turf grass is still an excellent flooring choice for many areas of the outdoor home. It's a relatively sturdy and forgiving living ground cover that tolerates a fair amount of use from children and pets. Grass is comfortable to the feet and soothing to the eye. With its deep green color and fine texture, a healthy lawn makes a perfect backdrop for ornamental shrubs, trees, and flowers. A lawn is also relatively inexpensive, especially if you start it from seed.

But today there's no rule that your entire landscape must be covered with grass. There are good reasons to opt for other flooring surfaces.

A grass lawn requires quite a bit of regular maintenance in order to retain its healthy look; on average, about two hours per week. If lawn work isn't your idea of enjoyable exercise, consider other flooring options, or at least reduce the size of the lawn. A lawn is difficult to maintain where foot traffic is too heavy, or where it's abused by pets, children, bicycles, or other vehicles. These areas are best suited to a different flooring surface, such as stone paving or loose-fill materials. And finally, grass requires lots of sunshine and water to thrive. In shady areas of your yard, trying to grow healthy, thick turf grass is an exercise in futility. In damp climates, frequent rain can make lawn grass muddy and unusable. In areas that enjoy a good balance of sun and rain, a lawn may need to be mowed twice each week.

Ground cover. If you're set on the idea of a living floor covering, remember that you still have choices other than grass. Mosses, violets, ivies and other vines, and low-growing perennial flowers all make wonderful ground covers, especially in shady areas where grass is hard to grow. Alternative ground covers are also the best choice on irregular or sloped yards where mowing is a tricky chore.

In shady spots and other areas where grass won't thrive, don't fight the inevitable. Use an alternate ground cover, instead. In this landscape, ferns, hostas, and other shade-loving plants form the floor beneath a group of trees.

Be aware though, that some of these ground covers are a bit more tender than turf grass and will suffer if the foot traffic gets too heavy.

Loose-fill materials. Gravel, wood chips, bark, and sand are good floor coverings for many areas where grass isn't practical. Sand or smooth gravel is a durable, forgiving surface for a child's play area, and wood chips, bark, or cocoa bean mulch can be a good choice for areas that can't be mowed, such as the ground under a deck or around a group of shrubs. These materials also work well for pathways, though they should be confined by a boundary of bricks, lumber, or another edging material.

Paths & driveways. Poured concrete and asphalt are traditional flooring materials for sidewalks and driveways that receive heavy foot and vehicle traffic—and for good reason. These materials are easy to shape and can tolerate heavy use for many years without much maintenance. Paving large expanses with either concrete or asphalt is a job for professionals, however, which adds significantly to the cost. And neither asphalt nor concrete is a very attractive surface. For this reason, other materials are

growing in popularity. Manufactured paver brick, for example, provides an attractive color and texture in a landscape, and is almost as durable as concrete. Ordinary concrete can also be colored or given a decorative finish to make it more attractive. An existing concrete driveway or path can also be given a face-lift with a mortared layer of thin paver brick.

You have more options when choosing surfaces for paths. Concrete and paver brick often are used, but other possibilities include cobblestone, flagstone, gravel, sand, bark chips, or shredded wood.

In some landscapes where most of the floor surfaces are given over to other ground materials, lawn grass forms the floor for pathways running between the various living areas.

Patios. A patio or terrace paved with concrete, brick, or natural stone provides a hard, durable, easy-to-maintain floor for many outdoor rooms. It's a great choice for social spaces, in areas where basketball or tennis will be played, and as a floor surrounding a swimming pool. When built with stone or brick, a patio provides a degree of elegance that

few other flooring choices can match. But a stone or brick patio is one of the more expensive flooring choices, and building one yourself takes quite a bit of time and effort. A patio requires a perfectly flat base, so it requires extensive preparation if your yard is uneven.

A concrete patio can be attractive as well as durable. This patio includes redwood dividers and a brushed aggregate finish to create pattern and texture.

Decks. A wood deck is suitable for most of the same applications as a patio and has several advantages. A deck is generally cheaper than a stone or brick patio. It can be built on uneven or steeply sloped terrain where a patio isn't practical. A deck can also be elevated well above the ground—built adjacent to a second-story interior room, for example. A deck requires a bit more ongoing maintenance than a brick patio, but it's considerably easier to care for than a turf-grass lawn.

A deck is a perfect way to create horizontal floor space on an uneven or sloped yard. In this landscape, the natural wood finish and vertical rail pattern complement the style of the house.

Walls

Each of the rooms in your outdoor home should have boundaries that define the space. Without walls of some type, your landscape will appear random, sprawling, and impersonal. In some rooms, these walls will be literal—a fence or garden wall that creates a solid physical barrier, but in other outdoor

A low hedge makes a good transitional wall between lawn grass and planting areas. A low hedge creates boundaries without interrupting the view.

rooms the boundaries will be more symbolic. A low row of shrubs or bed of flowers can serve to separate living spaces more gently than is possible with a solid barrier.

Walls in all their various forms serve obvious practical functions, but the ornamental, aesthetic benefits are just as important. Practically speaking, a garden wall—or the modern counterpart, a fence or hedge—provides security and privacy, offers shelter from wind and sun, and muffles neighborhood noise. Retaining walls have the vital job of holding back earth on a sloped yard. Aesthetically, outdoor

TIP:

Many people are surprised to learn that a sturdy, solid fence doesn't do much to block strong winds. When a strong breeze hits a solid wall or fence, it surges up over the obstacle, then sharply downward, creating a swirling gust that can ruin plants. A better choice as a wind block is a hedge or staggered board fence that breaks up a strong gust into small, harmless eddies.

walls give you a chance to introduce new textures and patterns into your landscape. They can provide a good backdrop for decorative plants and can introduce an important vertical element into your landscape.

Traditionally, landscape walls are installed on the property lines between homes, but remember that you can also use walls to separate different living areas within your yard. A fence can screen off a utility space from the rest of the yard, for example. A trellis trained with vines can help turn a deck or patio into a quiet retreat isolated from the other sections of your yard.

It's important to remember that any solid fence or wall will block your view, as well as the views of your neighbors. When planning the walls of your outdoor home, make sure you're not sacrificing a pleasant view of the surrounding neighborhood. And it's a good idea to consult with neighbors before building a high fence or wall that will affect their view.

A brick garden wall adds a touch of elegance to any landscape. In this example, shrubs and flowers soften the transition from the wall to the lawn.

Fences. A fence is the most common wall choice for today's outdoor home, for good reason. Precut wood pieces, including pickets, rails, and even entire fence panels, are relatively cheap and easy to find at your local home center or building supply store. Metal brackets make it easy to build a basic, traditional fence, and it takes only a bit of imagination to design and build a truly unique fence.

Garden walls. A garden wall made of brick or stone is a classic landscape feature that sends a message of wealth and luxury. Properly built, a mortared stone or brick wall will last for many decades and won't require much upkeep. But a traditional 6-ft.-high garden wall built from mortared brick or stone isn't very practical for most of us. Hiring someone to build such a wall is very expensive, and doing it yourself can take literally hundreds of hours.

Roses and other flowering shrubs can create a low ornamental hedge. With its thorns, a rose hedge can also be quite effective as a security wall.

A low, curved retaining wall creates an effective border between two outdoor living spaces. A border of shrubs or flowers softens the transition.

A healthy evergreen hedge creates privacy and serves as an elegant backdrop for decorative flower beds. However, a hedge requires regular maintenance in order to look its best.

A raised planting bed, built with retaining walls, can help define boundaries of an outdoor living space and it also introduces visual interest in a yard that is otherwise flat. This boulder retaining wall would look most natural in an informal landscape.

But there are several ways to borrow some of the aesthetic appeal of a traditional mortared stone wall without the big expense. You can use natural stone to build a dry-laid wall without mortar, for example. Or, you can build a wall from decorative concrete block.

Hedges. Shrubs planted in rows can create a living wall with wonderful color and texture. Although a hedge doesn't provide the same security as a fence or garden wall, it can create a dense visual screen, and works better than a fence for diffusing wind and absorbing noise.

A hedge is more difficult to maintain than a fence, however. It needs to be watered and fertilized frequently, and must be pruned twice a year to maintain its shape. And shrubs are prone to damage from insects and diseases.

Retaining walls. A retaining wall serves several functions in a yard with a steep slope. First, it helps prevent erosion. And by turning a slope into a series of terraces, retaining walls can add usable level space to your yard. If the slope is high enough to require several narrow terraces, each of the level spaces can be planted with ornamental flowers and shrubs.

Berms. A berm is a low ridge of earth that can define the boundaries of an outdoor room. On a corner property adjacent to a busy street, for example, a berm can provide much-needed privacy and can deflect noise upward. You can plant the berm with flowers, shrubs, or trees; or top it with a fence to increase privacy.

Border gardens. A border garden is a long, decorative planting area filled with perennial and annual flowers, and sometimes ornamental shrubs. In addition to lending its beauty to your yard, a border garden creates a symbolic wall that establishes boundaries without blocking the view. In its classic sense, a border garden is positioned on the boundary between two different properties, but these days a perennial border can be used to separate spaces within the yard, as well.

Doors & Windows

Like the rooms inside your house, outdoor living spaces should be planned with doors, to allow people to move about, and windows that frame views to the outside world.

The form of these doors and windows depends on the nature of the walls. In a traditional fence or garden wall, the doors can be fully functional gates, and the windows can be framed openings. In a landscape where border gardens form the walls, doors can be implied by a gap between planting beds where lawn grass flows from one living space to another. Where the adjacent scenery is pleasant, you can design fully open "picture windows" that give unobstructed views of the surrounding neighborhood.

Some landscape doors are mostly decorative in function. Many archways, arbors, and pergolas are designed as doorways to greet the eye. These structures imply movement and provide a visual accent for your landscape. You can also position an archway to create a picture frame effect, outlining a decorative accent or an attractive view.

Trompe l'oeil is a classic ornamental painting technique that is enjoying renewed popularity. In modern practice, the technique usually involves painting murals of open doors or windows onto a solid fence or garden wall. Trompe l'oeil murals generally work best in small garden spaces, where they serve to make the space look larger.

A gate can serve both a practical function, as a security door, and a decorative design function.

Lattice screens can incorporate openings that serve as windows to the outside world. In this deck, an opening in the privacy screen draws attention to a pleasant view.

A masonry wall or fence painted with a trompe l'oeil mural can make a space seem larger. Such murals can either be quite realistic, or deliberately surreal and fantastic, like this one.

Ceilings

It's often assumed that open sky will serve as the ceiling for a landscape, but this isn't the only choice, nor is it always the best one. In a climate that is often rainy, or one that's very hot and sunny, it can be difficult to enjoy the outdoors unless there is some type of overhead shelter.

At least a portion of your outdoor home should have a ceiling that protects you from the elements. Shade trees or a vine-covered arbor can create comfortable, cooling shadows and can even absorb a light rainfall. A canvas or rigid plastic awning extending out from the house offers shade and better rain protection.

Shade trees should be selected carefully. Some trees, such as lindens and maples, will cast such dense shade that only the most shade-tolerant plants and ground covers can be grown beneath them. Other shade trees that are more airy, including locusts and ginkos, are better choices in many instances.

A screened-in porch or gazebo not only provides overhead protection, but also keeps out insects,

which can be a big problem in many regions of the country. Each year, thousands of open decks are converted to screened-in porches after the homeowners grow tired of swatting mosquitoes and other pests. Such shelters can be permanent structures, or you can make use of a portable tent shelter, which can be erected whenever it's needed.

As with other landscape elements, ceilings can serve ornamental as well as practical functions. The wood framing of a pergola or arbor, for example, creates a symbolic ceiling that gives texture and pattern to the vertical dimension of a landscape.

A pergola provides a ceiling structure that gives an outdoor living space a feeling of full enclosure. The effect works well for passageways and for private retreats.

Colorful cloth strips draped across a wood frame break up direct sunlight during midday hours. When energized by a light breeze, such a ceiling adds both movement and sound to your landscape.

A gazebo provides both a ceiling and walls. In regions where mosquitoes or other flying insects are a problem, a gazebo creates a pleasant haven.

Utilities & Fixtures

You wouldn't dream of building a house without electrical service and plumbing, but you'd be surprised at how many people ignore these utilities when it comes time to design their outdoor home.

Utilities. At the very least, your landscape should include one or two hose spigots and electrical receptacles mounted on the house or garage. But better still is a landscape where most of the rooms are served with an underground sprinkler system or water spigot, and with GFCI receptacles fed by underground electrical circuits.

Without wiring and plumbing, the usefulness and convenience of your landscape is seriously limited. Including sufficient utility services in your new outdoor rooms also gives you many options for adapting the landscape as your needs change over the years.

As with most elements of the outdoor home, plumbing and wiring serve both practical and decorative functions in the landscape. Electrical service lets you power motion-sensor security lights and use electric hedge trimmers and other accessories. It can also power decorative landscape lighting and the

pumps on a fountain or whirlpool tub. Underground plumbing lines let you install a drinking fountain, garden utility sink, or labor-saving sprinkler system. Plumbing can also supply water to an ornamental waterfall or pond.

Another useful utility is a natural gas line, which can fuel a cooktop, barbecue, or outdoor fireplace.

Fixtures. Many outdoor rooms serve functions that require appliances and other fixtures. Let the purpose of the room dictate your choices.

Front rooms are often served by decorative low-voltage lights. If you plan to prepare meals in your outdoor home—and almost everyone does—you'll

An underground sprinkler system reduces watering chores and keeps your outdoor home green and fresh. Once found only in the yards of expensive homes, sprinkler systems now can be constructed from kits that use affordable materials and are designed for do-it-yourself installation.

Floodlights help improve security around your home and can extend the use of active spaces, such as tennis or basketball courts, into the evening hours.

Landscape lighting makes your landscape more attractive and safer at night. Installing low-voltage landscape lights is an easy and inexpensive do-it-yourself project.

want dining areas to include the equipment that makes this possible. For occasional use, a simple portable barbecue unit may be all you need. But if outdoor dining and entertaining play a big role in your lifestyle, you'll probably need a more elaborate setup, which can include a built-in gas cooktop, refrigerator unit, a sink with running water, and storage cabinets.

Another popular fixture is a decorative brick fireplace that burns either wood or natural gas. A fireplace can be used for food preparation, of course, but it can also serve as an cozy focal point for social gatherings on cool evenings. For this reason, a recreation space often includes a fireplace or fire pit.

A whirlpool hot tub gives an added dimension to a recreation space. Other fixtures you might consider for recreation areas include ornamental light fixtures and low-voltage wiring for outdoor stereo speakers.

Ornamental light fixtures are a good choice for private retreats and hobby areas as well. These spaces are also well served by including an ornamental water feature, such as a pond or fountain.

Kids' spaces and sports areas generally don't require much in the way of appliances and fixtures, other than light fixtures to make evening use of the space practical.

Dining areas may require electrical service, plus plumbing and gas lines. This full-featured outdoor kitchen even includes a built-in refrigerator.

A hot tub inset in a deck creates a wonderful space for relaxation or small, intimate social gatherings.

Most ornamental water features require both plumbing and electrical wiring. This waterfall uses a small electric pump to recirculate the water.

Path lights can be integrated into any landscape style— formal, or rustic.

Furnishings

Once the basic elements of your outdoor living spaces are planned, it's time to turn to the furnishings and decorative accents. Furnishings play a huge role in the practical function of outdoor living spaces and, along with decorative features, they do much to influence the overall style and mood of your landscape.

Furniture. As with all the other landscape elements, the benches, chairs, tables, and other furniture in your outdoor rooms should be practical, and should help contribute to the overall style or look that you've selected.

Let common sense guide your choice of furnishings. An eating area or entertaining space almost certainly needs one or more tables and should have enough chairs or benches for family and friends. Furniture for these spaces should be durable and easy to clean. A private retreat, on the other hand, may require little more than a stylish and comfortable bench or chair. A children's play space calls for play structures and furnishings chosen for their entertainment value as well as their sturdiness and safety.

If your space and budget allow, it's best to choose durable, permanent furniture for your outdoor rooms. Stone, teak, redwood, cedar, and wrought iron are the materials of choice for permanent outdoor furnishings, because these materials are very attractive as well as durable.

But in many homes it's necessary for some outdoor rooms to serve different functions at different times of the day, which makes large, heavy pieces of furniture impractical. A wood deck might serve as a children's play space during the day, but as an adult social area at night. In these instances, portable furniture is a good option. The stereotypical folding lawn chairs made from metal or wood

Lounging furniture is important for recreation spaces and private retreats. A simple hammock and glider swing set the tone for this area dedicated to relaxation.

Outdoor furniture can take many forms, from a comfortable wicker rocker to a stone garden bench that lends an architectural touch to a landscape.

are still available, of course, but new, more stylish products are quickly replacing them. New plastic-resin furniture, which is light, sturdy, inexpensive, and attractive, may be ideal for you.

Accents. If you plan well, much of the visual appeal in your landscape will come from the functional elements of your outdoor home—the wood and stone used in the walls, floors, furnishings, and so forth. But some landscape elements exist solely for their decorative appeal rather than their practical function. Your choice of accents will do much to make the landscape reflect your personality.

Flower gardens and other planting beds often serve as landscape decoration, as do potted plants, statuary pieces, wind chimes, water gardens, fountains, and other water features.

When decorating a landscape, try to appeal to all the senses—not just the visual. One of the major appeals of a water feature, in addition to the sparkling, reflected light, is the musical sound of running, splashing water. Many flowers are chosen for their scent, and wind chimes for their enchanting tones.

A simple birdbath can add visual appeal in many ways—as a piece of garden sculpture, as a water feature that reflects light, and as an attraction for birds. Such permanent features anchor and balance the living landscape, which changes constantly.

A large water feature, such as this pond with a fountain, makes a dramatic statement in a landscape. Such features aren't practical in every landscape. They're best suited for homes with classic styling and lots of yard space—and for homeowners with ample budgets. But there are hundreds of more modest water features that can provide the same effect when used in a small yard.

Baskets of flowers are a versatile way to decorate your outdoor rooms. Here, flower baskets suspended from an iron frame fill in a "wall" created by a border garden and sharpen the boundary between spaces.

Materials

The materials used to build the walls, ceilings, floors, and other elements of your outdoor home have far-reaching effects. These selections will influence your landscape's look and style, its durability and maintenance needs, and its overall cost.

Professional landscape designers and contractors often categorize the various materials as either "hardscape" or "softscape" materials.

Hardscape materials include those used to build the nonchanging structure of the landscape. They include natural and manufactured stone, wood, and durable plastics. Softscape materials are the living components of a landscape: the turf grass, flowers, trees, shrubs, and other plants that make up the outdoor home.

Each building material has its own qualities—both good points and drawbacks—and knowing these qualities helps you create a landscape that meets your practical needs and budget.

Keep three issues in mind when choosing the hardscape and softscape materials for your outdoor home: visual appeal, cost, and installation requirements. When planning your landscape, you'll need to constantly weigh the relative importance of these three considerations.

Although there are exceptions, it's an unfortunate truth that the most attractive building materials are usually the most expensive, as well. One way to make top-of-the-line materials more affordable is to do the installation work yourself. The cost of a cut-stone garden wall is reduced by about 40% if you build it yourself rather than have a stonemason do the work. Saving money by doing the work yourself will only be practical, however, if you feel confident of your do-it-yourself abilities.

On the following pages we'll describe the qualities of many different building materials available to you. The choices you make ultimately will be based on your personal taste, your budget, and your skills as a do-it-yourselfer.

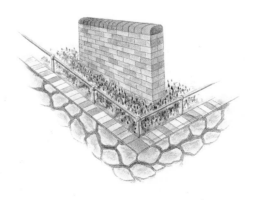

Bark mulch

Cedar bark wood chips

Teak

Cedar lattice

Redwood

Pine

Wood

Wood is perhaps the most versatile of all outdoor building materials. It can be used to form outdoor floors (decks, walkways), walls (fences, retaining walls), ceilings (pergolas and screens), outdoor furniture (benches and tables), and decorative accessories (planters and sculptures). Since it originates from living plant material, wood always looks natural in an outdoor home. It blends with almost any architectural style and looks especially good in a setting surrounded by trees. And wood is usually less expensive than stone or brick.

For do-it-yourself convenience, many precut and preassembled products are available, including posts for decks and fences; pickets, rails, and panels for fences; balusters and flooring boards for decks; and stringers and railings for stairways. You'll pay more for this convenience, but it can save you quite a bit of construction time.

Not all lumber is suitable for outdoor use. If ordinary pine framing lumber is left exposed to the elements, it will be consumed by rot and insects within a few years, in most climates. Unless you live in a very dry region, you'll need to use wood that resists these threats. Remember, though, that no wood is entirely safe from rot. Any wood left exposed to the elements requires some maintenance.

Redwood is an attractive, relatively soft wood that has natural resistance to moisture and insects. It is often used for exposed surfaces on a deck, for fences, and for outdoor furniture. Today, most redwood lumber is harvested from commercial forests rather than from old-stand forests, so you can use redwood without feeling guilty about plundering the environment. But it can be difficult to find a supplier that sells redwood at an affordable price. Few home centers carry redwood lumber, so you'll probably need to buy from a lumberyard that caters to contractors.

Cedar is another attractive soft wood that resists insects and decay. Like redwood, cedar enjoys many applications in the outdoor home, including fences, planters, decks, arbors, and screens. Cedar is also less expensive and easier to find than redwood. Most home centers carry a wide selection of cedar, both in dimensional boards and in convenient preassembled panels for fencing and screens.

When shopping for cedar or redwood, look for wood identified as "heart" or "heartwood" on the grade stamp. In both species, the heartwood, which is darker in color, has better resistance to decay than

Redwood deck photo courtesy of California Redwood Assn.

Wood blends well with most other landscape building materials, both natural and manufactured. In this landscape, the tall privacy fence and archway successfully blend with boulder retaining walls and a decorative iron gate.

the lighter colored sapwoods.

Teak and white oak are hardwoods that are sometimes used for top-of-the-line outdoor furniture. These woods, which are also used in shipbuilding, have a dense cell structure that resists water penetration. Because these woods are expensive, it isn't practical to use them for building large structures, such as a deck or fence. Instead, it's better to use these premium woods in accent pieces, such as benches or large planters.

Pressure-treated pine is the wood of choice for most outdoor construction, since it's stronger, cheaper, more durable, and more widely available than redwood and cedar. Most pressure-treated pine has a noticeable green color, but the wood can either be stained or left to weather to a pleasing gray.

Despite popular fears, the chemicals in pressure-treated pine don't easily leach into the soil, nor are they easily absorbed through the skin. But you should take some commonsense precautions when building with pressure-treated lumber: Avoid prolonged skin contact with the fresh sawdust, and avoid breathing the dust when you cut it.

Bark, wood chips, and shredded wood can be used for a loose-fill flooring surface around shrubs and in planting areas, and in pathways. In communities where a park service or urban forestry department is responsible for clearing dead trees, wood chips may be available free of charge at city collection sites.

Apply a coat of sealer-preservative or staining sealer to all sides of outdoor structures. Make sure sealer is applied to all end-grain. Even pressure-treated lumber is vulnerable to moisture and rot.

PRESERVING WOOD

Although redwood, cedar, and pressure-treated pine do resist rot, keep in mind that they won't survive indefinitely unless they are periodically treated with a good wood sealer/preservative. Choose a product from a well-known manufacturer, and apply the preservative every other year or so.

For planters, chairs, and other accessories, you can brush the sealer on. For large structures, such as a deck or arbor, it's easier to apply sealer with a pressure sprayer.

43

Soil & Stone

Natural stone is a classic building material for landscapes, used for everything from underground drainage systems to luxurious ornamental garden walls. Natural stone comes in a variety of forms, ranging from microscopic sands to enormous boulders weighing hundreds or thousands of pounds.

Although stone can be very important to the hardscape of your landscape, soil is even more crucial to the growth and health of grass, shrubs, trees, and other plants. The "dirt" that supports your plants is actually a complicated mixture of finely ground stone minerals, clay, silt, organic materials, and living organisms. It serves the crucial role of supplying air, water and nutrients to plant roots. Soil is also the anchor that keeps plants in place. You may be lucky enough to have plenty of good topsoil in your landscape, but it's more likely you'll need to bring in additional topsoil for various uses as you build your outdoor home.

Soil, sand, gravel, and stone are best purchased at aggregate companies and stone yards, which sell these materials in bulk at reasonable prices. Though nurseries and garden centers carry these materials, you may find the cost to be steep at these stores.

BUILDING STONE

Natural stone is one of the finest building materials you can use in your landscape. It has a beautiful natural color and texture, and a timeless elegance that no other material can match. Stone is also durable; it's not uncommon for a stone landscape wall or walkway to last longer than the home itself.

These exceptional virtues come at a price, however. Natural stone is one of the more expensive building materials you can choose. It's also very heavy, and is rather difficult to work with.

Natural stone includes a wide range of materials, ranging from rounded boulders used for building

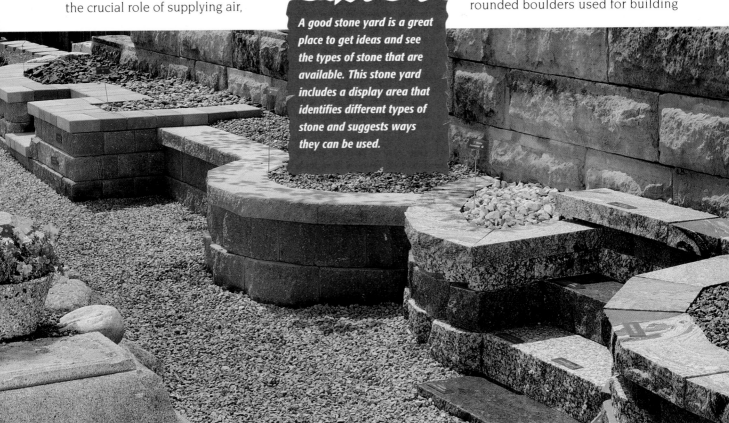

A good stone yard is a great place to get ideas and see the types of stone that are available. This stone yard includes a display area that identifies different types of stone and suggests ways they can be used.

Dollars & Sense

TYPE	TYPICAL USE	COVERAGE	ESTIMATED COST
Limestone flagstone, 1"	Paved surfaces	150-200 sq. ft./ton	$1.50-$2.50 per sq. ft.
Granite flagstone, 2"	Paved surfaces	80-90 sq. ft./ton	$3-$4 per sq. ft.
Bluestone flagstone, 1"	Paved surfaces	140 to 160 sq. ft./ton	$2-$3 per sq. ft.
Limestone, 3"-6" thick	Walls	20 sq. ft./ton	$7-$8 per sq. ft.
Granite , 4" thick	Walls	20 sq. ft./ton	$12-$13 per sq. ft.
Bluestone, 2"-6" thick	Walls	20 sq. ft./ton	$15-$16 per sq. ft.
Boulders, 6"- to 18"-dia.	Retaining walls	16 to 18 sq. ft./ton	$2.50-$3 per sq. ft.
Gravel, 4" thick	Base for paving	50 sq. ft./ton	$15-$20 per ton
Sand, 4" thick	Base for paving	50 sq. ft./ton	$10-$12 per ton
Black dirt, 6" layer	Planting areas	50 sq. ft./cu. yd.	$9-$11 per cu. yd.
River rock gravel, 6" layer	Loose fill	50 sq. ft./ton	$9-$10 per ton

retaining walls to carefully cut granite, marble, or limestone paving bricks. In its various forms, natural stone can be used in almost every element of the outdoor home, including flooring surfaces, ornamental walls, structural retaining walls, and walkways. Natural stone is also used for purely decorative features, such as rock gardens, ponds, fountains, and waterfalls.

Natural stone is sold in many different forms, so you'll need to know the following terms when you visit your local stone dealer.

Fieldstone, sometimes called *rubblestone*, is any loose stone collected from the earth's surface, rather than extracted from a quarry. Fieldstones can range in size from massive boulders to relatively small stones picked up from a river bed or field (only with permission, of course). Small, round fieldstones used for paving floor surfaces are known as *cobblestones*.

When purchased from a stone yard, fieldstone is usually sorted according to size, shape, and color. Fieldstone can be used to build retaining walls, ornamental garden walls, and rock gardens, where it creates an informal, natural look.

Cut stone refers to pieces of granite, marble, or limestone that have been cut to roughly square surfaces and edges. At some stone yards, these rocks will be known as *ashlars* or *wall stones*. Cut stone works well for stone garden walls, either mortared or dry-laid. It is quite expensive, however, so the use of cut stone is sometimes limited to a decorative cap placed atop a brick or concrete block wall.

Flagstone is uncut sedimentary rock with naturally flat surfaces. Some stone yards refer to these stones as *steppers*. Flagstone is used mostly for patios and walkways, and for stepping-stones. It can be dry-set, or installed with mortar. Limestone, sandstone, slate, and shale are the most common types of flagstone.

GRAVELS & SANDS

Gravel consists of small aggregate stone sold in bulk. It is sorted according to color, size, and stone type for a variety of different landscape purposes, both structural and decorative. Limestone- or sandstone-based gravel is used to form a base layer under concrete, asphalt, or brick paving. It's also used as an informal driveway or pathway surface.

Quartz- or granite-based gravels can be used as a loose-fill surface for informal pathways, where it lends a pleasing color and texture to the landscape.

River rock is quartz or granite gravel that has been smoothed by running water. It's generally used for decorative purposes, often as a flooring surface under a deck or bed of shrubs. It also makes a good surface for pathways. River rock that's been screened to include very small pieces of aggregate is called *pea gravel*, an ideal flooring surface for children's play areas.

Sand is actually nothing more than natural stone reduced to very small crystals through millions of years of weathering. If you examine a handful of sand under a microscope, you'll see that it consists of fine particles of granite, quartz, limestone, and other minerals. Sand is used to form a base drainage layer under patios, walkways, and driveways, and as a loose-fill flooring material for children's play areas. Like gravel, sand is available in different forms for different uses. Fine silica sand is preferred for children's sandboxes, while coarser sand provides one of the ingredients in poured concrete.

Interlocking
retaining wall
blocks

Molded
paver slabs

Paver
bricks

Exposed aggregate
paver slabs

Concrete
paver slabs

Manufactured Stone

Manufactured stone offers certain advantages over natural stone that make it a better choice for many applications. Concrete and brick are almost always cheaper than natural stone, and they are more uniform and easier to work with. Although traditional poured concrete isn't as attractive as natural stone, there are new masonry materials that can rival natural stone for elegant visual appeal.

CONCRETE BLOCKS & BRICKS

Concrete blocks and bricks are available in a growing selection of sizes and styles for use in your outdoor home. Many of these products are well suited for do-it-yourselfers, because their weights are manageable and installation is easy, though time-consuming.

Decorative block is used to make screen walls and is available in several colors. A decorative block wall is one of the most economical choices for a stone landscape wall.

Concrete paver slabs, available in several shapes and sizes, can be used for laying simple walkways and patios. They're available with a standard finish, with a smooth aggregate finish, or colored and molded to resemble brick. Concrete paver slabs are relatively inexpensive and quite easy to work with. They're usually laid in a bed of sand and require no mortar. The surface is generally finished so the smooth gravel aggregate is exposed.

Paver bricks resemble traditional kiln-dried clay bricks, but are more durable and easier to install. Paver bricks are available in a variety of colors and geometric shapes for paving patios, walkways, and driveways. They have largely replaced clay bricks for landscape use, and can be set into a bed of sand with no mortar required.

Edging blocks are precast in different sizes for creating boundaries to planting areas, lawns, and loose-fill paths.

POURED CONCRETE

A long-standing favorite for driveways, walkways, and patios, poured concrete has obvious landscape applications. It's much less expensive than natural stone, and because it's poured while in a semi-liquid

Dollars & Sense

Use the following chart as a guideline for estimating the cost of various paving materials. These costs are for materials only and assume you're doing the installation yourself. Having a professional install the materials will add to the cost.

MATERIAL	COST	DIY LEVEL
Poured concrete path or patio, 3" thick	$.75 to $1 per sq. ft.	Moderate
Poured concrete driveway, 6" thick	$1.50 to $2 per sq. ft.	Difficult
Concrete paver slabs, sand-set	$2 to $3 per sq. ft.	Easy
Concrete paver brick, sand-set	$2.50 to $3.50 per sq. ft.	Easy to moderate
Decorative block garden wall	$6 to $10 per sq. ft.	Moderate to difficult
Concrete edging brick	$.80 to $1.20 per linear ft.	Easy

state, concrete can be formed to fit curves and other shapes, such as a large landscape pond or fountain. Concrete is also exceptionally strong.

Concrete is often criticized for its harsh, industrial look. But these days it's possible to tint concrete or give it a decorative surface finish that makes it quite attractive in a landscape.

For walkways and small paving projects, you'll probably find it easy enough to pour and finish concrete yourself. Large surfaces are more challenging, however. For a large driveway, for example, you may want to hire professionals to do the work.

When building with concrete, you have several choices. For small jobs, it's easiest to buy premixed bags of concrete, which you simply mix with water. For larger jobs, you may want to rent a power mixer and blend your own concrete using gravel and sand, bags of Portland cement, and water. For very large jobs, it's best to order premixed concrete from a local dealer. Concrete is priced and delivered by the cubic yard. The cost for premixed concrete ranges from $80 to $100 in most regions. Use this chart to estimate how many cubic yards of concrete you'll need:

SLAB THICKNESS	COVERAGE/CUBIC YARD
3"	110 sq. ft.
4"	80 sq. ft.
6"	55 sq. ft.

Poured concrete can be colored and molded to resemble paver brick or natural stone. Many concrete contractors offer this service, but there are also kits that let you do it yourself.

A sand-set brick paver patio is a project most patient do-it-yourselfers can tackle successfully. It's a time-consuming project, but not difficult.

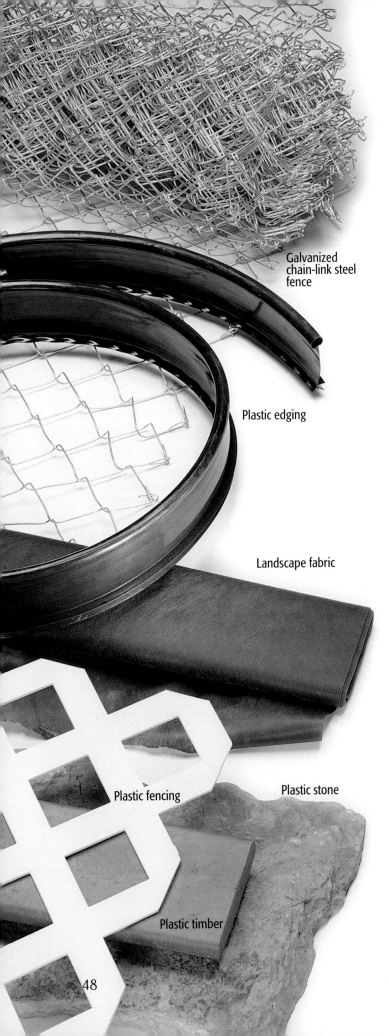

Galvanized
chain-link steel
fence

Plastic edging

Landscape fabric

Plastic fencing

Plastic stone

Plastic timber

Metals & Plastics

Some of the most important materials in your landscape are used on elements that go largely unseen. Durable metals and plastics are used for underground utilities, garden edgings, and a host of other applications.

METAL

Connectors, including the nails, screws, bolts, connectors, post anchors, hinges, and latches that hold together wooden decks, fences, gates, and gazebos, must resist the effects of the weather. For this reason, connectors should be made of galvanized steel or another corrosion-resistant metal, such as aluminum.

Fencing made of galvanized chain-link steel can be used to create a very secure outdoor wall. Traditional wrought iron, though less common today, is still used for fencing, railings, and patio furniture. Wrought iron lends elegance to your landscape, but it's quite a bit more expensive than other forms of fencing. Iron also requires periodic inspection and maintenance to keep it from rusting.

PLASTICS

Although some people still criticize the use of plastics in the landscape, knowledgeable landscape designers and builders recognize that plastics now serve vital structural and decorative purposes. Plastics are lightweight, easy to work with, durable, maintenance-free, and inexpensive—ideal for the do-it-yourselfer.

Plastics can be attractive, as well. The laughable

Underground utility lines, including plumbing pipes and electrical circuits, now use plastics extensively. Local Building Codes will dictate which materials you may use.

48

pink plastic flamingo has given way to stylish resin patio furniture and elegant lightweight planters, sold at the most exclusive landscaping stores. Consider the following items when planning your landscape:

Furniture made of plastic resins is inexpensive, lightweight, durable, and easy to clean.

Planters and pots made from plastic are much lighter and less brittle than clay pots. New pots made from polyethylene foam are difficult to distinguish from classic clay or concrete urns.

Underground plumbing pipe is easy to install and never corrodes. Plastic PE and PVC pipes make it possible for do-it-yourselfers to install plumbing fixtures and sprinkler systems that could once be tackled only by professionals.

Electrical cable sheathed in durable vinyl plastic brings electrical service to the outdoor home. Buried vinyl cable can last for many decades and is relatively easy for a do-it-yourselfer to install.

Landscape fabric laid beneath mulch or ground cover allows water to penetrate the ground but keeps weeds from sprouting.

Fencing materials made from textured vinyl include a variety of posts, rails, and pickets in several colors. Even at close inspection, these products look remarkably like painted wood. Unlike wood, however, plastic vinyl fencing materials will never need to be repainted or restained.

Plastic lumber made from blends of recycled plastic is just as strong as wood, but it has no flaws, such as knots or cracks. Plastic lumber is

Many types of plastic outdoor furniture are made from recycled plastics, such as that from milk cartons and soda containers. If you're concerned about the environment, look for labels that identify plastic furniture made from recycled materials.

available in standard sizes, ranging from 1"-thick decking boards to 4 × 4 posts, and in several colors. It can be used in virtually every application where wood is appropriate: decks, walkways, planters, fences, and arbors.

Edging materials let you create boundaries around planting beds and mulched areas. These flexible plastic products are easier to install and less expensive than traditional brick edgings.

Dollars & Sense

This chart shows how plastics compare to natural materials for some common landscape elements. In many instances, plastic materials are both cheaper and more durable than natural materials.

ELEMENT	TYPICAL COST	AVERAGE LIFESPAN
Adirondack chair, wood	$229	6 years
Adirondack chair, plastic resin	$79	12 years
Cedar fence, 6 ft. tall	$5/ft.	8 years
Plastic resin fence, 6 ft. tall	$20/ft.	20 years
Brick garden edging	$1/ft.	15 years
Plastic garden edging	$.35/ft.	15 years
Clay planter, ornate	$59	4 years
Polyethylene planter, ornate	$43	7 years

Plants

Plants are perhaps the most important of all the materials used in the outdoor home. While the hardscape materials are more or less unchanging, plants bring the outdoor home to life and make it a unique space.

Plants serve obvious practical functions—lawn grass as a flooring surface, hedge shrubs as walls, trees as a ceiling canopy, and so forth—but their ornamental function is even more important. Plants give a landscape its character. Knowing some basic information about plants—such as their climate ratings—makes it much easier to plan your outdoor home efficiently.

On the following pages, you'll be introduced to the different categories of plants you can use in your landscape: annuals, perennials, ground cover, and trees and shrubs. Included in the descriptions are lists of recommended plant varieties for different situations. These lists are by no means complete, but the plants we're recommending are both attractive and easy to grow. No matter where you live, some variety of each plant species should be available at local garden centers.

The ideal conditions for growing plants is moist soil in a sunny location. Most plant species do very well in these circumstances. As the soil becomes drier or the site becomes more shady, it becomes harder to find plants that will grow well.

Very few plants thrive in total, deep shade. Even those plants described on the following pages as *shade tolerant* generally do best in partial shade—where they enjoy two to four hours of sun each day; or in filtered shade—where they receive strong reflected light or relatively bright light filtered through a high canopy of trees.

Trees, flowers, and other plants can be purchased at many places, ranging from grocery stores to large mail-order suppliers. In general, it's best to shop for your plants from a local full-service nursery that knows growing conditions and has knowledgeable salespeople on staff who can help you make wise selections.

Annuals

Annuals are plants that complete their life cycle in a single year. Growing annuals is a little more time-consuming than growing perennials, because they must be replanted every year. But annuals offer one major advantage: they provide spectacular, long-lasting color in the landscape. Unlike most perennial species, which have a peak bloom season lasting just a few weeks, many annuals bloom for virtually the entire growing season.

In addition, most annuals are rather easy to grow from seed. Not only is this an inexpensive way to grow plants, but it makes it possible to experiment with plant varieties available only through mail-order seed distributers. Most local nurseries carry a limited number of best-selling varieties, but there are hundreds or even thousands of options when you purchase seeds by mail.

Because they're not expected to live through winters, annuals usually don't carry a zone rating. Some flowers grown as annuals in northern climates are actually perennials in other regions, where the climate allows them to live through the winter. Geraniums, for example, are normally grown as annuals in cold climates, but are grown as perennials in climates where there is no killing frost. Some annuals, on the other hand, self-seed very easily where soil conditions are right. Since these annuals never need to be replanted, they are sometimes treated as perennials.

ANNUALS THAT SELF-SEED EASILY

Bachelor's button (*Centaurea*)

Cosmos

Flowering tobacco (*Nicotiana*)

Hollyhock (*Alcea*)

Larkspur (*Consolida*)

Love-in-a-mist (*Nigella*)

Marigold (*Tagetes*)

Poppy (*Papaver*)

Salvia

Snapdragon (*Antirrhinum*)

Sunflower (*Helianthus*)

Sweet alyssum (*Lobularia*)

Recommended Annuals

TEN GOOD ANNUALS FOR SUNNY AREAS WITH MOIST SOIL

Plant	Height	Color	Comments
Marigold (*Tagetes*)	1 to 4 ft.	Yellow, orange, red	Easy to grow from seeds
Petunia	1 to 2 ft.	Many colors	Thrives in almost any soil
Snapdragon (*Antirrhinum*)	1 to 2 ft.	Many colors	Also tolerates partial shade
Love-in-a-mist (*Nigella*)	12 to 18"	Blue-purple	Blooms late into autumn
Cupflower (*Nierembergia*)	6 to 15"	Purple	Perennial in the South
Hollyhock (*Alcea*)	5 to 9 ft.	Pastel flowers	Easy to grow from seed
Larkspur (*Consolida*)	1 to 4 ft.	Mauve, blue, white	Excellent for cut flowers
Geranium (*Pelargonium*)	9" to 3 ft.	Red, white, purple	Perennial in zone 10
Canterbury bells (*Campanula*)	2 to 4 ft.	Pink, blue, purple	Long-lasting blooms
Dahlia	1 to 6 ft.	Many colors	Perennial in zone 10

TEN GOOD ANNUALS FOR SUNNY AREAS WITH DRY SOIL

Plant	Height	Color	Comments
Nasturtium (*Tropaeolum*)	1 to 8 ft.	Bright yellow or orange	Good climber on trellises
Cosmos	2 to 7 ft.	Pink, yellow, orange, or white	Fernlike foliage
Moss rose (*Portulaca*)	2 to 6"	Many colors	Good in rock gardens
Alyssum (*Lobularia*)	4 to 8"	White, pink, or lavender	Fragrant blossoms
Cleome	3 to 5 ft.	Pink	Good background plant
Flowering tobacco (*Nicotiana*)	1 to 3 ft.	Pink, white	Fragrant; tolerates moist soil
Bachelor's button (*Centaurea*)	1 to 2 ft.	Purple, white, or pink	Good for cut flowers
Oriental poppy (*Papaver*)	1 to 4 ft.	Orange-red, white, red, or pink	Good in mixed borders
Scarlet salvia	1 to 3 ft.	Lavender or red	Tolerates alkaline soil
Larkspur (*Consolida*)	2 to 4 ft.	Blue, rose, or white	Good for cut flowers

FIVE GOOD ANNUALS FOR SHADY AREAS WITH DRY SOIL

Plant	Height	Color	Comments
Forget-me-not (*Myosotis*)	5 to 8"	Blue, pink, or white	Good for rock gardens
Larkspur (*Consolida*)	2 to 4 ft.	Blue, rose, or white	Won't tolerate deep shade
Honesty (*Lunaria*)	2 to 3 ft.	Purple	Tolerates alkaline soil
Browallia	1 to 2 ft.	Purple or white	Also tolerates moist soil
Bachelor's button (*Centaurea*)	1 to 2 ft.	Pink, blue, purple, or white	Won't tolerate deep shade

FIVE GOOD ANNUALS FOR SHADY AREAS WITH MOIST SOIL

Plant	Height	Color	Comments
Impatiens	6" to 2 ft.	All colors except green, blue	Prolific bloomer
New Guinea impatiens	1 to 2½ ft.	Many colors	Tolerates partial sun
Browallia	1 to 2 ft.	Purple or white	Good in container gardens
Wax begonia	6" to 1 ft.	Red, pink, or white	Tolerates acidic soil
Pansy (*Viola*)	6" to 1 ft.	Many colors	Won't tolerate deep shade

Perennials

Perennials are plants that live more than one year. Turf grasses, trees, and shrubs are all perennials, but the term usually refers to a large group of ornamental flower species. When choosing perennials for your landscape, it's important to pick plants that are "hardy" for your region and can survive the winter. For convenience, perennials are categorized according to the USDA climate zone map. Make sure you choose plants with a hardiness rating that is no lower than your temperature zone. If you live in zone 5, for example, you can grow plants rated for zones 2 through 5, but plants rated for zones 6 through 10 may not survive your winters.

The best source for perennials is a good local nursery, which will be certain to carry only those plants that are hardy in your region. Perennials can also be purchased from mail-order suppliers, but mail-order catalogs sometimes exaggerate the zone hardiness ratings to increase sales. If you purchase by mail order, first check with local nurseries or a university arboretum to make sure the plants are truly hardy in your climate.

In general, perennial flowers require less work than annuals, since they return each spring and don't need to be replanted. But it's important to remember that perennials, too, have an average life expectancy. Some (known as biennials) rarely last more than two years, while other perennials can last for many decades. If you seek a low-maintenance landscape, pick perennials known for their long lives.

In general, perennials aren't as showy and colorful as annuals, and have a shorter bloom period. A perennial border offers subtle, elegant beauty that is quite different from the dramatic display of a bed of annual flowers. Serious gardeners generally prefer perennials over annuals.

BULBS

Bulbs are a class of spectacularly colorful perennial flowers that are planted from a thickened root structure rather than from seed. The term "bulb" is used to describe a variety of root structures, including true bulbs (tulips, daffodils), tubers (begonia), corms (gladiolus), and rhizomes (iris). Many of these plants are available in potted form, but it's cheaper to buy bulbs in bulk and plant them yourself. Reputable mail-order suppliers are good sources for quality bulbs.

Like other perennial plants, bulbs are rated for hardiness according to temperature zone. If you plant bulbs that are not hardy in your zone, you'll need to either dig them up and store them each fall, or resign yourself to planting new bulbs each year.

Recommended Perennials

FIVE GOOD PERENNIALS FOR SUNNY AREAS WITH MOIST SOIL

Plant	Zone	Height	Comments
Monkshood (Aconimum)	2	3 to 5 ft.	Blooms late summer, fall; tolerates shade
Daylily (Hemerocallis)	3	1 to 4 ft.	Blooms early to late summer; tolerates partial shade
Siberian iris (Iris siberica)	3	2 to 4 ft.	Blooms early summer; attractive grasslike foliage
Bellflower (Campanula)	3	6" to 3 ft.	Long bloom season; many species available
Garden phlox	4	3 to 4 ft.	Blooms summer, early fall; easy to grow; long-lived

FIVE GOOD PERENNIALS FOR DRY, SUNNY AREAS

Plant	Zone	Height	Comments
Dianthus (pinks, carnations)	2	6" to 2 ft.	White, pink, or red blooms, early summer to fall
Black-eyed susan (Rudbeckia)	3	2 to 4 ft.	Gold blooms in summer; good cutting flowers
Purple coneflower (Echinacea)	3	1 to 3 ft.	Purple blooms in summer; good cutting flowers
Stonecrop (Sedum)	3	6" to 3 ft.	Blooms spring or fall; attractive foliage; long-lived
Coreopsis	4	1 to 3 ft.	Blooms spring to late summer; tolerates heat

FIVE GOOD PERENNIALS FOR SHADY AREAS WITH DRY SOIL

Plant	Zone	Height	Comments
Periwinkle (Vinca)	2	6 to 12"	Blooms spring to early summer; good ground cover
Foxglove (Digitalis)	4	2 to 4 ft.	Blooms in midsummer; tolerates clay soil
Fern (various species)	3	2 to 5 ft.	Tolerates deep shade; spreads quickly
Cranesbill (Geranium)	2	6 to 18"	Blooms late spring, summer; good for woodland gardens
Spotted nettle (Lamium)	3	6" to 1 ft.	Blooms late spring to summer; good ground cover

FIVE GOOD PERENNIALS FOR SHADY AREAS WITH MOIST SOIL

Plant	Zone	Height	Comments
Astilbe	4	2 to 4 ft.	Blooms early to midsummer; good near water gardens
Bleeding Heart (Dicentra)	3	2 to 3 ft.	Blooms late spring to early summer; good cut flower
Hosta	3	6" to 3 ft.	Grown for foliage rather than flowers; very long-lived
Cardinal flower (Lobelia)	2	3 to 4 ft.	Blooms early to late summer; good in marshy areas
Cranesbill (Geranium)	2	6 to 18"	Blooms late spring, early summer; good in woodlands

FIVE GOOD BULBS FOR SPRING BLOOMS

Plant	Zone	Height	Comments
Tulip (Tulipa)	3-8	8 to 24"	Many varieties available; good planted in masses
Daffodil (Narcissus)	4	up to 18"	Many varieties available; naturalizes in lawns
Hyacinth (Hyacinthus)	5	10"	Very fragrant; bright, unusual flowers
Crocus	3	2 to 8"	Earliest of all bulbs; can be naturalized in lawns
Bulb iris (Iris reticulata)	5	4 to 20"	Delicate, colorful blooms; attractive, grasslike foliage

FIVE GOOD BULBS FOR EARLY- TO MIDSUMMER BLOOMS

Plant	Zone	Height	Comments
Asiatic lily (Lilium x)	3	2 to 5 ft.	Long bloom period; long-lasting bulbs
Giant allium	4	3 to 5 ft.	Huge lavender flower balls; good filler for background
Tuberous begonia	10	9 to 8"	Spectacular blooms, many colors; does well in shade
American lily (Lilium x)	4-8	4 to 8 ft.	Red, pink, orange, and yellow blooms
Gladiolus	9	2 to 4 ft.	Blooms 8 to 10 weeks after planting

FIVE GOOD BULBS FOR LATE SUMMER AND FALL BLOOMS

Plant	Zone	Height	Comments
Oriental lily (Lilium x)	3	3 to 7 ft.	Spectacular blooms; very fragrant
Gladiolus	9	2 to 4 ft.	Must be dug and stored for winter in cooler climates
Caladium	10	8" to 2 ft.	Tolerates shade; dig and store for winter in cool climates
Tiger lily (Lilium lancifolium)	3	4 to 6 ft.	Orange flowers spotted with purple; very easy to grow
Freesia	9	1½ to 2 ft.	Many colors; blooms 10 weeks after planting

Ground Cover

In most outdoor homes, large portions of the floor areas are carpeted with turf grass or another living ground cover. These low-growing perennial plants tolerate a certain amount of foot traffic, though some species are more durable than others in this regard. On steep slopes and in other problem areas that receive little foot traffic, low-growing shrubs or larger perennials plants, such as daylilies, can be used as a ground cover.

TURF GRASS

Turf grass is the most popular living ground cover, but it has very specific cultural needs that must be met in order for the lawn to thrive:

• A grass lawn generally needs at least four hours of direct sun each day. Areas that receive less direct sunlight than this should be planted with another ground cover. In cooler, wetter climates, grass does very well with day-long sun exposure, while in hotter, dryer climates, a grass lawn may be baked unless it gets a few hours of shade each day.

• A grass lawn doesn't do well where foot traffic is very heavy, such as children's play

Any plant with a low, mat-forming growth habit can serve as a living ground cover. In this landscape, fragrant thyme adds pleasing color and texture to an outdoor floor.

spaces or natural pathways across the yard.

• A grass lawn needs a fair amount of water. If you want to grow a lawn in a dry climate, you must be prepared to irrigate frequently or install a sprinker system.

If your conditions are suitable for grass, you have two options for creating a lawn. Laying rolls of commercially grown sod gives you faster results, but planting grass seed is much cheaper. In arid climates where sod must be grown in a controlled environment, a sod lawn can be prohibitively expensive. Creating a lawn by seed also allows you to pick grass species that will do well in special conditions, such as in deep shade or in play areas that are used heavily.

OTHER GROUND COVERS

Alternative ground covers are the best choice where heavy shade or other conditions make it hard to grow grass. There are several good ground covers that thrive in shade and never require mowing.

Increasingly, homeowners are opting for ground covers other than grass, even where there is plenty of sun to support a lawn. If you have a steep slope that's difficult to mow, or if you simply dislike lawn work, consider covering the floor areas of your outdoor home with a different ground cover. Remember, though, that few ground covers tolerate foot traffic as well as turf grass.

GROUND COVERS FOR SHADY AREAS

• Pachysandra
• Ajuga (bugleweed)
• Hosta
• Lamium
• Periwinkle (*Vinca*)
• Wintercreeper (*Euonymus*)
• Lilyturf (*Liriope*)

GROUND COVERS FOR SLOPES

• Daylily
• Crown vetch (*Coronilla*)
• Rugosa rose (*Rosa*)
• Creeping juniper (*Juniperis*)
• English ivy (*Hedera*)
• Virginia creeper (*Parthenocissus*)

Trees & Shrubs

Shrubs and trees are a class of perennial plants that have woody stems. They serve obvious practical functions in the outdoor home—trees provide a ceiling of shade; shrubs create privacy walls. But trees and shrubs also serve important decorative functions. Flowering shrubs and trees add bright color, while evergreens contribute mass and shape to the overall composition of your outdoor home.

Shrubs and trees are categorized as either *deciduous* or *evergreen*. Deciduous trees and shrubs lose their leaves each fall and grow new leaves in the spring. Many deciduous trees and shrubs provide vibrant fall color just before shedding their leaves. Evergreens keep their leaves year-round, and help provide color and mass to the winter landscape.

It's crucial that you think about the mature size of the trees and shrubs you're considering. One of the most common landscaping mistakes is to plant trees and shrubs too close together, or too close to buildings and other structures. Ornamental trees planted next to your home's foundation may look fine for a few years, but eventually they'll outgrow the site, blocking light to your windows and possibly damaging your foundation. When planning the location of trees and shrubs, make sure to position them as though they're already full grown.

The distinction between trees and shrubs is not always clear. Some plants sold as shrubs require regular pruning to keep them from becoming small trees. Before you purchase trees and shrubs, make sure you understand the care and maintenance needs of the varieties you are considering.

You'll have several options for purchasing trees and shrubs for your landscape.

Bare-root plants have had the soil removed from their roots after being dug from the ground. They're generally purchased and planted in the spring before the leaves appear and are less expensive than plants sold in containers. Mail-order sources usually sell only bare-root plants, since they can be shipped at reasonable expense. Bare-root plants require careful planting, however.

Container plants are sold in the pots in which they have been grown. Available throughout the growing season, container specimens can be planted any time the soil can be worked. Container-grown trees are relatively inexpensive, but it takes quite a while for them to achieve good size.

Balled-and-burlapped plants, also called B & B, have had their roots pruned to form a compact fi-

Many ornamental trees and shrubs create beautiful spring color. Shrubs and trees also add shape and definition to a landscape.

brous root ball that is wrapped in burlap. B & B plants are sold throughout the growing season and can be planted any time the soil can be worked. B & B trees and shrubs are generally larger (and more expensive) than container-grown plants and will reach adult size relatively soon.

Spade-planted trees are mature plants that are dug and planted with a large tree-spade machine. Spade-planted trees are a good option if you want a mature-looking landscape immediately. Spade-planted trees cost hundreds or even thousands of dollars, however. For this reason, most people find it practical to invest in just one or two spade-planted trees for important locations in the landscape, then use B & B or container-grown plants for other areas.

Principles

This section of *Creative Landscapes* will give you a quick but comprehensive introduction to the artistic, or aesthetic, principles that professional architects and designers use when planning residential landscapes. With these insights, you'll be ready to begin the rewarding and fun process of creating plan drawings for your new outdoor home.

Don't be intimidated by the idea that you'll be serving as your own landscape designer. Although landscape professionals are highly trained specialists in their fields, much of their knowledge is based on principles and concepts that almost anyone can understand and apply. You'll be surprised at just how many design principles are based on good old-fashioned common sense.

In the first chapter, "Design Concepts," you'll learn seven simple concepts that will help guide your landscape planning decisions. Applying these principles makes it quite easy to design a successful landscape.

In "Landscape Styles," you'll see how a landscape can be designed around certain popular themes that create a unified look. Choosing a thematic style makes it easier to choose the best materials, plants, landscape structures, and layout for your outdoor home. The chapter includes a short catalog of popular landscape styles that you can use as a guide for designing your own landscape.

IN THIS SECTION

Design Concepts

Over the years, architects and designers have learned that people are more likely to enjoy landscapes that are composed and decorated using certain familiar patterns and themes. You probably already understand many of these design concepts, even if you've never heard labels attached to them.

Whenever you spot a landscape that you instantly enjoy, take a minute to identify the elements that please you. Maybe it's the complementary blues and yellows in a perennial flower bed, or the texture and sweeping lines of brick walkways and edgings. Perhaps it's the creative use of space, or the consistent use of stone throughout the landscape. Once you understand why certain yards appeal to you—and why others don't—you'll be in a good position to plan your own outdoor home.

Don't be intimidated by complicated terms such as "axis," "rhythm," "line," and "nucleus" that you might hear from landscape experts. In reality, all those lofty terms can be summarized by a handful of simple, commonsense ideas we'll talk about on the following pages: *purpose, simplicity, unity, balance, movement, interest, and harmony*. If you keep these seven ideas in mind while designing and planning your outdoor home, success is almost guaranteed.

Initially, you may find that two or three of these design principles ring especially true, while others aren't quite as clear. If this is the case, then just focus on the concepts that are most meaningful to you, and don't worry about the rest. As you work on your design ideas, these other principles will gradually become more understandable.

And don't worry if some of the principles in this chapter seem to contradict one another at first. At one point, for example, we'll say that a landscape should be simple, restrained, and unified, while on another page we tell you that variety makes a landscape more interesting. Be patient. Later, as you work toward a final design for your landscape, you'll begin to see that these principles don't disagree at all, but serve to complement one another. In a very simple landscape design, for instance, you might choose to build all the features with natural stone, but you can still include variety by using a strikingly different type of stone in one or two places.

A final word: Don't feel obliged to follow any set of design "rules" when planning your outdoor home. The only goal is to create an outdoor home that expresses your personality and suits your lifestyle.

Purpose

The single most important design principle is that of function, or *purpose*. It's also the principle most often neglected. A professionally designed landscape can be visually stunning, but fail nonetheless because it doesn't serve the owner's needs.

Each separate space or "room" in your outdoor home should be designed to fulfill one or more definable purposes or goals. For an entry space leading to the front door of your home, the purpose might be simple visual appeal. For a secluded backyard patio, the primary goal might be privacy.

Knowing the intended purpose of a space is crucial to the planning process. A deck used primarily for subathing, for

Well-chosen furnishings can help define the purpose of an outdoor living space.

example, should be placed where it will receive afternoon sunlight, while a deck used for family meals and entertaining is enhanced by positioning it to enjoy the shade of an overhanging tree.

As you design the various rooms of your outdoor home, consider the purpose of each space and make a list of the elements that will help fulfill that function. A play area for young children, for example, might require a location that is visible to supervising adults; a forgiving flooring surface, such as smooth gravel; a secure fence or wall that prevents youngsters from wandering off;

Shelter, security, and proximity to adult supervision are important for children's play areas.

Redwood deck photo courtesy of California Redwood Assn.

trees or an awning that provides sheltering shade; and play equipment and furnishings that appeal to kids.

Remember, too, that some outdoor living spaces have more than one purpose. An expansive front yard area may serve as decoration much of the time, but may occasionally be the site for yard games or social gatherings. And the purpose of an outdoor room may change over time—from season to season, or over several years. A summer patio can become a winter room for bird-watchers. Or a children's play area can be turned into a gardener's hobby area after the kids are grown. Recognizing that the purpose of an outdoor room may change over time helps you plan your landscape effectively.

Space. Make sure the physical size of the space is suitable for the purpose. Except for utility spaces, any outdoor room that receives regular use should provide a minimum of 100 square feet of space. Even a space used by only one or two people won't be comfortable unless it is roughly 10 ft. × 10 ft. or larger in size. But it's also a mistake for an outdoor room to be too large. A very large deck or patio, for example, can make people feel lost unless it is subdivided to provide smaller, more intimate areas.

Boundaries. In a well-planned landscape, clearly defined boundaries separate the living areas. Sometimes these boundaries are formed by physical barriers, such as fences or walls. But boundaries can also be implied by a curving row of low shrubs, or a bed of flowers. Yards without boundaries between areas seem aimless and lacking in purpose.

Transitions. Give special attention to the transitions between outdoor

Brick edging creates an effective transition between a lawn and perennial flower garden, and also simplifies maintenance by making the lawn easier to mow.

rooms. Smooth, gradual boundaries are more pleasing than abrupt transitions.

For example, the transition between a concrete slab and a grass lawn can be much improved with a narrow bed of perennial flowers or shrubs, or with an edging of paver bricks. Good designers understand that abrupt transitions between materials are moderated by the addition of a third material.

Shelter. Depending on the climate in your region, an outdoor room may require shelter from sun, wind, rain, or insects in order to fulfill its purpose. In some regions, a simple canopy of trees or an awning extending from the house may provide all the shelter you need, while in other areas, a gazebo with a shingled roof and insect screens may be necessary.

Utilities. Some spaces in your outdoor home may require electrical and plumbing lines. A deck or patio without lighting won't function very well for nighttime social gatherings. And a flower garden without a plumbing line for watering the plants isn't very practical. You may also want to consider telephone, television, and sound system wiring for some of your outdoor rooms.

With its simple elegance, this front room perfectly serves its purpose: to greet and welcome guests into the home.

Utilities, such as a sprinkler system, plumbing line, or electrical circuit can be crucial to the function and purpose of an outdoor room.

Simplicity

Here is a concept that can't be stressed strongly enough: Good landscape designs are simple. A simple, restrained landscape is easier and cheaper to plan and build, it's more attractive to look at, and it's easier to maintain. The more complicated the landscape, the greater its chances for failure.

Despite its many benefits, simplicity can be difficult to achieve. Sheer enthusiasm leads many do-it-yourselfers (and some professional designers) to force as many different kinds of plants and materials into a landscape as possible. The results are usually disappointing—a visual hodge-podge of colors, textures, shapes, and sizes.

Let's start with visual appeal. A landscape composed in a simple fashion—
with smooth lines,
large masses,

and repeated use of two or three hardscape materials—is soothing to the eye and has a calming effect. A landscape that makes consistent use of one material in garden walls, walkways, and patios is much more pleasing than a yard that mixes many different materials, which compete for visual attention.

The same guidelines apply to softscape materials—the plants. A landscape that makes clever use of a few different flower species is almost always more pleasing than a yard packed full of dozens of different species of trees and plants. Similarly, an individual

Wherever possible, use similar building materials for the different elements of your outdoor home. This landscape makes extensive use of brick for walkways, patios, and retaining walls.

flower garden is more pleasing when the plants are massed together into a simple, strong arrangement.

In addition to visual appeal, simplicity has practical benefits. A landscape with a few well-chosen elements usually costs less to create than one that uses many different materials. Buying materials in bulk can sometimes earn you a discount, while you'll often pay a premium price for small quantities. A simple landscape is also easier to create, since there are fewer installation techniques to master.

And finally, a simple landscape is easier to maintain, which is an important consideration if your lifestyle doesn't afford you a lot of free time. A yard with intricate lines and many planting areas filled with flowers will probably demand several hours of

Ornate architectural styles usually look best when juxtaposed against very simple landscape designs. In this landscape, natural stone walls and walkways echo the building materials used in the house, and creeping vines on the walls and ground unify the scene. For interest, the space includes a single mass of flowers in a contrasting color.

A simple landscape is restful, inexpensive to construct, and easy to care for. It's also one of the most appealing landscapes you can create.

yard work each week, while simple shrub beds can be tended in a weekly half-hour session.

TIPS FOR KEEPING YOUR LANDSCAPE SIMPLE

• Use no more than two or three types of hardscape materials, if possible. Using natural stone for all walkways, patios, retaining walls, and edgings, for example, is one way to foster visual simplicity.

• Limit the number of plant species in your landscape. Unless you are a dedicated hobby gardener, try to limit yourself to one or two tree species, three or four different shrub species, and six to eight types of flowers.

• Be restrained in your use of color. Using broad splashes of a few complementary colors is more effective than a kaleidoscope of many different hues.

• Be conservative in your use of accents and furnishings. One key decorative accent provides a valuable focal point; many decorations make a landscape look confused and haphazard.

This landscape uses a very simple and restrained color scheme to create a restful atmosphere. Using related colors that lie close together on the color wheel (page 74) is one way to foster simplicity in your landscape design.

Unity

As a design principle, the term *unity* refers to the art of making a landscape fit in visually with its surroundings. A good landscape complements not only your home, but the surrounding neighborhood and the larger community as well. Unity makes a landscape seem natural and creates a more comfortable, reassuring environment. In addition to being unified with its surroundings, your outdoor home should have internal unity—the individual rooms of your landscape should complement one another.

SOME GUIDELINES FOR ACHIEVING UNITY:

• Build your landscape using building materials also used in your home. If your house is made of brick, for example, use brick for paved surfaces and garden walls. If it's not practical to use exactly the same materials, try to select materials with colors that match those found in the house. On a house with brown roof shingles, for example, you might build a retaining wall with sandstone or interlocking block in a matching shade of brown. If your house has Victorian detailing, you might copy some of these ornamental touches in the design of a wood fence and gate.

• Use repetition to unify the rooms of your outdoor home. Making sure that adjacent outdoor spaces share colors or patterns will help to visually unify your landscape. An informal hallway of stepping-stones running between adjacent rooms is another way to create unity. Or, you can repeat key shrubs or flowering plants from room to room. A classic way to create this unity is by using a continuous carpet of lawn grass flowing from one outdoor living space to the next.

• Use rock and wood products that are indigenous to your region. These materials will be familiar and easy to obtain in your area, and using them will

The retaining wall and walkway in this landscape are built with the same stone found in the nearby hillside.

This landscape features steps and retaining walls built from brick that matches the materials used in the house. This is an excellent way to create unity.

make your landscape seem natural. If you live in a mountainous region, for example, a retaining wall built from granite boulders will seem more natural than one built from sedimentary sandstone. In addition, indigenous materials are likely to be cheaper than those imported from far away.

• Pay attention to transitions between the house and yard, between the different rooms of the landscape, and between your landscape and adjacent properties. If you can make these transitions gradual rather than abrupt, you'll have done much to im-

Good designers understand that abrupt transitions between materials are moderated by the addition of a third material. In this yard, a low hedge improves the transition between lawn grass and concrete paving.

prove the sense of unity. A well-planned foundation planting of shrubs and flowers, for instance, is essential for unifying the house with the rest of the landscape.

• Repeat the decorating scheme of your indoor home. If the interior of your home is decorated in a Colonial style, for instance, mimic this theme in your landscape. Also try to use building materials that echo those used inside the house. If your kitchen uses slate floor tiles, for example, an adjoining outdoor patio can use similar paving to create a sense of unity. Designing in this way will make your landscape seem like a natural extension of your home when you look out upon it from the indoors.

• Build your landscape using trees, plants, and other materials that you see in other nearby yards. If your neighborhood is filled with stately oaks, filling your yard with birch trees will make it look rather unnatural. Taking your design ideas from those used successfully by your neighbors can also make your landscape seem larger and more majestic. Neighbors planning their landscapes together can create a truly wonderful effect.

Choosing familiar plants also has a practical benefit: if they are growing well in your neighbors' landscapes, you can be fairly certain these plants will thrive in the conditions found in your yard.

A neighborhood in which several landscapes feature similar trees, flowers, and building materials has a wonderfully unified atmosphere. Everyone benefits when neighbors design their landscapes in cooperation with one another.

Consider the topography and natural history of your region and neighborhood when designing your landscape. The style of this home and landscape is perfectly suited to the mountainous, forested region in which it is located.

Balance

The term *balance* is often used to describe the proper proportioning of visual "weight" in a landscape. In a perfectly balanced landscape, all the elements are arranged symmetrically. Symmetrical balance is appropriate for certain formal landscape styles, but in most instances it's best to seek an asymmetrical balance, in which the overall visual weight is roughly balanced, but without perfect symmetry. For example, if your house forms a large visual mass at one side of your yard, you can balance it by positioning a large shade tree (or a group of several

Even a small space can balance many different family activities.

smaller trees) on the other side of the yard.

A well-planned outdoor home also is balanced in function. Areas designed for active family life should be balanced with one or two quiet areas where an individual can retreat in privacy. Spaces designed for kids should be offset by spaces planned with adult needs in mind. An outdoor home needs areas dedicated to pure visual appeal, but it also needs areas devoted to practical functions, such as storage and maintenance.

The concept of *scale* is closely related to that of balance. Scale refers to the relative size of elements within a landscape. In a balanced landscape, the scale of the various elements is consistent and logical. A very large yard calls for large trees, wide paths, and spacious areas of lawn. In a very small yard, on the other hand, dwarf tree species and potted plants might be more appropriate.

Regardless of the overall size of your landscape, elements that will normally be viewed at a distance should be larger or more coarsely textured, while small, fine-textured elements should be nearby, where they can be fully appreciated. In a border garden surrounding a patio, for example, position large, coarse shrubs and tall flowers with large blooms in the background, and place low plants with small blooms near the front of the garden.

The term *balance* usually describes visual weight in a landscape, but it can also describe a state of equilibrium between any pair of opposing principles, elements, or functions. Whenever one "look" threatens to dominate a landscape, it's a good idea to consider balancing it with an opposite to save your landscape from monotony. Balance large areas of subdued, monochromatic color by creating some spots of dramatic color. Strong horizontal lines, such as walkways and decks, can be countered with a vertical element, such as a fence, arbor, or row of columnar shrubs or trees.

OTHER EXAMPLES OF VISUAL BALANCE:

• **Coarse textures balanced by fine textures.** Lawn grass is a fine-textured surface that should be balanced by coarse-textured elements, such as a stepping-stone path or a broad-leafed tree or shrub.

Lawn grass is very fine-textured, and should be balanced with plants with larger leaves and a coarser texture. In this outdoor room, an edging of hosta provides this balance.

Your landscape should be balanced in terms of function. Include areas that appeal to all members of the family. This yard includes rooms dedicated to adults, as well as play areas for children.

• **Straight lines balanced by curved.** Most homes and building sites are square and have straight edges. Designing curved pathways or planting areas with sweeping edges can do much to balance the

This apple tree trained against a fence (a technique called espalier) *shows how vertical lines can be balanced by horizontal lines.*

landscape and save it from monotony.

• **Conformity balanced by surprise.** A landscape that is otherwise relentless in its uniformity can be brought to life by including one or two surprising focal points. A formal, symmetrical Colonial landscape, for instance, becomes more interesting if it includes a single piece of strikingly modern sculpture.

• **Softscape balanced by hardscape.** Too much of anything is bad—in your outdoor home as in any aspect of life. A landscape should be a balance of living plants (softscape) and structural building materials, such as wood, stone, and brick (hardscape). Good landscape

A small, unusual piece of statuary can provide balance to an otherwise traditional garden.

designers suggest that hardscape flooring surfaces make up about half of your landscape, with the rest carpeted with lawn grass or other plants. A yard with nothing but plants looks wild and incomplete; a landscape consisting of nothing but brick, wood, and stone looks sterile and lifeless.

Movement

The concept of *movement* is critical to an outdoor home, both for practical and aesthetic reasons. The idea of movement has more implications than you might first realize.

PHYSICAL MOVEMENT

Like the inside of your house, an outdoor home must provide the means for people to move between the different spaces. Just as a house includes hallways, doors, and stairs, a landscape uses sidewalks, driveways, garden steps, and gates to control movement. Proper placement of these traffic paths is just as important outdoors as it is indoors. Well-planned gates and walkways provide easy access to the different living areas, while directing traffic efficiently. On a kitchen deck used for outdoor meals, for instance, it's best to position the deck stairs so the natural path from the door of the house to the yard doesn't conflict with the dining space.

Consider the purpose of each outdoor room when planning the position, layout, and materials for the physical pathways. For example, in a utility area running from a side entrance to the garbage collection area, a basic concrete sidewalk running in a straight line is most practical. In a room devoted to ornamental gardening, on the other hand, it might be better to create a meandering stepping-stone path that carries the visitor on a leisurely tour of the landscape's most interesting features.

VISUAL MOVEMENT

In landscapes, a sense of visual or symbolic movement is just as important as physical movement. Unlike the interior of your house, the outdoor home is a dynamic space with many elements that constantly change—from morning to night, from season to season, and from year to year. For this reason, it's

This landscape incorporates several types of literal and figurative movement. Pathways and stairs lead people between the outdoor rooms. Visual movement is implied by the archway and in the angles of the retaining wall timbers.

important that your landscape be designed so there are strong, continuous visual lines—pathways that lead the eye and intrigue the mind.

Visual pathways can be created in a number of ways. Mulched planting areas that extend around the entire outdoor home can gently lead the eye around the landscape and provide a sense of unity. Shrubs and flowers repeated throughout the landscape can also lend a sense of visual movement. A floor of lawn grass that occasionally narrows to form pathways between different outdoor spaces also serves this important function.

Don't forget vertical space when planning for visual movement. Because most of the visual lines in a landscape are horizontal, a few well-planned vertical elements can help provide contrast and interest. Picket fences, ornamental flowers with a tall growth habit, and columnar-shaped trees and shrubs can all provide vertical movement in a landscape.

TIME

Another type of movement to consider when planning your outdoor home is the passage of time. Think carefully about how the function and look of your landscape will change as morning moves into afternoon, as summer moves into fall and winter, as this year gives way to the future. The sun's position in the sky will change over the course of each day and over the passage of the seasons, which can have a clear impact on how you use your landscape. The deck you use for sunbathing on June afternoons, for example, may receive no sun at all in September. The trees and many other softscape materials you plant this year will grow steadily larger, which can dramatically change the look of your landscape, and sometimes even its function. Within a decade, a row of "shrubs" planted as a privacy screen may become overgrown shade trees that shed leaves into your swimming pool and block the sunlight needed to grow grass.

Also consider your personal time budget when planning your outdoor home. Do you enjoy yard work and welcome it as an enjoyable way to exercise and relax? Or do you prefer a low-maintenance landscape that frees you for other activities?

DECORATIVE MOVEMENT

Finally, elements that create literal motion can be an important source of visual interest in a landscape. Including a small fountain or circulating waterfall is one way to create interesting motion in your landscape. A colorful canvas awning, a wind sock, tall grasses, or a quaint whirligig that catches the wind can also provide this benefit.

In midsummer, a landscape will be at its most complex and colorful. Design simplicity is an important virtue at this time of year.

In autumn and winter, muted earth tones will dominate the landscape. Now, texture and shape become more prominent than color.

Interest

It's possible to create a landscape that doesn't quite succeed even though it dutifully applies all the design concepts discussed on the previous pages. A landscape can be unified, balanced, harmonious, simple, and perfectly suited to its purpose—but it can still be dull.

To create interest, design your landscape so each living space has some element chosen for its ability to draw the attention of the physical senses, the intellect, or the emotions.

SENSORY INTEREST

Elements that appeal to the bodily senses—sight, sound, touch, and smell—are very helpful for creating interest in a landscape.

Sight. Because sight tends to be the most dominant of the senses, the techniques for creating visual interest in a land-

Strikingly colorful flowers in many contrasting hues provide the interest in this yard.

scape receive much attention.

• Use contrasting colors, textures, and patterns. In a yard dominated by the fine texture and uniform color of lawn grass, for example, introducing some coarse-textured hardscape materials and bright flowering plants can make the landscape much more interesting to the eye.

• Create surprise in your landscape by introducing one or two unexpected features. In very formal, symmetrical landscapes, for instance, a colored, reflective gazing ball can add a touch of surprising abstraction. A great way to create the feeling of surprise and mystery is to lay out

The reflective gazing ball is a traditional accent piece currently enjoying a comeback.

your landscape so that some areas aren't immediately visible to the eye. A path that curves around a grove of trees and disappears into a hidden area is sure to draw visitors toward its mystery.

• Provide variety in your selection of building materials, plants, and accents. Many landscape accessories are designed for the sole purpose of lending visual interest to your yard. Landscape ponds, garden statues, trellises, and arbors are some accessories you might consider. Use them sparingly, though, because variety can very easily become clutter.

Sound. Though it receives less attention than sight, sound is very effective for creating interest in a landscape. A fountain or self-circulating waterfall adds the musical sound of cascading water to the outdoor home. Wind chimes and songbirds can also provide appealing sounds.

A water feature, such as a birdbath, creates interest in many ways. Water reflects sunlight, creating bright highlights in your landscape. The musical sound of running or splashing water appeals to the hearing. And water features draw birds and other wildlife to your landscape.

Many outdoor rooms feature a single accent piece to provide interest. Here, a decorative urn planted with flowers is the focal point of the landscape.

Smell and touch. Including a few fragrant flowers, trees, and shrubs in your landscape is a wonderful way to add interest. Be selective, though, because too many aromatic plants can be overwhelming. The sense of touch can be courted by clever use of building materials, especially in flooring surfaces. The texture of a stone or gravel walkway can be quite pleasant to the feet. Sunlight and wind also offer tactile appeal, and should be considered as you plan your landscape.

INTELLECTUAL INTEREST

A landscape can create interest by appealing to the mind. A well-chosen statue or pot can ignite the imagination and pique the intellect. Plant tags identifying the species of various flowers and shrubs can also stimulate thought. For an amateur naturalist, a landscape designed to welcome birds and animals can be greatly appealing. If you're among this group, you might want to include a birdbath and feeders, or a flower garden that will appeal to butterflies.

EMOTIONAL INTEREST

Elements chosen for their nostalgic or sentimental value create strong emotional interest in a landscape. Family keepsakes, such as an antique mailbox, garden tool, or planter, can be good accent pieces. A set of child's handprints can turn a plain concrete sidewalk or driveway into a fond reminder of family history. Plants, too, can create emotional interest— either for personal or historical reasons. In some families, treasured plants are handed down from generation to generation. Other plants seem to possess an inherent emotional appeal. Rose bushes, oak trees, crocuses, and daffodils are among the many plants that speak directly to our emotions.

A garden statue can be the perfect stimulus for emotional and intellectual interest in a landscape.

Harmony

Harmony is achieved by making sure all the hardscape and softscape elements in your landscape complement one another. In short: the plants and building materials used in your outdoor home should all look good when viewed together.

The key to creating harmony in the outdoor home is to think carefully about how each element will relate to the overall landscape picture. Paving materials, walls and fences, furniture, plants, light fixtures, and decorations should all be chosen with an eye to the overall image of your landscape.

One way to develop a harmonious landscape is by starting with the big picture and gradually moving to the fine details.

REGIONAL HARMONY

Most modern communities feature a wide range of architectural styles, and the range of landscape styles is often just as broad. But it's likely there will be a few landscape styles that feel most natural in your region. It's helpful to look at natural landscapes for clues about how to create a landscape that is in harmony with your region. Designing your yard to resemble the natural habitats in your area is a good way to create harmony. If you live in a forested area, in other words, consider a woodland landscape. If you live in Nebraska, a prairie-style landscape is a natural fit. There

are exceptions to every rule, but in general it's best to avoid a landscape style that sharply contrasts with the surrounding countryside. In an arid Southwest community, a yard planted with towering evergreens will not only be difficult to maintain, it also might look rather silly.

ARCHITECTURAL HARMONY

The next place to look for guidance in creating a harmonious landscape is your house. Look at the overall architecture of your home and the construction materials that were used to build it, and let this information guide your landscaping decisions. If your home is faced with natural flagstone, for example, a landscape that uses natural stone in its patios and walkways will look more harmonious than one that uses paver bricks. Basic construction style plays a part, too. A very formal, symmetrical landscape will clash badly if designed around a rustic, cottage-style home, while an informal, English-style landscape will look quite natural.

COLOR HARMONY

The term "harmony" sometimes has a different meaning among designers talking about the use of color, but we'll define harmonious colors as any group of colors that enhance or complement each other rather than clashing. Color harmony is a strong consideration for garden designers choosing plants, but it should also be considered when choosing colors for building materials and accessories.

The theory behind color harmony is complicated, involving the science of light wavelength and temperature, but there's really no reason to worry about the technical explanations. Using the classic color wheel—a graphic model that designers use to show the relationship of colors—designing a harmonious color scheme is quite simple.

In general, color harmony in the landscape is achieved by using hues that are either related or complementary, while avoiding color combinations that contrast or clash.

Related colors are those located adjacent to one

The ultimate goal of any landscape is achieving harmony between the manmade and natural elements. In this outdoor room, the statue with its outspread arms is in perfect harmony with the soaring branches of the surrounding trees.

Choosing related colors creates a restful, reassuring look in the landscape. This garden features flowers in related shades of blue and purple.

opposite one another on the color wheel. Complementary pairs exaggerate and enhance one another: purples look brighter when contrasted with yellows, for example. Complementary color schemes are good

Contrasting colors, when used selectively, can create surprise and interest in a landscape. In this garden, pink foxgloves contrast sharply with the predominant yellows and oranges.

another on the color wheel. Because these colors reflect areas of the light spectrum that are close together in wavelength, the eye and brain easily process the visual image. The effect is soothing and reassuring. For this reason, a design using related colors is ideal for quiet, private areas of the landscape. An outdoor room that features different shades of green and blue, for example, is likely to be a very restful environment.

Complementary colors are those that fall

for active, social areas of the outdoor home, such as a children's play area or recreational deck.

Contrasting colors are those that are neither related nor complementary. On the color wheel, contrasting colors have three colors between them. Contrasting colors often clash and are jarring to the eye, so it's generally best not to juxtapose them. Sometimes, however, contrasting colors can be used effectively to add surprise, drama, and interest in a landscape.

A landscape that makes good use of living things and natural materials is always harmonious.

Landscape Styles

Style in landscape design is a product of careful decision making. A sense of style is nothing more than the ability to choose the right building materials, plants, and furnishings, and arrange them in a way that creates a coherent "look" or theme. All it takes is patience, along with a basic understanding of practical design principles, which you learned in the last chapter. As you begin to make these important choices, it's helpful to keep the following ideas in mind:

Eclectic vs. Traditional: If you're adventurous, it's possible to create your own landscape style by choosing and arranging diverse elements in any fashion that pleases you, with little regard to tradition. Landscapes designed in this highly personal way are said to be *eclectic* in style, and they can be quite beautiful and unique. They can also be quite comical and bizarre. The success or failure of an eclectic landscape depends entirely on the taste and skill of you, the designer.

Another, perhaps safer, strategy is to model the look of your yard after one of several dozen traditional landscape styles (several of these are described on the following pages). Some landscape styles are modeled after historical periods, while others mimic different geographic looks. Following an accepted style makes it easier to achieve a look of harmony, but you should also make sure your landscape has at least a few personal touches.

Many great landscapes blend the traditional and eclectic approaches. Choose an overall style that fits the look of your home and the context of your neighborhood, but use materials, plants, and furnishings that have strong personal appeal to you.

Formal vs. Informal: Depending on your personality, you may prefer a very orderly, symmetrical landscape, or a more freewheeling, informal yard. If you have no strong personal preference, then you can let your house style guide your decision.

Formal landscapes often work best for homes that fit historical styles. A Colonial or French chateau-style home, for example, is a natural fit for a formal landscape. Formal landscapes make strong use of geometric shapes, and they have a strong central line (or axis) that creates a feeling of permanence. Formal styles tend to be symmetrically balanced, with shapes and lines that are mirrored from side to side.

Informal landscapes often work best for more modern homes. Informal styles use sweeping, curved lines and often include rolling lawns. They often include natural wooded areas and may include elements of surprise. Informal landscapes usually require less maintenance than formal landscapes, which may be an important consideration for you.

A Catalog of Traditional Styles

Colonial Style

Home style: This landscape style is best suited for a large yard and a large, two-story home finished in brick or lap siding. Homes that have an entryway with pillars or columns blend well with Colonial landscapes.

General layout: Colonial landscapes generally feature a formal main entry, often edged with symmetrical plantings of shrubs or flowers. The secondary entry and garage are frequently hidden. Driveways may be hidden behind shrubs to preserve large expanses of unbroken lawn, carefully edged and manicured. Planting areas are often rounded, featuring large, smooth curves.

Building materials: Flooring surfaces are often paver brick or natural stone. Garden walls may be constructed from brick or natural stone, and fences made from wood pickets or wrought iron are typical. Planting areas are often mulched with wood chips and edged with brick.

Plants: Large, deciduous shade trees indigenous to the region are common; oaks, sycamores, maples, and lindens are good choices. Boxwood hedges are often used, as are neatly trimmed deciduous shrubs.

Accessories & decorations: Themes of patriotism and heritage are common, including national flags and historical statuary.

Cottage Style

Home style: Smaller, bungalow-style homes built before 1950 are a natural match to this landscape style, although the look can be adapted to fit all but the most formal of architectural styles.

General layout: Much of the floor space in this landscape style is given over to ornamental plantings. Planting areas are often laid out and edged quite formally, but the plant arrangements within these beds are usually very diverse and informal. Grass meanders through the various outdoor rooms, serving more as a pathway material than as a traditional lawn. Even small landscapes make plentiful use of pathways, gates and archways. Many cottage landscapes include several quiet sitting areas, carefully positioned to provide spots for quiet reflection and relaxation.

Building materials: Natural stone or sand-set brick flooring surfaces are common in cottage landscapes. Garden walls normally use dry-fit natural stone. Fences are built from wooden pickets and are often painted white.

Plants: These landscapes often include small ornamental trees and flowering shrubs; climbing roses are another favorite feature. Flower gardens are plentiful and large, and tend to include older heritage or "heirloom" species, such as delphinium, foxglove, snapdragon, hollyhock, clematis, and English rose. To emphasize the cozy, miniature scale of the cottage architecture, the edges of the landscape are sometimes planted with very large trees that sharply contrast with the small house structure.

Accessories & decorations: Natural ponds, birdbaths, and light-hearted statuary of people or animals are regular features of cottage landscapes. Ornamental stone or metal lanterns are sometimes used. Wood furniture in classic English styles will complement this landscape.

Estate Style

Home style: Estate landscapes are best suited to large, formal-style homes situated on very spacious suburban sites. In the city, a two-story brick home set well back from the street can also support an estate style landscape. Architecture influenced by classic French or Italian influences often calls for this landscape treatment.

General layout: The overall landscape effect is one of formality and symmetry. The landscape strives to make the front entry the focal point, and circular drives looping past a formal entry are common. Lawn areas are carefully manicured and have perfectly rounded curves. Landscape elements are usually large and bold to match the scale of the home. Where space allows, an estate-style landscape can be framed with wooded areas.

Building materials: Paver brick driveways, walkways, and edgings are typical, though mortared natural stone is sometimes used. Landscape walls are often made of iron fencing or brick.

Plants: Large trees and shrubs are used to create shape and mass in the landscape and balance the weight of the house. Ornamental flower beds are often planted with bright bedding annuals arranged for bold geometric effect. Shaped hedges and shrubs are common features.

Accessories & decorations: Sizable fountains and statuary are often seen in this landscape style, as are large formal ponds. Large, decorative planting urns may be featured, and wrought-iron or teak furniture is popular. Driveways and walkways are often lined with landscape lighting.

COLONIAL

COTTAGE

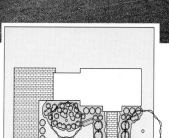

This traditional landscape shows many features of the Colonial style: symmetrical layout, deciduous hedges, and native shade trees. The driveway and garage are blocked by shade trees and large shrubs to preserve the balance of the front yard.

In classic cottage landscape fashion, this yard includes a wide variety of colorful flowers and shrubs. The use of natural stone in the planting areas, and the painted picket fence and archway, are also typical in cottage landscapes.

ESTATE

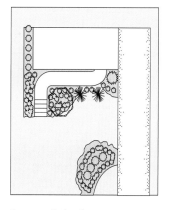

Estate-style landscapes are most appropriate for large, formal homes on expansive sites. Here, the sweeping curves of the lawn and planting areas are consistent with the estate style.

Ranch Style

Home style: Modern, one-story rambler-style homes are compatible with this landscape style.

General layout: The overall style of this landscape is simple and understated to be consistent with the uncomplicated architecture of the house. Overall, the lines of the landscape are low and horizontal, although one or two vertical elements may be included for contrast. A small courtyard or patio surrounding the front entry is a common feature. Foundation plantings are usually minimal.

Building materials: Wood fences may use split rails or horizontal boards to match the horizontal lines of the house. Poured concrete, paver brick, and wood decking are popular flooring choices and should be chosen to complement the materials used on the exterior of the house. Retaining walls are usually constructed from landscape timbers or rough-textured concrete block products.

Plants: Low-spreading shrubs and trees are the most commonly used plants. Ornamental flowers are used with restraint, and are often limited to low-maintenance species.

Accessories & decorations: Pioneer or western themes are often used, as shown by the popularity of brick barbecues and stone fire pits. Flowers in pots or hanging baskets are common.

Natural Woodland

Home style: Rustic-style homes and modern split-levels can both be appropriate for a woodland landscape. Houses with stained or natural wood siding lend themselves well to this style.

General layout: Woodland landscapes are decidedly informal in look. Lawn areas typically mimic the appearance of a woodland meadow, with soft meandering borders that gradually give way to shrubs and shade trees. Lawns are often inset with islands of ornamental shrubs and flowers in natural-looking arrangements.

Building materials: Natural stone and wood decking are the most commonly used flooring surfaces. Where a solid wall is needed, unpainted wood fencing is the most common choice, but rubblestone garden walls are also used.

Plants: Towering trees, both deciduous and evergreen, are common features of this landscape style. Softscape flooring choices often include ground cover other than grass, especially in shady areas. Boundaries between outdoor rooms are often formed with ornamental shrubs chosen for their wild, exuberant look. Flower beds are large and diverse, and are often planted with wildflowers or related hybrid species. Herb and vegetable gardens are common.

Accessories & decorations: Birdbaths, animal feeders, rustic benches, and adirondack chairs are traditional furnishings. A stone fire pit is a good addition.

Victorian

Home style: Large, two-story wood houses built near the turn of the century can readily accommodate this landscape style. Houses with porches, steep roofs, and painted "gingerbread" detailing are especially well suited to a Victorian landscape.

General layout: Victorian landscapes are usually dramatic, to complement the boldness of the house architecture. But to avoid visual competition with the ornate trim and sharp angles of the house, the lines of this style usually follow smooth, simple curves.

Building materials: Painted wood is a favorite building material in Victorian landscapes, and fences, gazebos, and other structures often echo the same detailing and colors found in the house trim. Natural stone is another popular building material, and is often used for walkways.

Plants: The Victorian era was a period of intense botanical exploration, and a true Victorian landscape reflects this in a broad selection of colorful, old-fashioned perennial flowers. Large beds of massed annuals are also common, planted in colors that complement the house trim. Fragrant flowers planted near the porch can make it a delightful place to relax. Flowering shrubs, especially rhododendrons and azaleas, are popular in Victorian landscapes.

Plantings around the foundations are kept minimal, to avoid covering up the trim details and preserve the view from the porch, but one or two large trees placed out in the yard can help balance the visual weight of the house. Weeping trees, such as willow and some varieties of flowering crab, are traditional features of Victorian landscapes.

Accessories & decorations: Hanging pots of bright flowers often adorn the porches of Victorian homes. Classic wood or simple wrought-iron furniture is a good fit in these landscapes, and ornamental pots and statuary are frequently used as accents.

Water features, such as a large fountain in the front or a pond in the backyard, are often a part of this landscape style.

RANCH

In this adaptation, low foundation plantings complement the low design of the house. Although the plant selection here is more diverse than is typical, the use of low-maintenance perennials is consistent with the style.

WOODLAND

Woodland landscapes typically use towering trees and are quite informal and rustic in appearance. Wood and natural stone are favorite building materials, and ornamental plants are usually shade-tolerant species.

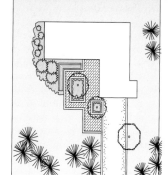

VICTORIAN

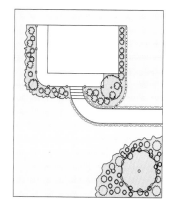

Victorian landscapes, like the one shown here, are colorful yet simple. The lines are smooth and curved, and old-fashioned plants predominate. Painted wood and natural stone are the most popular building materials in this landscape style. Hanging baskets and flowering shrubs are common decorative elements.

81

Contemporary Style

Home style: Modern architectural styles with strong angular lines lend themselves to this landscape type. Traditional ramblers and split-level homes can also be well-suited to a contemporary landscape style.

General layout: The overall effect of a contemporary landscape style is often abstract. Dramatic, free-flowing lines predominate in these landscapes, a strategy that helps unify the yard with the architecture of the house. Extensive foundation plantings are typical. Planting areas tend to have bold geometric or rounded shapes, and are used with hardscape edgings. Long, wide walkways are often included, styled to boldly lead the eye to the main entry.

Building materials: Paver brick, wood decking, and poured concrete are typical flooring choices. Retaining walls are usually built from wood timbers or textured concrete block chosen to complement the building materials used in the house. Fences are usually constructed with natural wood and vertical picket styling.

Plants: Shrubs, ground covers, and small flowering trees are used extensively; ornamental flowers are used with restraint. Low-maintenance plants are typical in these landscapes. Shade trees with striking bark or attractive textures are popular; choices include pine, birch, honey-locust, mountain ash, ginko, and palm. Weeping trees are also popular. A small flowering tree is often included for accent.

Accessories & decorations: Modern, contemporary furnishings and accents are appropriate, since older, traditional styles usually look out of place. Abstract fountains and statuary can be used to good effect. Landscape lighting with dramatic uplighting effects is common.

Country Farm Style

Home style: Large, two-story homes with traditional, painted lap siding work best for this landscape style. Homes with open porches—especially wrap-around porches—are well suited for country farm landscapes.

General layout: The overall effect in a country farm landscape is informal and down-to-earth. Large landscape elements, such as large trees, vegetable gardens, and flower beds, are usually included in order to balance the visual weight of the home. Lawn areas tend to meander through the outdoor rooms, mimicking the look of a flowing meadow, and may be interrupted with large island planting areas. Lawn areas gradually give way to border areas planted with prairie flowers and grasses, or with woodland shrubs and trees. Foundation plantings are usually rather narrow and restrained.

Building materials: Wood and natural stone predominate in paved floor areas and for walls. Natural split-rail fences are common in backyard areas, while painted fences with horizontal rails are popular in front yards.

Plants: Fruit trees, vegetables, and herbs are more common here than in most other landscape styles. Shade trees are large to balance the weight of the house. Columnar trees are sometimes planted in rows bordering the edge of the yard to mimic the look of a farm windbreak. Flowers tend to be heritage varieties, such as foxglove, delphinium, snapdragon, and hollyhock.

Accessories & decorations: Rural, rustic themes are popular. Antique farm implements are common decorations, as are wooden mailboxes, yard signs, and weather vanes.

Mediterranean Style

Home style: Italian, Spanish, Mexican, and southern California architectural styles lend themselves to this type of landscape. Many one-story stucco homes are a natural fit for Mediterranean-style landscapes.

General layout: Mediterranean landscapes with Italian and Spanish influence are often multilevel, though California and Southwest variations are often flat. The entry area is often given over to a courtyard or large patio, and there may be several paved patio areas in the landscape.

Building materials: Textured concrete and geometric paver bricks are popular for paved flooring areas. Brick or stucco garden walls are often used in this landscape style, as is wrought-iron fencing.

Plants: Species that tolerate dry conditions are best suited to this landscape. Low-maintenance ground covers are often used instead of grass in lawn areas. Small fruit trees, such as citrus or olive, are common features, and small shade trees are sometimes inset into patios. Bright annual flowers planted in large pots add spots of color to the landscape.

Accessories & decorations: Terra-cotta planters are popular features, and stone benches are also common. Spanish and Italian styles can make extensive use of statuary, ornamental urns, and water features, such as fountains and formal pools. Landscape lighting is a common feature, and it often includes uplighting of trees and other elements.

CONTEMPORARY

This modern home uses several elements typical in contemporary landscapes: low shrubs, extensive foundation plantings, and small specimen trees with attractive bark. Most contemporary landscapes are conservative and restrained in their use of color.

COUNTRY FARM

In a country farm home, the landscape generally uses large masses to balance the weight of the house. Here, extensive foundation plantings help the house blend into the landscape, but the shrubs are kept low to preserve an open view from the porch.

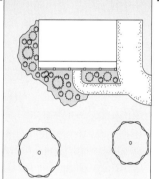

MEDITERRANEAN

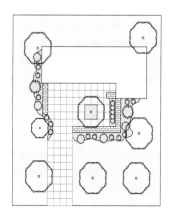

Like most Mediterranean landscapes, this California-style home makes extensive use of brick and stone paving. The entry courtyard, with its potted plants and spacious, spreading shade tree, is also typical of this landscape style.

Making Plans

Now that you've learned a bit about the basics of landscape design, you're ready to start the hands-on process of creating working plans for your new outdoor home. The best way to do this is by working through the following chapters in order. Refer back to the Design Basics section for help if you find yourself stalled at any point. By the time you finish this section, you'll have a complete plan package for building your new landscape, including a full-color final design, working plans with all specifications, a demolition plan, and planting maps.

It pays to take your time with this process. A leisurely approach to planning yields better results than rushing the work. Many professional landscape designers tell their clients to spend a full year thinking about and refining their landscape plans before the hands-on construction work begins. At the very least, we think it's a good idea to spend several weeks—or even months—to develop a plan. This may seem like a long time, but you'll probably find that it passes very quickly, since the process is a lot of fun. Planning your yard is a great way to spend free time when you can't be outdoors. During cold winter months or on rainy afternoons, what could be better than dreaming about your new landscape?

IN THIS SECTION

Gathering Information

Now that you have an understanding of the landscape elements and the principles of design, you're ready to begin creating an actual plan for your new landscape. The first step in this process is to develop a foundation of facts and ideas.

Some of the most important information will come from looking at the needs and opinions of you and your family. Unless your landscape is designed with all users in mind, it won't succeed completely, so make sure everyone in the family is considered. A landscape with elaborate flower beds and many shrubs might please you, but it may disappoint your teenager, who was hoping for a basketball court. You might love the look of a huge green lawn, but it might not look so great to the family member who must mow it each week.

Some people have no trouble visualizing a new landscape and expressing their tastes. But if you have difficulty with this, there are many sources of information that can stimulate ideas. Magazines, books, and television programs can help crystallize your opinions, and visits to public gardens and arboretums can be especially useful.

As you plan your outdoor home over the next few weeks, carry a camera with you. Take snapshots of private yards and public landscapes that appeal to you. Stop and talk to homeowners whose yards catch your eye. Avid do-it-yourself gardeners and landscapers almost always enjoy sharing their ideas.

You'll need to determine an appropriate budget for your landscape. Planning can't proceed unless you have a realistic idea of how much a landscape should cost—and how much you can afford to spend.

Creating a great landscape will also depend on how well you know your own yard and understand its relationship to the surrounding neighborhood and community. Careful observation and measurement of physical dimensions, sun and shadow patterns, and other details will be crucial to your landscaping plans. A good plan also takes into consideration the appearance of surrounding properties and the opinions of your neighbors. Your community government may also have something to contribute to your landscaping plans, in the form of local Building Codes. These regulations provide guidelines for creating a safe landscape that meets community standards.

Brainstorming

Dreaming up ideas for your new outdoor home is one of the most interesting and enjoyable steps in the entire design process. Ideas are the building blocks for designing a good landscape. Now is the time to let your imagination roam. Don't edit yourself at this stage—just let your fantasies take over.

Not everybody is comfortable daydreaming with wild abandon. If your imagination is a bit tame, the following step-by-step sequence will give you several ways to feed the design process.

Step A: Poll Your Family

Start by inviting everyone in your home to talk about their favorite outdoor pastimes. Encourage them to think not only about the activities they enjoy right now, but also those they might like to try in the future. The youngster who now is content to play in the sandbox may want a skateboard ramp in a few years. Or, if retirement beckons in the near future, you might want to plan for

A notepad and camera are good tools for documenting landscape ideas you discover.

a garden space in which to spend those well-deserved leisure hours.

Step B: Choose Your Outdoor Rooms

Once you have an idea of the different activities your yard should support, decide how many defined spaces you'll need to meet these needs. If yours is a small household, you might get by with just two or three distinct areas. But a large, growing family may need five or more rooms in its landscape.

It's possible to design a space so it can serve one function today but can be converted easily to another use in a few years. This is a good option if you have limited space. A timber play structure for kids, for example, might eventually lose its children's swings and slides in favor of an old-fashioned porch swing, climbing vines, and hanging flower baskets.

Remember, too, that one outdoor room can serve several functions. A patio used as a play area for small kids can become a comfortable spot for adult socializing after the children are asleep for the night.

Step C: Define the Elements

Now it's time to begin choosing the materials you want to use for the floors, walls, ceilings, and other elements of your outdoor rooms. Keeping a separate list for each space, jot down the materials you'd like to feature in your landscape. Refer to the chapters on Elements (page 28) and Materials (page 40) if you need a refresher on the options. It's a good idea to list two or three possible selections in each category, since there's a good chance that your plans may change as you balance fantasy against reality.

Step D: Evaluate the Existing Features of Your Yard

Take note of existing yard features that could be retained in your new design. If possible, utilize any features that are attractive and still adequate to their purpose as you redesign the landscape. If a concrete patio adjacent to the dining room still serves its function, for example, there's no reason to demolish it. The more elements you can keep, the cheaper and quicker it will be to create your new landscape.

If you don't want to keep the current structures, consider using the building materials elsewhere. Rubble from a concrete walkway could be used to form a dry-laid retaining wall. Or, sod removed to lay a pea-gravel floor in a children's play area can create a new grass floor in another area of the landscape.

Step E: Search for New Ideas

Originality is a virtue, but there's nothing wrong with borrowing good ideas from other sources. Keep a camera handy when you drive or walk, and take snapshots of landscape elements that appeal to you.

When planning your landscape, consider how features can be adapted for different uses as your lifestyle changes over the years. Once the kids outgrow this timber sandbox, it can be easily converted into a raised planting bed for ornamental flowers or vegetables.

On routine commutes to your workplace or local shopping areas, vary your route each time so you have new landscapes to study.

Public parks, home and garden trade shows, university arboretums, and historical buildings can all be great sources of landscape ideas.

Step F: Comparison Shop

Once you have a list of the elements you're considering for each outdoor room, begin calling and visiting landscape stores and building supply centers to learn how much these building materials cost. In most cases, prices are quoted by the unit—by the piece, by the cubic yard, by the ton, and so forth. The salespeople can help you translate these quantities into practical terms. A ton of cut stone, for example, might be sufficient to build 20 square feet of dry-laid garden wall.

Now is also the time to begin shopping for trees, shrubs, sod, and other softscape materials that you're considering for your landscape. The quality and prices of plants vary tremendously, so be diligent as you look for suppliers.

File away this information for the moment. When you begin to lay out the actual measurements for your landscape, your notes will help determine the quantities needed and the overall cost for all the hardscape materials and plants you'll need.

TIP:

Use this technique to test different landscape ideas: Make simple sketches of your yard by enlarging a photograph on a photocopier, then tracing the outline of the house and other permanent fixtures onto drawing paper. Next, find magazines or catalog photos of plants and landscape features, and trace them into the drawing to see how they might look in your yard.

Budgeting

Before you begin to dream in earnest, it's a good idea to figure out how much you can (or should) spend on your outdoor home. It's easy to get discouraged at this stage, but don't let the dollar amounts scare you off. In fact, you can probably afford more landscape than you first think.

All-new landscapes. Professional landscape designers and real estate professionals say that it's reasonable to spend 10% to 15% of the total home value on professionally installed, all-new landscape, whether it's a first-time landscape for a newly constructed home or a complete demolition and reconstruction of an established yard.

If you do the work yourself, however, the total cost of an all-new landscape will be closer to 5% to 10% of your home's value. On a $200,000 home, this means you can expect to pay $10,000 to $20,000 for an all-new, do-it-yourself landscape.

Remodeled landscapes. Your costs may be considerably less if you're planning a "remodeled" landscape that will preserve some of the features of your present yard. When you do the installation yourself, it's possible to do a fairly extensive landscape renovation while spending 3% to 5% of your home's market value—$6,000 to $10,000 on our hypothetical $200,000 home.

Even this amount can seem like a very large sum, but there are many creative ways to make your landscape more affordable.

Many landscaping materials are available free of charge. For example, your community may have a wood chip pile or compost site where you can obtain mulch. Stone for landscaping can sometimes be scavenged from building sites. Demolition sites can provide second-hand brick and concrete rubble.

BORROWING

Like any home improvement, a landscape project can be funded with a home improvement loan or second mortgage. Or, you can refinance your principal mortgage to provide the money needed to remodel your outdoor home. Any interest you pay on a home improvement loan or mortgage will be tax deductible. There are other types of loans you can use to pay for a landscaping project, but in most cases the interest rates are higher, and the interest can't be deducted. A loan officer at your bank or credit union can explain the tax implications of any loan you want to consider.

PAYING OUT-OF-POCKET

Unlike most home improvements, a landscape can

be renovated over a period of several years. Once you have a complete landscape plan, for instance, you might choose to complete just one outdoor room each year. Spending $1,000 to $2,000 annually, you can gradually build your landscape. You'll also save a considerable amount of money over the long run, since you won't be paying interest on borrowed money. If you choose to use this strategy, you may want to develop separate budgets for each room of your outdoor home.

CUTTING COSTS

Sales. It's possible to trim thousands of dollars off the cost of your landscape by shopping creatively. Like any retail business, building supply centers and landscape suppliers hold sales from time to time. In areas where landscaping is a seasonal business, look for bargains during the off-season months when retailers are trying to reduce inventory.

Discounted plants. Plants are often cheaper when purchased very early or very late in the growing season. In early spring, nurseries often hold special

TERM OF LOAN IN YEARS

Interest Rate	3	5	7	10
8.00%	31.34	20.28	15.59	12.13
8.25%	31.45	20.39	15.71	12.26
8.5%	31.56	20.51	15.83	12.39
8.75%	31.68	20.63	15.96	12.53
9.00%	31.79	20.75	16.08	12.66
9.25%	31.91	20.87	16.21	12.80
9.5%	32.03	21.00	16.34	12.93
9.75%	32.14	21.12	16.47	13.07
10.00%	32.27	21.28	16.60	13.22
10.25%	32.38	21.37	16.73	13.35
10.5%	32.50	21.49	16.86	13.49
10.75%	32.62	21.62	16.99	13.63
11.00%	32.73	21.74	17.12	13.77
11.25%	32.85	21.86	17.25	13.91
11.5%	32.97	21.99	17.38	14.05
11.75%	33.09	22.11	17.51	14.20
12.00%	33.21	22.24	17.65	14.34

This table shows you the monthly payments on a loan. To calculate your payments, you'll need to find the interest rate and the payback term of the loan, then find the corresponding index number in the chart. When you multiply this index number times the amount of your loan, in thousands, you'll discover what your monthly payments will be. Let's imagine that you're borrowing $10,000 at 10% interest, and you'll be paying it off over 5 years. Your monthly payment would be $212.80.

sales to draw in customers and, in the late fall they often close out inventory by holding big sales. Make sure, however, that you don't buy diseased plants when you shop sales. If you're not ready to plant immediately, perennials and shrubs can be temporarily planted right in the pot until your landscape is ready for them.

Salvaging. With a little ingenuity, it's possible to obtain some building materials at no cost whatsoever. You can sometimes find fieldstone and other rock to use in retaining walls and other projects by scouting new-home construction sites. At demolition sites, you may be able to find brick that you can use in garden walls and pathways. Concrete rubble can be used to build retaining walls. If you see neighbors demolishing a fence or deck, ask if you can salvage the wood to use for planters or walkways.

Naturally, you should get permission from the owner or construction foreman before you collect building materials from any location.

Combining resources. Consulting with your neighbors might reveal ways to save costs. If your neighbors are also interested in doing some landscaping work, you might be able to buy large quantities of materials together to save money. Or perhaps you've got your heart set on a mortared stone wall but can't quite afford it. If your neighbor shares your enthusiasm, you might work out a plan to share the expense, since the wall will benefit both properties.

As you develop your landscape plan over the next chapters, keep notes on the costs of the building materials and accessories you are considering for each room of your outdoor home. Estimate the totals every so often to make sure you're not exceeding the overall budget you've set. The design process is about decision making. At times, you'll be forced to economize on some elements of your landscape in order to afford the elements that are most important to you.

Courtesies & Codes

In principle, we'd like to tell you that you're free to design your landscape however you see fit. In practice, however, it's not quite that simple.

Unless you live in a rural area or on a farm, there probably are local regulations you'll need to consider when planning your outdoor home. Building Codes often restrict the height of fences or garden walls. Some of these rules are designed to protect public safety, while other are intended to preserve certain aesthetic standards. For instance, some communities prohibit "prairie-style" landscapes with tall grasses that contrast sharply with the neighborhood norm of carefully mown lawns.

In addition, and perhaps more importantly, you should also consider the feelings and opinions of your neighbors when planning your landscape, since changes to your own yard often affect them, as well. The tall hedge you plant for privacy, for example, might cast dense shade over your neighbor's sunbathing deck. Though such legal cases are rare, disagreements over landscaping have escalated into court battles.

Good manners dictate that you should at least discuss your plans with your neighbors to avoid hard feelings. And you may find that this courtesy reaps unexpected rewards. For instance, you and your neighbor might decide to share the labor and expense by landscaping both your properties at the same time. You could also save money by buying materials in bulk and sharing the delivery charges. Or you might combine your resources on a key feature that benefits both yards—such as a stone garden wall or shade tree. When several neighbors put their heads together to create an integrated landscape plan for their yards, the results benefit everyone. Individual landscapes look larger when the surrounding yards share a complementary look and style.

Finally, you should check with your local utility companies to pinpoint the locations of any underground electrical, plumbing, sewer, or telephone lines on your property. The locations of these features can have obvious importance if your landscape plans require digging or changes to the grade of the property. It costs nothing to have the utility companies identify the locations of these lines, and it can keep you from making an expensive and potentially life-threatening mistake.

On the following pages, you'll find some common legal restrictions for typical landscape projects.

FENCES

Good fences are said to make good neighbors, but in truth, few landscaping projects are more likely to offend a neighbor than a tall fence that suddenly interrupts a view they've grown to expect. If you consult them regarding no other feature, make sure to talk to your neighbors about any plans you have for a new fence or garden wall.

• **Height:** The maximum height of a fence may be restricted by your local Building Code. In some communities, backyard fences are limited to 6 ft. in height, while front yard fences are limited to 3 or 4 ft., or may be prohibited altogether.

• **Setback:** Even if not specified by your Building Code, it's a good idea to position your fence a foot or so inside the official property line to avoid any possible boundary disputes. Similarly, don't assume that the fence marks the exact boundary of your property. Before digging an elaborate planting bed up to the edge of your neighbor's fence, for example, it's best to make sure you're not encroaching on someone else's land.

• **Gates:** Gates must be at least 3 ft. wide—4 ft. if you plan on pushing a wheelbarrow through them.

DRIVEWAYS

• **Width:** Straight driveways should be at least 10 ft wide; 12 ft. is better. On sharp curves, the driveway should be 14 ft. wide.

• **Thickness:** Concrete driveways should be at least 6" thick.

• **Base:** Because it must tolerate considerable weight, a concrete or brick paver driveway should have a compactible gravel base that is at least 6" thick.

• **Drainage:** A driveway should slope ¼" per foot away from a house or garage. The center of the driveway should be crowned so it is 1" higher in the center than on the sides.

• **Reinforcement:** Your local Building Code probably requires that all concrete driveways be reinforced with iron rebar or steel mesh for strength.

SIDEWALKS & PATHS

• **Width of sidewalks:** Traditional concrete sidewalks should be 4 ft. to 5 ft. wide to allow two people to comfortably pass one another.

• **Width of garden paths:** Informal pathways may be 2 ft. to 3 ft. wide, although stepping-stone pathways can be even narrower.

• **Thickness of slab:** A poured concrete sidewalk should be 3" to 4" thick.

• **Base:** Most Building Codes require that a concrete or brick sidewalk be laid on a base of compactible gravel at least 4" thick.

• **Reinforcement:** Your local Building Code may require that standard concrete sidewalks be reinforced with iron rebar or steel mesh for strength.

• **Surface:** Concrete sidewalks should be textured to provide a nonslip surface.

• **Drainage:** Concrete sidewalks should be crowned or slanted ¼" per foot to ensure that water doesn't puddle on the surface.

• **Sand-set paver walkways:** Brick paver walkways should be laid on a 3"-thick base of coarse sand.

STEPS

• **Proportion of riser to tread depth:** The relationship between step rise and depth (run) is important. In general, steps should be proportioned so that the sum of the depth, plus the riser multiplied by two, is between 25" and 27". A 15" depth and 6" rise, for example, is a comfortable step (15 + 12 = 27); as is an 18" depth and 4" rise (18 + 8 = 26).

• **Railings:** Building Codes may require railings for any stairway with more than three steps, especially for stairs that lead to an entrance to your home.

Fences should be set back at least 1 ft. from the formal property lines.

Driveways should be at least 10 ft. wide to accommodate vehicles.

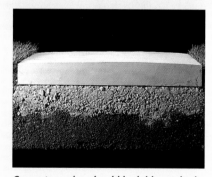

Concrete paving should be laid on a bed of gravel to provide drainage.

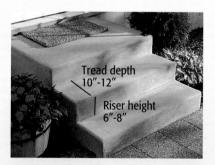

Concrete steps should use a comfortable tread depth and riser height.

CONCRETE PATIOS

• **Base:** Concrete patios should have a subbase layer of compactible gravel at least 4" thick.

• **Thickness:** Concrete slabs for patios should be at least 3" thick.

• **Reinforcement:** Concrete slabs should be reinforced with wire mesh or a grid of rebar.

GARDEN WALLS

• **Footings:** In many communities, mortared brick or stone garden walls more than 4 ft. in height require poured concrete footings that extend below the maximum winter frost line. Failure to follow this regulation can result in a hefty fine or a demolition order, as well as a flimsy, dangerous wall.

• **Drainage:** Dry-set stone garden walls installed without concrete footings should have a base of compactible gravel at least 6" thick to ensure the stability of the wall.

SWIMMING POOLS

• **Fences:** Nearly all Building Codes require a protective fence around swimming pools to keep young children and animals away from the water.

• **Location:** In some areas, Building Codes require that below-ground swimming pools be no closer than 10 ft. from a building foundation.

LIGHTING

• **Courtesy:** Neighbors may have a legitimate complaint if you install floodlights that shine onto their properties, so consider this when planning your lighting installation. Consulting neighbors during planning is a good way to prevent disagreements of this type. Choose neighbor-friendly fixtures with heads that limit the glare.

• **Safety:** Switches for landscape lighting fixtures may be no closer than 10 ft. from a pool, hot tub, fountain, or other water feature. In addition, many local Building Codes require that all outdoor circuits be protected by ground-fault circuit-interrupters (GFCIs).

FLOWERS

Neighbors and your local government may have something to say about the most basic of landscape elements—ornamental flowers.

Codes: Local ordinances and state law may prohibit the use of some flower species, especially those invasive species that threaten natural plant life.

Courtesy: Some flowers, such as violets, have such an aggressive growth habit that they can take over a lawn—both yours and, more importantly, your neighbor's. It's also possible that a neighbor might be allergic to some plants. Highly scented shrubs, such as lilacs, may be so unbearable to some people that it ruins their enjoyment of the outdoors. Planting your garden with bright flowers that draw bees will not be appreciated by a neighbor who is allergic to bee stings.

Safety: A surprisingly large number of plants contain toxins that can be poisonous if ingested. If small children will be playing in your yard, make sure to avoid such plants. Foxglove, monkshood, English ivy, nightshade, castor bean, and mistletoe are some of the common plants that pose some danger to small children.

TREES

• **Courtesy:** Consult your neighbors, especially if you're planning to plant one or more large trees in your yard. Trees cast shade, shed leaves and drop debris, and your neighbor will feel the impact of these events. Most neighbors welcome an attractive new shade tree, but check this out before finalizing your plans.

Concrete patios require reinforcement with steel mesh or rebar.

Frost line

Mortared garden walls need to be supported by concrete footings.

A pool requires a protective fence to keep neighborhood children and animals from falling in.

Codes: Certain tree species may be restricted by your community. In areas ravaged by Dutch elm or oak wilt disease, for example, these tree species may be prohibited.

• **Planting locations:** Regulations may restrict where you can plant trees. For example, boulevard areas that you routinely mow and care for actually belong to the city, which may determine what you plant in these areas. Local Building Code may also prohibit planting trees and shrubs near sewer lines or water mains.

• **Safety:** Your community has the power to force you to trim or remove large shade trees that pose a hazard or inconvenience. So, it makes practical sense to plant trees that are likely to experience good health and slow growth. Resist the temptation to plant fast-growing trees for quick shade. Within ten years or so, you'll be faced with cutting down trees that have rampantly taken over your landscape. Slow-growing species are much stronger and durable than fast growers, and they generally are more attractive, as well.

RETAINING WALLS
• **Height:** For do-it-yourself construction, retaining walls should be no more than 4 ft. high. Higher slopes should be terraced with two or more short retaining walls.

• **Batter:** A retaining wall should have a backward slant (batter) of 2" to 3" for dry-set stones; 1" to 2" for mortared stones.

• **Footings:** Retaining walls higher than 4 ft. must have concrete footings that extend down below the frost line. This helps ensure the stability of the wall.

PONDS
• **Safety:** To ensure the safety of children, some communities restrict landscape ponds to a depth of 12" or 18" unless surrounded by a protective fence or covered with heavy wire mesh.

DECKS
• **Structural members:** Determining the proper spacing and size for structural elements of a deck can be a complicated process, but if you follow these guidelines, you will satisfy Code requirements in most areas:

BEAM SIZE & SPAN

Beam size	Maximum spacing between posts
two 2 × 8s	8 ft.
two 2 × 10s	10 ft.
two 2 × 12s	12 ft.

JOIST SIZE & SPAN

Joist size	Maximum distance between beams (Joists 16" apart)
2 × 6	8 ft.
2 × 8	10 ft.
2 × 10	13 ft.

• **Decking boards:** Surface decking boards should be spaced so the gaps between boards are no more than 1/4" wide.

• **Railings:** Any deck more than 30" high requires a railing. Gaps between rails or balusters should be no more than 4".

• **Post footings:** Concrete footings should be at least 8" in diameter. If a deck is attached to a permanent structure, the footings must extend below the frost line in your region.

Slopes are best handled by installing a series of short retaining walls rather than one tall wall.

Building Codes require that railing balusters be spaced no more than 4" apart to keep small children from slipping through or being trapped between them.

The Yard Survey

As a starting point for creating a landscape plan, you'll need to accurately measure the features of your yard and note them on a rough sketch, called a *yard survey*. The survey is just a reference tool you'll use to draw the site map (page 100), so it doesn't have to be drawn to perfect scale. A rough sketch of your yard will work just fine, but the noted measurements must be exact.

Plan on spending at least a full afternoon measuring your yard, and enlist the aid of a helper, if possible. Before you begin, have your local utility companies come to mark the locations of any underground utility lines such as telephone, cable TV, electrical lines, and plumbing pipes. This will be crucial information, especially if your new landscape is likely to include any digging or earthmoving.

Step A: Sketch a Yard Survey

1. Start by making a rough survey map of your yard and all its major features on a sheet of paper. Then, label the important points on the map with key letters. Corners of the property and all buildings, walkways, and slabs should be labeled, as well as utility lines, trees, and large shrubs.

2. With your survey map in hand, go outdoors and mark each point with its key letter, using stakes or note cards.

3. Choose one straight line to use as a baseline. A property line is often the best place to start, provided it's straight. Measure this line, using a 100-ft. tape measure. Jot down the measurement, identifying it with the key letters that mark the ends of the line. To ensure accuracy, make sure the tape measure is horizontal when you measure. If your site is sloped, use stakes, string, and a line level to establish a horizontal line to measure.

4. Measure and record the remaining straight lines of your landscape, including the edges of your house, garage, driveway, and sidewalks. If your yard, home, driveway, and sidewalk are all square and perpendicular to one another, these measurements may provide all the information needed to draw a site plan.

Step B: Measure the Remaining Points

To accurately measure points that can't be located relative to the baseline or another straight line, use a method called *triangulation*. Triangulation involves locating a feature by measuring its distance from any

TOOLS & MATERIALS

- Notepad
- Pencils
- 100-ft. tape measure
- Stakes
- Strings
- Line level

A: *Sketch your yard and all its main features on a sheet of paper, and assign a key letter to each point. Measure all straight lines and record the measurements on a notepad.*

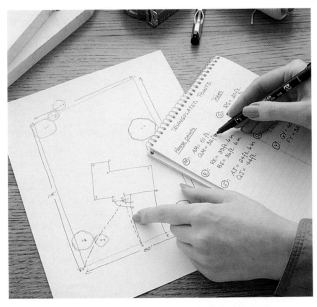

B: *Take triangulated measurements to determine the locations of other miscellaneous features, such as trees and shrubs, that don't lie along straight lines.*

two points whose positions are known. If your house isn't square to the property boundaries, for example, you can pinpoint the corner of the house by measuring from two points along a straight property boundary you've already established. The position of trees in the yard can also be triangulated by measuring from both ends of a straight property boundary. When you later create a scaled plan drawing, these triangulated measurements will let you accurately position these points on your drawing.

Step C: Measure Irregular Features

1. To estimate curved or irregular boundaries, take a series of perpendicular measurements from a straight line on the site, such as the edge of your house or garage. If no straight reference line is available, you can stake a string in place on the site, measure its location, and use it as the reference line. Measure at 2-ft. intervals along the reference line to the boundary in question. Make sure the tape measure is perpendicular to the reference line at each measuring point. Note all these perpendicular measurements on the sketch.
2. Measure and mark the locations of utility lines and shade patterns on your sketch. Also mark any low-lying areas that hold moisture after a rainfall.
3. Note any additional features that may influence your landscape design, such as the direction of prevailing winds and the quality of view around your

yard. It's helpful to look at your yard at several different times during the day, since sunlight and wind patterns usually change from morning to evening.
4. Mark compass directions on the sketch.

Step D: Measure & Sketch Elevations

Elevations are drawings that show vertical landscape features, as viewed from the side. Elevation drawings are especially important if you're planning to build structures along sloped areas of your yard. If you'll be installing a retaining wall, for example, you'll need elevation sketches in order to plan the project. You'll also need elevation drawings to properly plan fences, decks, arbors, and other vertical features.
1. Measure the vertical drop of a slope by using stakes and string. Drive a short stake at the top of the slope and a long stake about 6 ft. away from it. Attach a string to the stakes, using a line level to make sure it's perfectly horizontal.
2. Measure the distance between the string and the ground at 2 ft. intervals along the string.
3. For long hillsides, continue this process to the bottom of the slope, setting pairs of stakes at 6-ft. intervals. Estimate the grade of the hill by measuring down from the horizontal strings.
4. Make a rough sketch of the slope on a notepad. Record all the measurements on the sketch. The elevation sketch will be used for reference when you draw site plan elevations and working drawings.

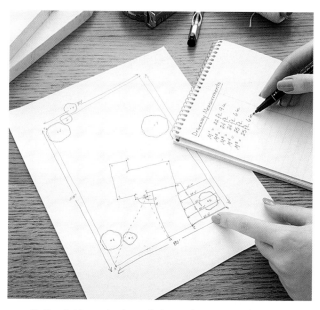

C: *To plot irregular boundaries and curves, make a series of measurements from a straight reference line.*

D: *Make elevation sketches to record the vertical measurements of slopes and any areas of your landscape that will have vertical design features.*

Drawing Plans

Equipped with a strong sense of your needs and preferences, and supported by a clear understanding of your site, you're now ready to start drawing up detailed landscape plans.

Good landscape plans make it possible to determine your final budget and develop a practical schedule for completing the work. If you plan to build the landscape yourself, the plans will help you organize your work efficiently; if you intend to hire contractors to do some or all of the work, landscape plans will make it possible for them to give you accurate bids on the work.

Your final landscape plans will include several different scale drawings, each showing a different aspect: a *site map* that establishes the position of all elements in the existing site; a *bubble plan* that indicates how the new living spaces will be laid out on your site; a *final design* that shows all the features of the new landscape, illustrated in color; a *demolition plan* that shows the elements that will be removed; and *working plans* that indicate measurements and provide other information that will be needed for the actual construction process.

At each stage in the design process, you may find it useful to create elevation drawings that show important elements of the landscape from a side view. There's no need to draw elevations representing every part of your yard; but wherever your landscape has vertical elements or includes a significant slope, an elevation drawing will be helpful.

It's best to approach this important part of the planning process with a sense of adventure—the best landscape plans are the result of playful exploration and fearless trial and error. Take your time, experiment with many different layouts, and don't be afraid to make mistakes. A plan drawing is only paper, after all, and can easily be changed.

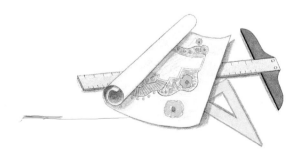

Creating a Site Map

TOOLS & MATERIALS

- Calculator
- Drafting triangle
- Ruler
- Compass
- Drafting pen or pencil
- Yard survey (page 96)
- Drafting paper

With your yard survey and measurements in hand (page 96), you can create an accurate site map drawn to scale. The site map is an overhead view of your yard—the basis for the finished landscape design.

A scale of ⅛" = 1 ft. is common for site maps and landscape plans. At this scale, you'll be able to map a yard as big as 60 ft. × 80 ft. on a sheet of 8½" × 11" drafting paper; or an 80-ft. × 130-ft. yard on an 11" × 17" sheet. If your yard is too large to fit on one sheet of paper, simply tape several sheets together.

Step A: Convert Measurements & Draw Straight Boundaries

1. Translate all the actual measurements noted on your yard survey to scale measurements. To calculate each scale measurement, multiply the actual measurement times the scale you've selected (see the chart, right, for decimal multipliers). If you're using a ⅛" scale, for example, an 80-ft. property line will be represented by a 10" line on your scale drawing (80 ft. × .125).
2. Select one straight line from your yard survey to

DECIMAL MULTIPLIERS

Use the following decimal equivalents when converting actual measurements to scale measurements.

Scale	Multiply actual measurements by:
⅛" = 1 ft.	.125
¹⁄₁₆" = 1 ft.	.0625
¼" = 1 ft.	.25
½" = 1 ft.	.5

act as your base line. Measure and draw in this base line on the site map, using a ruler.
3. Using a drafting triangle and ruler, measure and draw in any lines perpendicular to the base line.

Step B: Scribe Arcs to Mark the Triangulated Points

To locate each triangulated point on your site map, use a compass to scribe intersecting arcs from the reference points already drawn on the map.

1. Adjust the compass arms to equal the scaled measurement of one side of the triangle. Place the tip of the compass on a reference point, then scribe an arc.
2. Readjust the arms of the compass to equal the scaled measurement of the other side of the triangle, and scribe a second arc that intersects the first. The intersection of the arcs marks the triangulated point.
3. Mark the remaining triangulated points.

Step C: Outline the Buildings

A: *Convert the measurements made when you created the yard survey into scale measurements. Outline your yard by drawing the straight boundaries to scale.*

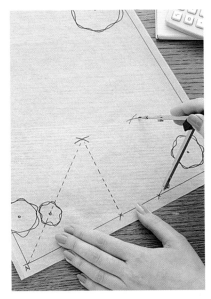

B: *Using a compass to scribe intersecting arcs, determine the locations of all points measured by triangulation during the yard survey.*

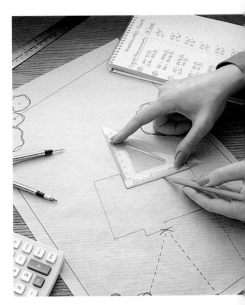

C: *Use a drafting triangle and ruler to mark the edges and corners of the house, garage, and any other permanent structures within the boundaries of the yard.*

Converting actual measurements to scale measurements often produces decimal fractions, which then must be converted to ruler measurements. Use this chart to determine equivalents.

DECIMAL FRACTION	RULER FRACTION
.0625	1/16"
.125	1/8"
.1875	3/16"
.25	1/4"
.3125	5/16"
.375	3/8"
.4375	7/16"
.5	1/2"
.5625	9/16"
.6875	11/16"
.75	3/4"
.8125	13/16"
.875"	7/8"
.9375	15/16"

Use the ruler and drafting triangle to mark the edges and corners of the house and any other buildings in your yard. If a structure lies at an angle to the main property boundaries, you'll need to establish two corners of a building, using the triangulation method, before you can outline the entire building.

Step D: Mark Curved & Irregular Boundaries

1. If you measured curved or irregular boundaries during your yard survey, establish them on the site map by laying out a series of perpendicular lines from an established reference point.
2. Connect the ends of the perpendicular lines with a line representing the curved or irregular boundary, then erase the reference lines.

Step E: Finish the Site Map

Use your elevation sketches (page 97) as a guide when indicating slope on your site map.

1. Where your yard slopes, draw in contour lines to indicate the pitch of the slope. Use tightly spaced contour lines to indicate a steep slope, and widely spaced lines to indicate a gradual slope. If your yard slopes at a rate of 1 ft. for every 8 horizontal feet, for example, the contour lines would be spaced 1" apart. A 45° slope, on the other hand, with a pitch of 1 vertical ft. for every horizontal foot, would be represented by contour lines spaced 1/8" apart.
2. Mark the locations of all entries and windows in your house and garage. This information will be helpful when you begin laying out the outdoor rooms of your landscape.
3. Mark the compass directions, prevailing wind patterns, the location of utilities, and any other relevant information on the site plan.
4. Make a key, indicating the scale at which the site map is drawn.

D: *Establish any curved or irregular boundaries by marking a series of lines perpendicular to an established reference line. Use the staggered ends of the lines as a guide to draw in the boundary.*

E: *Finish the site map by drawing in contour lines to indicate slope. Also mark compass directions, prevailing wind patterns, the location of utilities, and other pertinent information.*

Sketching Bubble Plans

A bubble plan is a rough sketch that divides your yard into the outdoor rooms you expect to include in the finished landscape. Some designers call these drawings *zone plans*. Drawing bubble plans is actually a test-phase—a chance to really stretch your imagination and have fun with the design process.

Draw several variations of your ideas, and include some suggestions that seem a little extreme. Sometimes taking an idea to extremes leads you to see entirely new possibilities that can then be adapted into more realistic versions. Even experienced professional designers may go through as many as a dozen bubble plans before settling on a favorite. To save time as you experiment with different layouts, you can sketch on photocopies of a tracing of your site map.

Once you have several promising bubble plans, invite the other members of your household to review the layouts and give their opinions. Agreeing on the layout for your outdoor home can prevent disappointments later on and can encourage family members to help during the construction process. Your reluctant teenager might be coaxed into helping dig garden beds if he or she knows it will reduce lawn-mowing chores.

Step A: Trace the Site Map & Make Photocopies

1. Tape a sheet of tracing paper over your site map. (If you have trouble seeing the map through the paper, try taping the sheets to a window to make the lines more visible.)
2. Mark the corner points of all the structures and features that will be retained in your new landscape. Don't trace elements you plan to remove or demolish.
3. Use a drafting triangle to outline the buildings and other structures, using a black pen.
4. When the tracing is complete, trace or photocopy it. You may need a dozen or more copies as you experiment with potential layouts.

Step B: Sketch Potential Layouts

1. Using a copy of your tracing, draw a loose pencil sketch, laying out the various rooms of your landscape. Wherever possible, draw smooth, curved lines to represent the boundaries of each space, using a curve template as a guide. Make sure you give adequate space for each outdoor room. A 10 × 10 area is

TOOLS & MATERIALS

- Site map (page 100)
- Drafting triangle
- Tracing paper
- Pencil
- Curve template
- Ruler
- Stakes
- String
- Cardboard

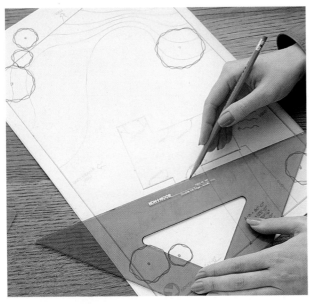

A: *Make a tracing of your site map that includes the property boundaries and any structures and features that will be included in your new landscape.*

B: *Experiment with layouts for your landscape by drawing several different bubble plans. Use smooth, flowing lines for the boundaries of each living space.*

the minimum that should be allowed for any room other than a utility space. Don't worry yet about the precise edges for decks, patios, and other hardscape features that will form your landscape.

2. Experiment with several variations. As you draw, try to visualize how your landscape will look when viewed from the windows and doors of your house, from the street, and from your neighbors' yards.

Step C: Test the Bubble Plans

1. Evaluate the merits of each bubble plan in the real world—by laying out the room boundaries in your yard. Use a rope or a garden hose to outline the floor of each living space.

2. Use cardboard cutouts, or stakes and string, to represent the walls of your outdoor rooms, including fences, hedges, and garden walls. Pay particular attention to the flow of traffic patterns between rooms as you lay out the walls.

3. Outline the walkways and paths as indicated on the bubble plan, again using cardboard cutouts,

DESIGN TIP:

If you have original blueprints from the builder or landscape architect who worked on your house or yard, these can be used as the basis for your site map, bubble plans, and plan drawings. Trace or photocopy the blueprints and use the copies to make your bubble plans.

stakes and string, and rope or a garden hose. Walk along these proposed pathways and imagine the views that will be created.

4. Position lawn chairs, benches, and other accessories in the spaces to get a feel for how well the plan works for the activities you imagine will take place in the various rooms.

5. Walk around the living spaces, envisioning the completed rooms and making sure the traffic patterns are unobstructed. If your observations suggest changes, adjust the bubble plan as needed.

Step D: Choose the Best Bubble Plan

Now, choose the bubble plan layout that gives the best "feel" to you and your family. Label the various living spaces to indicate their purpose. This bubble plan will be the starting point as you turn to the following pages to begin drafting a final design.

C: *Test different bubble plans in your yard by outlining the walls with rope or a hose, and by positioning cardboard cutouts to represent stepping-stones and walkways.*

D: *Select the bubble plan that best suits your needs and preferences. Redraw it carefully and label the various living spaces according to their purpose.*

Drafting a Final Design

After choosing a bubble plan that gives the best rough layout for your new landscape, it's time to develop a final design drawing—a carefully drafted color rendition of your new landscape, based on your site map and selected bubble plan. This drawing will show all the elements of your outdoor home, represented by standard landscaping symbols (page 107) and illustrated in color. It will display the promise of your new landscape, and it will guide and inspire when you begin the actual construction process.

A final design drawing requires careful, detailed work. Expect some trial and error as you transform the rough layout represented by your bubble plan into a polished, professional-quality design drawing. Have several photocopies of your site map on hand, because you'll almost certainly have a false start or two before arriving at a final design.

One of the keys to a professional landscape design is to use smooth, flowing lines rather than straight lines and sharp angles. Strive to establish a continuous flow through all the rooms in your landscape. Unavoidable straight lines, such as property boundaries and city sidewalks, can be disguised with flowing planting beds that have curved borders. Shrubs, trees, and flower beds can also form internal boundaries between different spaces in your landscape. In your final design, the boundaries of each living space should resemble the flowing curves found in your bubble plan.

Also strive for a feeling of continuity between the various rooms of your outdoor home. Many people

TOOLS & MATERIALS

- Colored pencils
- Drafting pencil
- Ruler
- Circle template
- Curve template
- Symbols (page 107 to108)
- Site map photocopies

A: *Outline the hardscape flooring and ceiling structures on a fresh copy of the site map.*

The landscape plan (left) includes the following labels: GROUND COVER WITH MULCH, WILD GRASS, GAZEBO, LOW SHRUBS, LOW EVERGREEN SHRUBS, RAILROAD TIES, STONE RETAINING WALL, PLAYSET, PEA GRAVEL, 6' EVERGREEN HEDGE, STONE WALK, BASKETBALL HOOP, DECK, COMPOST BIN, WINDOWS, CONCRETE SLAB, DOOR, WINDOW, DOOR, FENCE WITH ARBOR TOP GATE, WINDOWS, GROUND COVER AND ROCK, DOORS, STONE WALK, ANNUALS, PERENNIALS, EVERGREEN TREES

use lawn grass as the unifying element. As it leaves one room, the lawn can narrow into a hallway passing through planting beds, then widen as it enters the next space. Repeated use of the same building materials or the same types of shrubs or flowers can also provide unity.

Step A: Draw in the Floors & Ceilings

1. On a fresh copy of your site map, outline any permanent hardscape flooring features you'll be installing, such as patios, decking, and walkways. Use your bubble plan for reference when positioning these elements, and use standard landscape symbols (page 107) to represent these structures.

2. Draw in any hardscape ceilings that will be included, such as awnings, pergolas, or gazebos.

3. Add any shade trees that will form softscape ceilings. Make sure to use outlines that approximate the *mature* sizes of all trees.

Step B: Add the Walls

1. Draw in any walls that will form the boundaries of outdoor rooms. Some will be physical barriers, such as fences, hedges, or garden walls, but other boundaries are simply implied by a sweeping row of low

bushes or a planting area with gradual curves.

2. Make sure your boundaries include gaps or doors to direct traffic flow, and windows where you want to preserve or create an appealing view of the surrounding landscape.

3. Add detail to the transition areas, such as where the house meets the landscape, and where a sidewalk or driveway meets the lawn. Try to make these transitions soft and gradual, rather than abrupt. Where possible, soften fences and other straight walls by creating transitions that are smoothly curved. Planting beds are a good way to achieve subtle transitions.

4. Add in symbols and textures for all the remaining elements of your landscape, such as birdbaths, raised planting beds, landscape ponds, furnishings, and accents.

Step C: Finish the Design

1. Mark the locations of any permanent utility fixtures, such as landscape lights and hose spigots.

2. Use colored pencils to shade in the outlines for the various hardscape and softscape elements of your landscape plan. Start with the uppermost elements, such as tree canopies and arbors, and work down to the floors.

TIP:

If it's not practical for you to include full foundation plantings in your new landscape, concentrate on the corners of your house. Small beds of shrubs or flowers positioned at the corners of your house will do wonders for easing the transition into the outdoor home.

B: *Draw in the wall elements, including fences, garden walls, hedges, border gardens, and other planting areas. Also indicate gates and other "doors."*

C: *Add the symbols and textures for any remaining elements, then use colored pencils to finish the design.*

Drawing Elevations

Most drawings for a landscape plan are overhead "plan" or "map" views. These work fine for showing the overall layout of your landscape and the horizontal dimensions of its features. But for areas that have a vertical hardscape element, such as a fence, garden steps, elevated deck, arbor, or retaining wall, you'll also need an *elevation drawing*, which shows a side view of your planned landscape. Elevations are essential for estimating building materials and planning the construction of vertical elements.

It's not always necessary to draw the entire structure when making an elevation drawing. If you're planning a fence or garden wall on a flat yard, for example, you can draw the elevation for a small section representing the construction pattern that will be used throughout.

The process for making an elevation drawing is similar to creating a final design plan, as described

in the last few pages.

Step A: Outline the Elevations

1. Convert the actual elevation measurements taken when you conducted the yard survey (page 96), to scale measurements (page 100). If practical, use a scale of $\frac{1}{4}$" = 1 ft. or $\frac{1}{2}$" = 1 ft., which lets you show more detail than is possible in a $\frac{1}{8}$" scale.

2. On a blank sheet of paper, draw a side view of each elevation site to scale.

3. Use sheets of tracing paper taped over the site drawings to test different design ideas. When planning a fence or deck, for example, make one sketch for each different style you're considering. Or, when planning the treatment for a steep slope, compare the effect of building one tall wall as opposed to several terraced walls over the course of the slope.

Step B: Complete the Elevation

1. Once you've selected the best design, carefully draft a final elevation drawing on fresh tracing paper, then photocopy it. Use colored pencils or pens to add color to all elements of the drawing.

2. Mark down all important height and length measurements on the elevation.

3. Draw a key, indicating compass directions and the scale at which the elevation is drawn.

TOOLS & MATERIALS

- Calculator
- Drafting pencil or pen
- Drafting triangle
- Ruler
- Tracing paper
- Colored pencils

A: *Draw an elevation view of each site to scale, using a ruler and drafting triangle. Test design ideas by overlaying sheets of tracing paper on the elevation drawing, and sketching variations.*

B: *For each elevation, select the best design variation and make a photocopy of this tracing. Use colored pencils to add color to all elements of the drawing. Note the important measurements of all components.*

Landscape Symbols

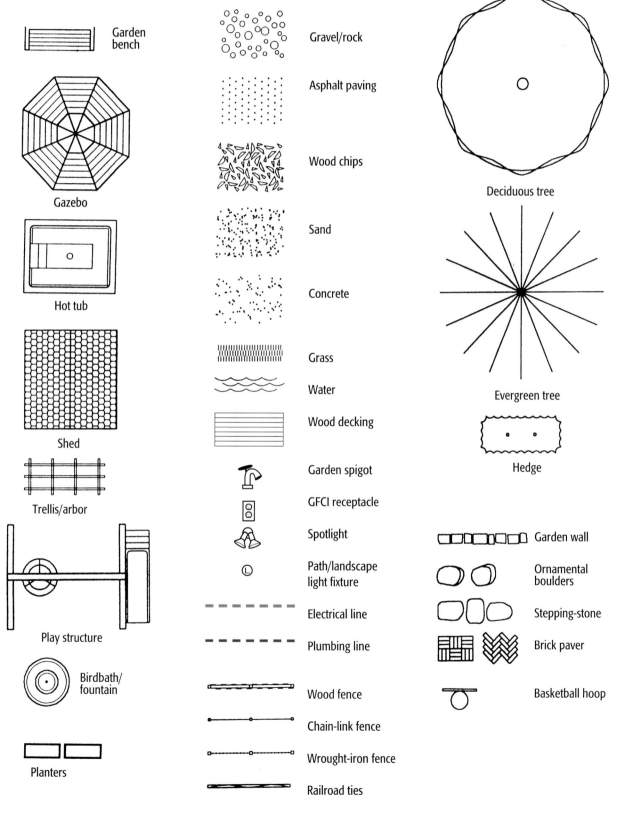

Garden bench

Gazebo

Hot tub

Shed

Trellis/arbor

Play structure

Birdbath/ fountain

Planters

Gravel/rock

Asphalt paving

Wood chips

Sand

Concrete

Grass

Water

Wood decking

Garden spigot

GFCI receptacle

Spotlight

Path/landscape light fixture

Electrical line

Plumbing line

Wood fence

Chain-link fence

Wrought-iron fence

Railroad ties

Deciduous tree

Evergreen tree

Hedge

Garden wall

Ornamental boulders

Stepping-stone

Brick paver

Basketball hoop

Creating Working Plans

By now, you're probably getting eager to start work on your landscape, but there's one small step left to complete: drawing up working plans.

Working plans for a landscape serve the same function as blueprints did for the contractors who built your house. A working plan is a bare-bones version of a plan drawing or elevation that includes only the measurements and specifications needed to actually construct the landscape. The goal now is to create working plans that contain all the vital measurements and specifications.

Working plans help you estimate the amounts of materials you'll need and make it easier to schedule and organize the work. Or, if you plan to hire landscape contractors or nursery professionals to work on your landscape, these plans will serve as the blueprint that guides their work.

Unless your landscape project is very simple, it's a good idea to create several working plans: a *demolition plan*, a *hardscape plan*, and one or more *planting maps*. If your project is very large, you may want to create a separate series of drawings for each of the different rooms in your outdoor home.

Step A: Create a Hardscape Plan

The hardscape plan includes the details of any major construction work your landscape will require.
1. Make a fresh tracing of your final design drawing (page 104) in pencil or black pen, featuring only the hardscape elements, such as paving, wood decking, fences, edgings, wiring, and plumbing lines. Make sure this drawing uses the same scale as your final design.
2. Use colored pencils to outline only the new hardscape elements.
3. Add dimension lines and measurements to indicate the sizes of all the new hardscape features.
4. In the margins of the hardscape plan, write down any information that will be helpful when you shop and place orders for materials. For paved surfaces, for example, you can indicate square footage, thickness of paving materials, supplier, and price.
5. Where necessary, draw side-view elevations for any

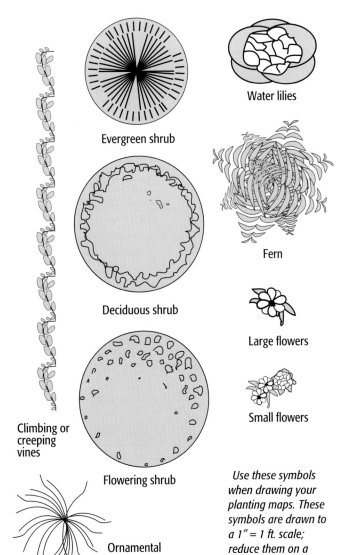

Evergreen shrub

Deciduous shrub

Climbing or creeping vines

Flowering shrub

Ornamental grass

Water lilies

Fern

Large flowers

Small flowers

Use these symbols when drawing your planting maps. These symbols are drawn to a 1″ = 1 ft. scale; reduce them on a photocopier if you're using a smaller scale.

A: *Create a hardscape plan that gives all measurements and other specifications you'll need to order the materials and build your landscape.*

details that can't be included in the overhead hardscape plan. On a sloped yard, for example, you may need an elevation to show the dimensions of terraces formed with retaining walls.

Step B: Create a Demolition Plan

The demolition plan will help you plan and schedule the major removal work, such as breaking up and removing old paving, cutting down trees, and stripping away grass.

1. Make a fresh tracing or photocopy of your site map (page 100), including all the current hard- and soft-scape features of your landscape.

2. In colored pencil or pen, highlight the elements that will be removed, demolished, or moved.

3. Note any information that is important for the demolition process. If trees need to be cut down, for example, indicate any obstacles, such as utility wires or neighboring buildings. If you'll be demolishing concrete or masonry, indicate how thick the slab is, and any rental tools that may be

needed. If you'll be moving sod or other plants from one spot to another, indicate their destinations.

4. Create a step-by-step sequence and schedule for the demolition tasks, and mark this sequence on the margins of the plan.

Step C: Create a Planting Map

Draw a planting map for each ornamental planting area you plan to include in your new landscape. Creating a separate map for each area will let you use a large, easy-to-read scale. You don't need to include large trees and shrubs that are already shown in your other working plans.

1. Draw the outline of each decorative planting area on a sheet of paper. Using a large scale, such as 1″ = 1 ft. will make it easy to see the detail in your planting map.

2. Using the symbols on the opposite page, mark the locations of all plants to be included.

3. Make notes indicating how many plants of each type you'll need. As you comparison shop, jot down the best sources for each plant type.

> **DESIGN TIP:**
>
> Design your planting areas so each ornamental species is repeated in groups of at least three plants. The same advice holds for shrubs and small trees. Groups of three or more look more natural than individual shrubs scattered around the yard.
>
> And avoid using too many different species of flowers. When you begin gardening for the first time, it's tempting to use many different plants, but such a landscape usually looks fragmented and confused. It's better to stick with five or six attractive, easy-to-grow species and use them consistently throughout the yard.

B: *Create a demolition plan that highlights the hardscape and softscape elements you'll be removing before building your new landscape.*

C: *Create planting maps for each border garden and planting bed you'll be installing. Note the species and number of plants in the margins.*

109

BUILDING YOUR OUTDOOR HOME

Part 2, Building Your Outdoor Home, will help you turn your landscaping dreams into reality. We wrote this part of the book especially for those of you who need background information, construction tips and techniques, and step-by-step instructions for common projects . It's designed to help you accomplish your goals, whether you're starting a new landscape from scratch or renovating an existing one.

Even though shaping the land, adding utilities, and constructing the hardscape aren't glamorous, they're essential parts of the process. And although landscape construction certainly doesn't produce instant gratification, it can be fun and the long-term rewards are more than worth the effort.

Many of these projects can be completed in one weekend, using tools you probably already own. Others require more time, rented tools or machinery, or specific skills such as plumbing or wiring. If you're not experienced in these areas, consult home improvement books, such as Black & Decker's *Complete Guide to Home Plumbing* and *Complete Guide to Home Wiring*.

As you get ready to break ground, we encourage you to relax and enjoy yourself. When possible, invite family and friends to help you with these projects. Take photographs of yourselves and the work in progress, and keep a scrapbook. You'll be building memories right along with landscape elements that you'll proudly use and enjoy for years to come.

Christian S. Paschke   *Jani Farris*

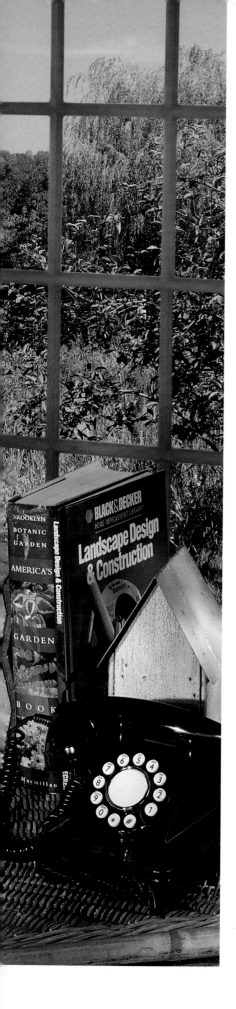

Building Basics

Creating a well-conceived landscape plan is the first step to building your outdoor home. But there's more to forming a landscape plan than drawing a detailed map of your new yard. The planning process also involves gathering information, making decisions and handling the logistical details that must be resolved before you begin to dig or build.

Early in the planning process, you'll need to decide what materials you're going to use to create the new landscape elements in your yard. For hardscape projects, such as landscape walls and floors, consider the look, durability and prices of available materials. With softscape features, such as hedges and garden beds, select plants that grow well in your climate and in the conditions of your yard. Once you've decided on materials, the next step is to determine quantities and locate suppliers.

Gathering the necessary tools is also part of the planning process. You probably already have many of the basic tools you'll need, but you may lack some of the more specialized tools. You'll probably need to rent some tools to complete certain projects, and locating and reserving them ahead of time will help you avoid frustration.

Researching local Building Codes and requirements, applying for work permits and checking with your neighbors allows you to make any necessary changes to your landscape plan before you begin working. Skipping this step can have unfortunate consequences, ranging from paying expensive fines to starting a project over from scratch.

Before you complete the planning, have your soil analyzed. Make sure to leave plenty of time for this step, as it takes anywhere from three to six weeks to get the results. The soil test report you receive will tell you how to amend your soil before you begin planting.

IN THIS CHAPTER

Materials

Wood, natural stone and manufactured stone are the primary materials for building landscape elements. Metal and plastics are secondary materials, used in the hardware you'll need for many projects, and for installing plumbing and electrical amenities.

WOOD

Home supply centers and lumberyards carry a variety of lumber and other wood landscape products. Cedar, redwood, cypress and pressure-treated pine are the best options for building outdoor structures because they are resistant to moisture and insect damage. Although these woods are outdoor-grade, they do require a coating of a high-quality wood sealer/preservative every two years to maintain the durability of the wood.

NATURAL STONE

Stone quarries, home supply centers and aggregate suppliers sell a large variety of natural stone in a range of sizes and shapes for different applications. *Cut stone,* also called ashlar, is used for creating walls, pathways and walkways.

Flagstone is quarried stone that has been cut into small slabs, typically less than 3 inches thick. It is frequently used for creating durable walkways, steps and patios.

Gravel is sold in two forms, rough and smooth, and is sorted by size. Rough gravel is used as a loose-fill material for paving floors and paths, and also for creating drainage features. Seeding aggregate, a smooth gravel, is used to texturize poured concrete. Compactible, or Class 5, gravel is commonly used as a base beneath paved surfaces.

Sand is another form of natural stone, commonly used for creating a mortarless bed for brick and stone, as well as floors in play areas.

Wood, stone, manufactured stone, plastic and metal materials are all used in landscape construction. These materials are often nonreturnable, so estimate the quantities you'll need before you buy.

Electrical and plumbing features, such as outdoor lighting and sprinkler systems, are constructed with metal and plastic materials.

MANUFACTURED STONE

A variety of concrete products are available in a wide range of sizes, textures and colors.

Poured concrete can have a smooth finish, but it can also be given a textured finish or even tinted.

Interlocking block is made from molded concrete that's designed to resemble natural stone. It's used for building retaining walls and raised garden beds.

Concrete pavers are made from poured concrete and are available in many shapes, colors and textures. Concrete brick pavers are frequently used in place of clay bricks for building patios, walkways and edging.

METAL

Metal hardware is required for many landscaping projects. Metals used outdoors must be strong and resistant to corrosion.

Connectors, such as nails, screws, post anchors and latches should be made from galvanized steel or another corrosion-resistant material.

Electrical materials include conduit, receptacle boxes and lighting fixtures. Choose materials that are outdoor-grade: galvanized thick-wall conduit, and receptacle boxes with a grounding terminal and watertight seals.

Plumbing materials, such as valves, pipes, pipe straps and spigots, are commonly made of copper or steel. Select Code-approved materials: pipes for outdoor use should be classified as *thick wall*.

TIP:

To protect your yard, place a tarp for sand, gravel or other materials as close to the work area as possible.

PLASTICS

Plastic hardware is commonly used for utilities, fixtures and edging.

Electrical hardware made from plastic includes plastic-coated electrical cable, receptacles, indoor receptacle and switch boxes and light fixtures.

Plumbing materials, including PVC pipe, PE (polyethylene pipe), valve boxes and sprinkler heads are made with high-grade plastics. PVC schedule 40 piping is used for underground plumbing lines, such as sprinkler system lines.

Flexible plastic edging is an inexpensive, easy-to-install edging material. For best results, buy a professional-grade edging that's been shipped and stored flat, rather than the less durable, coiled edging often sold at home centers.

ESTIMATING MATERIALS

The chart below can help you estimate the quantities of stone and masonry materials you'll need for landscape projects. Sizes and weights of materials may vary, so consult your supplier for exact specifications.

ESTIMATING STONE & MASONRY MATERIALS:

Sand, gravel, topsoil (2" layer)	Surface area (sq. ft) ÷ 100 = tons needed
Standard brick pavers (4" × 8")	Surface area (sq. ft) × 5 = number of pavers needed
Poured concrete (4" layer)	Surface area (sq. ft.) × .012 = cubic yards needed
Flagstone	Surface area (sq. ft.) ÷ 100 = tons of stone needed
Interlocking block (6" × 16" face)	Area of wall face (sq. ft.) × 1.5 = number of blocks needed
Cut stone (2-ft.-thick walls)	Area of wall face (sq. ft.) ÷ 7.5 = tons of stone needed

Plants

Plants add year-round color and texture to your landscape. Determining which plants are suited to the climate in your region and to the sun and soil conditions of your planting areas is an important part of developing your landscape plan. The information here will help you select healthy specimens of the best annuals, perennials and bulbs for your yard. Similar information on shrubs and trees can be found in "Hedges" (page 170) and "Trees" (page 172).

SUPPLIERS

In most cases, you'll find the best selection of plants at nurseries and garden centers. But, if you know what to look for, you can often find good deals on plants sold at discount retailers and mail-order catalogs. When ordering plants by mail, choose a supplier that has a guaranteed return or exchange policy.

ZONE RATINGS

The U.S. Department of Agriculture (USDA) zone map is designed to help you select appropriate plants for your climate (see page 117). The zones are numbered from 1-11, based on the average annual minimum temperature of each area. If you're buying plants locally, you'll find that nurseries and garden centers typically carry only plants suited to the zone in which they're located. If you're buying plants by mail, consult plant descriptions and the zone map to make sure the plants you select are suited to your area.

ANNUALS

Annuals complete their life cycle in one season. They grow much faster than perennials, but don't survive the winter. They're usually sold in small containers packed into large trays, or "bedding flats." Healthy annuals are compact, have plenty of buds and show good leaf color and root structure. Don't buy annuals with light-colored leaves, gangly stems or roots protruding from the container.

(left) Nurseries, garden centers and home supply stores carry a selection of annuals, perennials, shrubs and trees. Selection, price and quality of merchandise are factors to consider when deciding where to shop.

(opposite) Consult the United States Department of Agriculture zone map to choose specimens suited to your climate.

PERENNIALS

Perennials return each year, growing and spreading without having to be replanted. They usually are sold as container-grown plants. Good perennials have balanced foliage, sturdy flower stalks and firm roots. Avoid perennials with sparse growth, poorly defined flower stems, shriveled or pale leaves or mushy stems.

BULBS

Bulbs are unique perennials that grow from fleshy underground root or stem structures that store the necessary nutrients for plant development. They are usually packaged in bags or sold in bulk. Healthy bulbs are large, firm and plump. Don't choose withered, dried-out bulbs or those with visible spots of disease, insect damage or decay. In general, bulbs sold in net bags, or packaged in straw or peat moss to absorb moisture, are of better quality than those packaged in plastic.

Selecting healthy plants for your landscape is easy if you pay attention to a few visual clues. Healthy perennials and annuals (right) have a compact shape with lots of buds. Poor specimens (left) may have gangly stems and exposed roots.

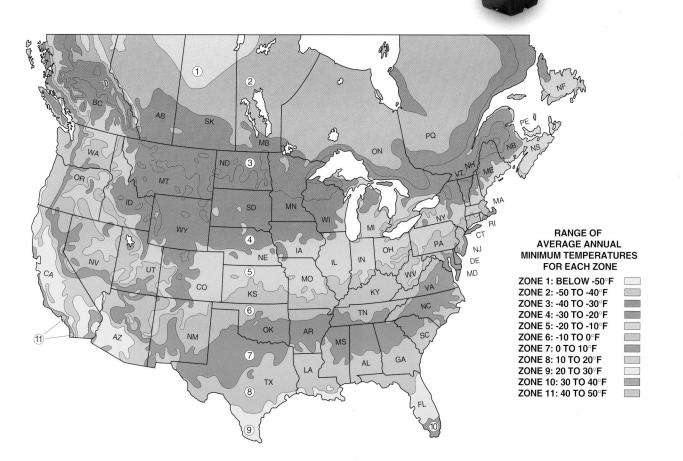

RANGE OF AVERAGE ANNUAL MINIMUM TEMPERATURES FOR EACH ZONE

ZONE 1: BELOW -50°F
ZONE 2: -50 TO -40°F
ZONE 3: -40 TO -30°F
ZONE 4: -30 TO -20°F
ZONE 5: -20 TO -10°F
ZONE 6: -10 TO 0°F
ZONE 7: 0 TO 10°F
ZONE 8: 10 TO 20°F
ZONE 9: 20 TO 30°F
ZONE 10: 30 TO 40°F
ZONE 11: 40 TO 50°F

Leaves

Grass

Peat moss

Compost

Straw

Manure

Soil

In addition to creating the foundation for your entire landscape, your soil provides the water and nutrients your plants, lawn, trees and shrubs need to develop large, healthy root systems. Very few yards, however, are blessed with perfect soil that provides an ideal growing environment. You'll probably need to amend your soil to improve its structure and nutrient levels. Whenever possible, amend the soil early in the landscaping process, when the task is easier and yields better results.

REQUESTING A SOIL TEST

To get the most accurate assessment of how to improve your soil, have it analyzed by a soil testing lab. For a small fee, a local lab or your state's agricultural extension service will conduct a detailed analysis of a soil sample from your yard.

In general, it takes anywhere from three to six weeks to receive the results of a soil analysis, so send the samples long before you plan to begin landscaping. Include written information with the sample, detailing what you've added to your soil in the past—such as fertilizers, lime, peat moss or compost. Also, include information on the specific plants you want to grow. The lab will provide a report that suggests specific amendments to add to your soil to support the plants you'll be growing.

HOW TO COLLECT A SOIL SAMPLE

For each area where you intend to plant, dig a 1-ft.-deep hole, using a clean shovel. Cut a ½"-wide slice from the top to the bottom of the hole, using the shovel. Remove the top ½" off of the slice, and place the remaining portion in a clean bucket. Repeat this process in at least five

Nitrogen is necessary for developing healthy leaf and stem growth.

Organic amendments are the best choice for improving the structure and nutrient levels of your soil.

Soil that's been amended properly has a structure that promotes a healthy root system. The roots of these annuals are deep and spread apart.

Recommendations for lawn growth tell you how to improve your soil to support a lawn.

Recommendations for vegetable and flower gardens specify how to amend the soil to foster successful gardens.

different areas of the planting site, mixing each of the slices together in the bucket.

Pour about one pint of the sample soil into a clean container, such as a locking plastic bag. Mail the sample and the written information to the soil testing lab.

HOW TO READ A SOIL TEST REPORT

The soil test report details your soil's texture, pH and nutrient levels. It will also tell you how to improve the soil in order to grow the plants you want.

Texture. Soil texture is categorized as loamy, sandy, silty, clayey or a combination of two of these categories, such as loamy-sand or silty-clay. *Loamy* soil is ideal for growing plants—it is composed of almost equal amounts of sand, silt and clay. Because sandy soil doesn't retain water or nutrients, plants must be frequently watered and fertilized. *Silty* soil holds moisture and nutrients fairly well. However, it cannot absorb a lot of water at once and requires frequent, light waterings. *Clayey* soil holds moisture and nutrients

well, but is too dense for root growth and too damp for plants that require well-drained soil.

The soil test report will suggest organic amendments, such as compost, manure or peat moss, to improve sandy, silty and clayey soils. In sandy and silty soils, organic material helps retain moisture for plant roots. In clayey soils, amendments help loosen the soil, improving breathability and drainage.

Soil pH is a value of the soil's acidity or alkalinity based on a scale from 0 to 14.0. The report will identify your soil's pH, and tell you the ideal pH for growing the plants you specified. If your soil is very acidic or alkaline, you may need to alter your plant selection.

Fertility is a measure of the quantity of nitrogen, phosphorus and potassium in the soil. The report will measure the presence of each element in parts per million (ppm), and rate each measurement as low, medium or high.

Specific recommendations. Amending poor soils with organic materials boosts nutrient levels and improves the soil's structure. The results of your soil test will suggest how you can amend your soil to foster lawn and plant growth. For detailed how-to demonstrations on applying amendments, see "Soil Preparation" (page 200). The process for amending soil for planting beds differs slightly and is covered in "Garden Bed" (page 208).

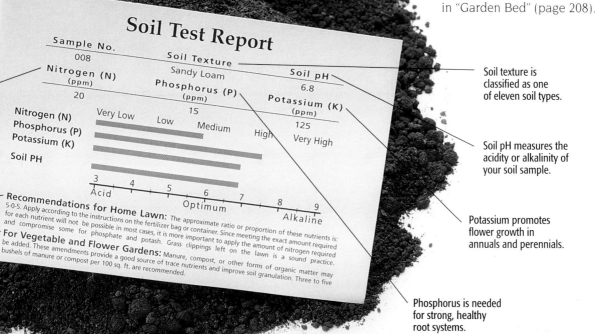

Soil texture is classified as one of eleven soil types.

Soil pH measures the acidity or alkalinity of your soil sample.

Potassium promotes flower growth in annuals and perennials.

Phosphorus is needed for strong, healthy root systems.

Tools

You probably already own many of the garden and household tools needed to complete the projects presented in this book. But, several projects require more specialized tools and machinery, which may be available at rental centers. You can also borrow tools from neighbors or friends. Whenever you rent or borrow tools, ask for a copy of the owner's manual and operating instructions as well.

If you buy new tools, invest in high-quality products whenever possible. Most hardware stores and home centers carry a wide variety of hand and power tools, in a range of prices. Read consumer publications and talk to experienced do-it-yourselfers to get information about dependable brands and useful features. To ensure your safety and prevent damage to your tools, always use a GFCI (ground-fault circuit-interrupter) extension cord when using power tools.

BASIC TOOLS:

- Hammer
- Maul
- Rubber mallet
- Power drill
- Screwdriver
- Hacksaw

- Carpenter's level
- Tape measure
- Garden shovel
- Trenching spade
- Wheelbarrow
- Garden hose

- Pressure sprayer
- Garden hoe
- Trowel
- Garden rake

SPECIALTY TOOLS:

- Reciprocating saw
- Jig saw
- Chain saw
- Circular saw
- Plate compactor

- Jackhammer
- Hand tamp
- Core aerator
- Vertical mower
- Power auger

- Fish tape
- Wire combination tool
- Line level
- Framing square
- Wood float

Buy the best quality tools you can afford. A quality tool can last a lifetime, which costs less in the long run than replacing a cheaper version three or four times.

To protect your investment, keep tools clean, dry and sharpened as necessary. Protect metal tools from rust by giving them a light coat of oil from time to time.

Planning Ahead

Before you begin building landscape structures, communicate your plans to neighbors, building inspectors and utility companies. Although it may seem inconvenient, making these calls gives you a chance to gather information and make any necessary adjustments to your landscape plans before work begins.

NEIGHBORS

Talk with your neighbors about your landscaping plans—this simple courtesy can prevent problems ranging from soured relationships to legal disputes. Show them sketches of your plan or pictures similar to the projects you're planning, especially projects that will affect their yards, such as building fences, walls, hedges or planting large shade trees.

An inexpensive line level is indispensable for many landscaping projects.

BUILDING CODES & REGULATIONS

Determine what your community's regulations and codes are before you begin landscaping. Many communities have standards that limit the dimensions and materials for landscape structures. Check local Building Code to determine the setback distance, a regulation that prohibits any structure from being built too close to property lines. If you're adding any structures that require concrete footings, such as fences, arbors or decks, check local Building Code to determine the depth required for the footings.

UTILITY LINES

Before beginning any project that involves digging or excavation, you must locate the buried utility lines in your yard. Your electric, telephone, gas, cable and water companies are required by law to inspect your site on request and mark the locations of buried lines. Call these companies several days before you plan to start digging.

BUILDING PERMITS & INSPECTIONS

You may need to obtain building permits and schedule inspections for some of the plumbing and electrical projects in this book. To obtain permits, you'll need to submit a drawing of the project for your local building inspector to approve. The inspector will tell you if there are specific materials you'll need to use for the project and suggest any necessary changes to your plan. Once you've received your permit, you'll need to display it in a front window of your home until the project has been completed.

Shaping

The topography of your yard—its shape, contour and the position of its natural features—is a fundamental element of your landscape. The basic shape of the land affects how you use your yard, its drainage patterns and the quality of its soil, as well as the amount of work involved in routine maintenance.

As you begin building your outdoor home, you may need to alter the shape of your landscape to make it more functional. Before tackling shaping projects, you'll need to become familiar with the basics of the process: demolition, grading, managing and creating slope and solving and preventing drainage problems.

In an established yard, you may need to remove elements to make space for new outdoor rooms and landscape features. Following professional techniques makes it easier to remove existing hardscape and softscape features, such as fences, patios, walkways, hedges and trees.

If water collects near your foundation or you have other drainage problems, you probably need to address issues of slope before you begin building the features of your outdoor home. By following some simple grading techniques, you can create slopes that direct water away from your house and eliminate soggy areas in your yard. In some cases, you may choose to install a dry well or create a drainage swale to channel and disperse excess water.

Steep slopes, or no slope at all, can present practical and aesthetic challenges that often can be managed by reshaping a yard's contours. Retaining walls can prevent erosion, simplify mowing and provide level planting space in areas that were previously unusable. Adding a berm can increase privacy, muffle sound and create visual interest.

Shaping projects often are simple, but they do involve quite a bit of physical labor. Although many people enjoy doing the work themselves, others prefer to hire a landscape contractor to help with part or all of it. Rented tools and equipment can make some jobs easier, as you'll see in many of the project descriptions that follow.

IN THIS CHAPTER

Demolition

The shaping process often involves relocating or removing landscape elements such as fences, walls, walkways or patios to make way for the new elements in your plan. Before you begin, develop a demolition plan, outlining what you're going to remove and what tools you'll need. With careful planning, you should be able to complete all the projects that require rental tools in one lease period.

You can also save money by using the materials from demolished structures in new projects. For instance, you can use sand-set paver bricks as garden edging (page 209), broken pieces of concrete to build a free-standing garden wall (page 168) or fence posts for creating raised garden beds (page 130).

Before you begin demolition, make plans for disposing of material that can't be reused. The solution may be as simple as renting a dumpster, or it may involve hiring a disposal contractor.

The following information outlines the tools and techniques you can use to remove wood, brick, stone and concrete structures from your landscape.

WOOD

Wood structures are among the simplest landscaping features to dismantle. The tools you'll need will depend on the structure and how it's built. You can dismantle decks and fences assembled with screws by removing the screws with a reversible drill or power screwdriver. For structures built with nails, use a crowbar to pry the individual boards loose. If you're not planning to reuse the lumber and can dispose of it in large sections, you might want to hire someone with a front-end loader to knock down an entire fence.

Removing the concrete footings used to anchor fence or deck posts can be a difficult task. Most footings are at least 18" deep—digging them up requires a lot of time and effort. In most cases, it's more practical to bury footings than to remove them. To bury a footing, remove 3" to 4" of the concrete surrounding the post, using a sledgehammer or a mason's hammer and chisel. Use a reciprocating saw to cut the post off flush with the remaining concrete, then cover the footing with soil.

To dismantle a fence that was assembled with nails, use a crowbar to pry the boards loose. After removing a board, hammer the exposed ends of the nails down against the board to prevent injury.

CONCRETE

The best way to remove small concrete structures, such as a step or walkway, is to break the concrete into small sections. If you're removing a walkway, you can easily accomplish this task with a 2 × 4 and a sledgehammer. Wedge the 2 × 4 under the edge of the concrete and pry it up. Strike the elevated portion of the concrete with the sledgehammer, splitting the concrete into large pieces.

Concrete patios and driveways are more difficult to remove. The easiest method for breaking up these structures involves using a rented jackhammer. You can also use a sledgehammer to break apart the concrete, but it's a time-consuming and labor-intensive job. When renting a jackhammer, ask the rental supplier to demonstrate the proper techniques for using the tool. Wear protective clothing, safety glasses and ear protection while operating a jackhammer.

BRICK & STONE

To remove dry- or sand-set brick and stone, all you'll need is a crowbar and some patience. On pathways and patios, simply pry up the bricks or stones. If you're using a crowbar to dismantle a dry-laid stone wall, start at the top of the wall and work down, carefully prying out each stone. If you're planning to reuse the material, discard any pieces that are crumbling or cracked.

To remove mortared walkways and patios, use either a jackhammer or a sledgehammer, following the same methods described above for removing concrete. This is, of course, very hard work, and you may want to enlist volunteers or hire helpers.

An easy way to demolish a mortared wall is to knock it over with a front-end loader. If you aren't comfortable operating such an intimidating piece of equipment, hire a contractor for the job. If that's not practical, use a sledgehammer and a wedge to break off sections of the wall. Starting at the top, force the wedge into a crack or joint, then strike it with the sledgehammer. When you reach the bottom of the wall, bury the foundation.

A. Mason's hammer
B. Sledgehammer
C. Wedge
D. Crowbar

Using a jackhammer is the easiest method for demolishing concrete patios and driveways.

Pry up the edge of a walkway with a 2 × 4, then use a sledge-hammer to break the concrete into manageable pieces.

125

Shrub & Tree Removal

Removing existing shrubs and trees is often a necessary part of the shaping process. Many times, shrubs and trees need to be removed to make way for new landscape features. It's also common to remove diseased or dying specimens to improve the appearance of the landscape.

Healthy shrubs and young trees (less than four years old) can sometimes be dug up and transplanted to another area of your yard. However, some species don't react well to being moved. Before you attempt to transplant a shrub or tree, check with your local nursery or extension service to make sure that moving the plant won't hinder its growth.

TOOLS & MATERIALS

- Basic tools (page 120)
- Hardhat
- Safety glasses
- Ear protection
- Bow saw
- Chain saw
- Wedge

HOW TO REMOVE SHRUBS & YOUNG TREES

If you're going to transplant a shrub or young tree, it's best to dig it up in the early spring when the plant is dormant. In order for the transplant to be successful, keep as much of the root ball intact as possible. Dig around the base of the tree, making a hole roughly the same diameter as the span of the branches. If the plant has a shallow root system, dig to a depth of 12"; plants with deeper roots require a depth of 18" to 24". To plant a transplanted shrub or tree, see the information on planting in "Hedges" (page 170) and "Trees" (page 172).

The simplest method for removing a shrub or young tree is to dig it up, using the same technique you'd use for transplanting. You can also cut it off at the base of the trunk, then dig up the stump.

HOW TO REMOVE MATURE TREES

If you need to remove a mature tree from your yard, one option is to have a tree contractor cut it down. If the tree is very large and located close to a house or building, this is the only good option. But if you're confident in your ability to use a chain saw and the

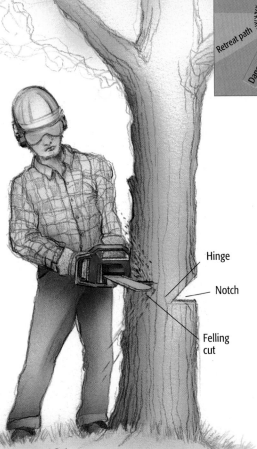

Hinge

Notch

Felling cut

A. *Use a bow saw to remove all of the limbs below head-level.*

B. *Remove a notch, then make a felling cut, leaving a 3" hinge in the center.*

tree has plenty of clearance space, you can save money by removing it yourself.

The first step in cutting down a tree is determining where you want it to fall. This area, called the *felling path*, should be roughly twice as long as the height of the tree and clear of any obstacles. You'll also need to plan two *retreat paths*, located diagonally away from the felling path. The retreat paths allow you to run away from the tree if it begins to fall in the wrong direction.

To guide the tree along the felling path, a series of cuts are made in the trunk. The first cut, called the *notch*, is made by removing a triangle-shaped section of the trunk on the side of the tree facing the felling path. A *felling cut* is then made on the opposite side, forming a wide *hinge* that guides the fall of the tree.

The following sequence outlines the steps professionals follow to fell a tree and cut it into sections. Before you begin, put on protective clothing, gloves, safety glasses, ear protection and a hard hat.

Step A: Remove Low Branches
Use a bow saw to remove any branches below head-level. Starting from the bottom of each branch, make a shallow cut up toward the center, then cut down from the top until the branch breaks away.

Step B: Make the Notch & Felling Cut
1. Using the chain saw, cut at a 45° angle, about ⅓ of the way into the trunk. **Do not cut all the way to the center of the trunk.** Complete the notch by making a straight cut about 6" below the first cut. Remove the triangle-shaped wedge.

2. On the opposite side of the trunk, make the felling cut. Using the chain saw, make a straight cut about 2" above the base of the notch, leaving a 3" hinge at the center. **Do not saw completely through the trunk.**

Step C: Insert the Wedge & Drop the Tree
Immediately after making the felling cut, insert a wedge in the cut. (The wedge prevents the tree from becoming unstable.) Secure the wedge by tapping it into place with a maul. Make sure that the area surrounding the tree is clear. Push the tree toward the felling path, and run along the retreat path.

Step D: Remove the Remaining Branches
Standing on the opposite side of the trunk from the branch, adopt an open, balanced stance. Hold the chain saw close to you and saw down until the branch separates from the tree.

Step E: Cut the Trunk into Sections
Stand to one side of the trunk and cut down ⅔ of the way through the trunk. Roll the trunk onto its side. Finish the cut from the top, cutting down until the section breaks away.

C. *Insert a wedge into the cut. Push on the tree to start its fall, then move out of the way.*

D. *Remove each branch by cutting from the top, using a chain saw or bow saw.*

E. *To cut the trunk into sections, saw ⅔ of the way into the trunk. Roll the trunk over, then complete the cut from the top.*

Grading

Unless your yard has the proper grade, or slope, rain-water can flow toward the foundation of your house—and possibly into your basement. An improper grade can also cause water to collect in low-lying areas, creating boggy spots where you'll have trouble growing grass and other plants. When graded correctly, your yard should have a gradual slope away from the house of about ¾" per horizontal foot.

Although the initial grading of a yard is usually done by a landscape contractor, you can do the work yourself to save money. The job is a bit time-consuming, but it isn't difficult. Typically, creating a grade at this stage involves spreading a 4" to 6" layer of topsoil over the yard, then distributing and smoothing it to slope away from the house.

Established landscapes often require regrading, especially if the house has settled. If you find signs of basement moisture problems or puddle-prone areas in the yard, you need to correct the slope. The measuring and grading techniques featured here will help you remove and distribute soil as needed.

TOOLS & MATERIALS

- Basic tools (page 120)
- Line level
- Grading rake
- Stakes
- String
- Tape
- Topsoil

HOW TO MEASURE & ESTABLISH A GRADE

Step A: Measure the Slope

1. Drive a pair of stakes into the soil, one at the base of the foundation, and another at least 8 ft. out into the yard along a straight line from the first stake.
2. Attach a string fitted with a line level to the stakes and adjust the string until it's level. Measure and flag the string with tape at 1-ft. intervals.

8' Level line

Measure at 1' intervals

A. To check the slope, level the string with a line level, then measure down at 1-ft. intervals.

3. Measure down from the string at the tape flags, recording your measurements as you work. Use these measurements as guidelines for adding or removing soil to create a correct grade.

Step B: Add & Distribute Soil

1. Starting at the base of the house, add soil to low areas until they reach the desired height.

2. Using a garden rake, evenly distribute the soil over a small area. Measure down from the 1-ft. markings as you work to make sure that you are creating a ¾" per 1-ft. pitch as you work.

3. Add and remove soil as needed, working away from the house until soil is evenly sloped. After you've completed an area, repeat steps A and B to grade the next section of your yard.

Step C: Lightly Tamp the Soil

Use a hand tamp to lightly compact the soil. Don't overtamp the soil or it could become too dense to grow a healthy lawn or plants.

Step D: Remove Debris

After all the soil is tamped, use a grading rake to remove any rocks or clumps. Starting at the foundation, pull the rake in a straight line down the slope. Dispose of any rocks or construction debris. Repeat the process, working on one section at a time until the entire area around the house is graded.

VARIATION: CREATING LEVEL AREAS

You may want to create some perfectly level areas for playing lawn sports such as croquet, badminton, volleyball and lawn bowling. Level areas also make safe play surfaces for small children and a good base for play structures.

Outline the perimeter of the area with evenly placed stakes. Extend a string fitted with a line level between a pair of stakes and adjust the string until it's level. At 2-ft. intervals, measure down from the marked areas of the string to the ground. Add and remove topsoil as necessary, distributing it with a garden rake until the surface under the string is level. Repeat the process until the entire area is leveled.

B. *Beginning at the foundation, use a garden rake to distribute soil, checking and adjusting the slope as you work.*

C. *Use a hand tamp to lightly compact the soil in the graded area.*

D. *Pull a grading rake in a straight line down the slope to remove rocks, clumps and debris.*

Raised Garden Beds

Raised beds are attractive, functional and easy to build and maintain. Especially if your yard has poor soil, raised beds are an ideal way to add ornamental or vegetable gardens to your outdoor home. If you build a raised bed properly, fill it with high-quality topsoil and water it frequently, growing healthy plants is practically foolproof. Because these gardens are elevated, they're perfect for children as well as disabled or older family members.

In addition to their functional appeal, raised beds can serve as strong design features. They provide excellent opportunities to repeat materials used in other landscape elements. You can build raised beds from a variety of materials, including brick, cut stone, interlocking block and landscape timbers.

As you plan your raised bed, think about the types of plants you want to grow and the amount of sunlight they need. Vegetables and most flowers need 6 to 8 hours of full sun during the day. If your yard doesn't have that much sun, plant it with woodland and other shade-loving plants.

Our version of a raised bed is 5 ft. × 3 ft., 10½" deep. To build this bed, you simply stack 4 × 4 cedar timbers flush on top of one another in three layers, and secure them with galvanized nails. Then you drill holes into the frame to provide drainage, which helps keep the plants healthy. Once the frame is complete, you line the bed and frame with landscape fabric to prevent weed growth and keep dirt from clogging the drainage holes. If you're planting shrubs or vegetables in your raised bed, put landscape fabric on the sides only, since these plants typically have deeper root growth than flowers.

TOOLS & MATERIALS

- Basic tools (page 120)
- Reciprocating saw
- Stakes and string
- 8-ft. 4 × 4 timbers (6)
- 6" galvanized nails
- Landscape fabric
- Galvanized roofing nails
- Topsoil
- Plantings
- Mulch
- Wood sealer protectant

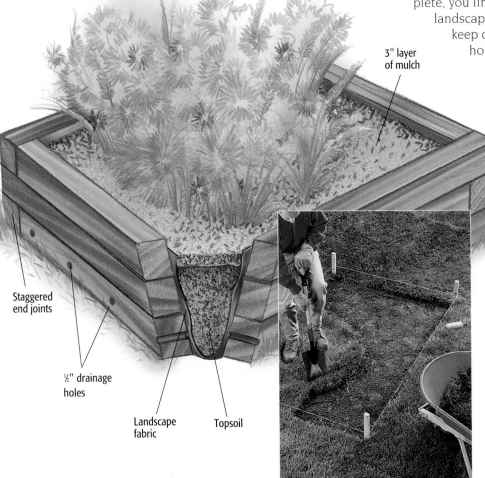

3" layer of mulch

Staggered end joints

½" drainage holes

Landscape fabric

Topsoil

A. *Use a shovel to remove the grass inside the outline, then dig a trench for the first row of timbers.*

B. *Level timbers in trench, then lay the next layer, staggering the joints. Drill holes and drive nails through the holes.*

HOW TO BUILD A RAISED BED

Step A: Prepare the Site

1. Outline a 5-ft. × 3-ft. area with stakes and string to mark the location of the bed. Use a shovel to remove all of the grass or weeds inside the area.

2. Dig a flat, 2"-deep, 4"-wide trench around the perimeter of the area, just inside the stakes.

Step B: Build & Level the Base

1. Measure and mark one 54" piece and one 30" piece on each 4 × 4. Hold each timber steady on sawhorses while you cut it, using a reciprocating saw.

2. Coat each timber with a wood sealer/protectant. Let the sealer dry completely.

3. Lay the first row of the timbers in the trench. Position a level diagonally across a corner, then add or remove soil to level it. Repeat with remaining corners.

Step C: Complete the Raised Bed

1. Set the second layer of timbers in place, staggering the joints with the joint pattern in the first layer.

2. Drill ³⁄₁₆" pilot holes near the ends of the timbers; then drive in the 6" galvanized nails.

3. Lay the third row of timbers, repeating the pattern of the first row to stagger the joints.

4. Drill pilot holes through the third layer, offsetting them to avoid hitting the underlying nails. Drive the nails through the pilot holes.

5. Drill ½" drainage holes, spaced every 2 ft., horizontally through the bottom layer of timbers.

6. Line the bed with strips of landscape fabric, overlapping the strips by 6".

7. Drive galvanized roofing nails through the fabric, attaching it to the timbers.

Step D: Fill with Soil & Plants

1. Fill the bed with topsoil to within 4" of the top. Tamp the soil lightly with a shovel.

2. Add plants, loosening their root balls before planting. Apply a 3" layer of mulch, and water the plants.

C. *Place the third layer of landscape timbers over the second, staggering the joints. Secure the timbers in place with nails. Drill ½" drainage holes through the bottom row of the timbers. Line the bed with landscape fabric.*

D. *Fill the bed with topsoil, then plant your garden. Apply a 3" layer of mulch and water the garden.*

131

Garden Steps

If you have a steep slope in a high-traffic area of your yard, adding garden steps makes the slope safer and more manageable. Or, if your yard has a long, continuous hill, you can add several sets of steps to get the same results. In addition to making your landscape more accessible, garden steps make your yard more attractive by creating visual interest.

Garden steps are built into an excavated portion of a slope or hill, flush with the surrounding ground. You can build steps from almost any hardscape mate-rial: stone, brick, concrete, wood or even interlocking block. Our version uses two materials: wood and concrete. The design is simple—the steps are formed by a series of wood frames made from 5 × 6 landscape timbers. The frames are stacked on top of one another, following the run of the slope. After the frames are set in place, they're filled with concrete and given a finished texture.

The exact dimensions of the frames you build will depend on the height of your slope, the size of the timbers you're using and how wide and deep the steps need to be. Gradual slopes are best suited to a small number of broad steps. Steeper slopes require a larger number of narrower steps. To keep the stairs easy to use, the risers should be no more than 6" high, and the depth of the frame, also called the *tread depth*, should be at least 11".

PLANNING YOUR STEPS

Drive a tall stake into the ground at the bottom of the slope and adjust it until it's plumb. Then drive a shorter stake at the top of the slope. Position a straight 2 × 4 against the stakes, with one end touching the ground next to the top stake. Adjust the 2 × 4 so it's level, then attach it to the stakes with screws (see diagram, left). Measure from the ground to the bottom of the 2 × 4 to find the total vertical rise of the stairway. Divide the total rise by the actual thickness of the timbers to find the

TOOLS & MATERIALS

- Basic tools (page 120)
- Hand tamp
- Reciprocating saw
- Staple gun
- Wood/ concrete float

- Masonry trowel
- Masonry edging tool
- Stiff-bristled brush
- Stakes and string
- 5 × 6 landscape timbers

- 12" spikes
- 3/4" galvanized pipe
- Plastic sheeting
- Compactible gravel
- Concrete mix

5 × 6 landscape timbers

Compactible gravel

Concrete

A. *Arrange the timbers to form the step frame and end nail them together, using 12" spikes.*

number of steps required. Round off fractions to the nearest full number.

Measure along the 2 × 4, between the stakes, to find the total horizontal span. Divide the span by the number of steps to find the tread depth. If the tread depth comes out to less than 11", revise the step layout to extend it.

HOW TO BUILD GARDEN STEPS

Step A: Build the Frames

Use a reciprocating saw to cut timbers, then assemble the step frames with 12" spikes. In our design, the front timber runs the full width of the step; while the back timber is 10" shorter than the front and fits between the side timbers.

Step B: Outline the Step Run

1. Mark the sides of the site with stakes and string. Position the stakes at the front edge of the bottom step and the back edge of the top step.
2. Outline the excavation for the first step at the base of the slope, using stakes and string. Remember that the excavation will be larger than the overall tread depth, since the back timber in the frame will be covered by the front timber of the next step.

Step C: Excavate & Install the First Frame

1. Excavate the area for the first frame, creating a flat bed with a very slight forward slope, dropping about ⅛" from back to front. The front of the excavation should be no more than 2" deep. Tamp the soil down

TIP: PLANNING YOUR GARDEN STEPS

To simplify the building process, take all necessary measurements, then make a sketch of the site. Indicate the rise, tread depth and width of each step. Remember that actual timber dimensions may vary from the nominal measurements.

firmly, using a hand tamp.

2. Set the timber frame into the excavation. Use a level to make sure that the front and back timbers are level, and that the frame slopes slightly forward.
3. Using a spade bit, drill two 1" guide holes in the front timber and the back timber, 1 ft. from the ends. Anchor the steps to the ground by driving a 2½-ft. length of ¾" pipe through each guide hole until the pipe is flush with the timber.

Step D: Add the Second Frame

1. Excavate for the next step, making sure the bottom of the excavation is even with the top edge of the frame you installed for the first step.

B. *Outline the area for the steps with stakes and string, then measure the height of the slope.*

C. *Excavate the area for the first step, and install the first step frame.*

D. *Excavate the area for the next step, and assemble the frame. Stake the second frame to the first with 12" spikes.*

Garden Steps (cont.)

VARIATION: BRICK-FILLED STEPS

If pavers are used elsewhere in your landscape, you may prefer to repeat that element by filling your wood step frames with sand-set pavers. Other variations you can try are shown on the opposite page.

2. Position the second step frame in the excavation, lining up the front of the frame directly over the rear timber of the first frame.

3. Nail the first frame to the second with three 12" spikes. Drill guide holes and drive two pipes through the back timber to anchor the second frame in place.

Step E: Place the Remaining Frames

1. Excavate and install the remaining steps in the run. The back of the last step should be flush with the ground at the top of the slope.

2. Staple plastic over the timbers to protect them while the concrete is being poured. Cut away the plastic from the frame openings.

3. Pour a 2" layer of compactible gravel into each frame, and use a scrap 2 × 4 to smooth it out.

Step F: Fill the Steps with Concrete

1. Mix concrete and shovel it into the bottom frame, flush with the top of the timbers. Work the concrete lightly with a garden rake to help remove air bubbles, but don't overwork it.

2. Screed the concrete smooth by dragging a 2 × 4 across the top of the frame. If necessary, add concrete to the low areas and screed the surface again until it is smooth and free of low spots.

3. Use an edging tool to smooth the cracks between the concrete and the timbers.

4. Pour concrete into remaining steps, screeding and edging each step before moving on to the next.

Step G: Finish the Surface & Cure the Concrete

1. While the concrete is still wet, create a textured, nonskid surface by drawing a clean, stiff-bristled broom across its surface. Brush each surface only one time, and avoid overlapping brush marks.

2. Remove the plastic from around the timbers.

3. When the concrete has hardened, mist it with water, cover it with plastic, and let it cure for one week.

4. After the concrete has cured, remove the plastic.

E. *Cover the completed framework with plastic. Pour and smooth a 2" layer of compactible gravel in each frame.*

F. *Shovel concrete into the first frame, then work it with a garden rake to remove air bubbles.*

G. *Texture the surface of the concrete by drawing a stiff-bristled broom across it in one sweeping motion.*

VARIATION: GARDEN STEPS

These wood-and-paver steps complement the colorful border that surrounds them.

These curving wood steps echo the informal tone of the rest of the landscape.

These attractive steps illustrate how effectively materials such as cement and stone can be combined.

These stone steps suit the rustic site perfectly.

The formality of these brick steps contrasts nicely with the riot of flowers.

Retaining Wall

Retaining walls are often used to manage steep slopes in a landscape. They not only prevent erosion, but also create flat space for a garden bed, patio or a hedge. Retaining walls are not limited to sloped yards, however. They can also be used to add the illusion of slope to a flat yard. After these decorative retaining walls are constructed, the area behind the wall is backfilled with soil for a planting area.

Interlocking block is the easiest material to work with when constructing retaining walls. The biggest advantage of interlocking block is that it doesn't require mortar. Blocks are available in many styles and colors that will blend with or provide an accent to your landscape. Some of these products have a natural rock finish that resembles the texture of cut stone, which adds a distinctive touch to a wall.

Although the wall itself does not require any type of fixative, the coordinating capstones are held securely in place by construction-grade adhesive. We've used coordinating capstones for this project, but you could also use mortared natural stone, which creates a pleasing contrast.

Limit the height of retaining walls to 4 ft. Taller walls are subject to thousands of pounds of pressure from the weight of the soil and water. They require special building techniques and permits, and are best constructed by professionals. If your slope is greater than 4 ft., build a series of terraced walls over the course of the slope, instead of a single, tall wall.

TOOLS & MATERIALS

- Basic tools (page 120)
- Rented plate compactor
- Stakes
- String
- Line level
- Landscape fabric
- Compactible gravel
- Interlocking block
- Perforated drain tile
- Gravel
- Hand tamp
- Construction-grade adhesive
- Capstones
- Caulk gun

HOW TO BUILD A RETAINING WALL

Step A: Excavate the Site

1. Excavate the slope to create a level area for the retaining wall. Allow at least 12" of space for the gravel backfill between the back of the wall and the hillside.
2. Use stakes to mark the front edge of the wall at the ends, and at any corners or curves. Connect the stakes with string, and use a line level to check the string, adjusting until it's level.

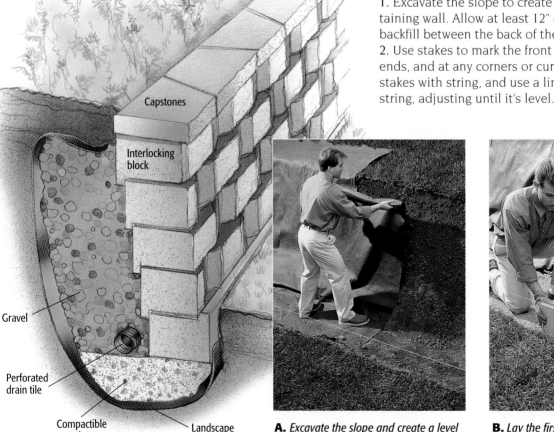

Capstones

Interlocking block

Gravel

Perforated drain tile

Compactible gravel

Landscape fabric

A. *Excavate the slope and create a level trench at the base. Line the excavation with strips of landscape fabric.*

B. *Lay the first row of interlocking block over the compacted gravel base in the trench, checking with a level as you work.*

3. Dig a trench for the first row of block. Make the trench 8" deeper than the thickness of the block. Measure down from the string as you work to make sure the trench remains level.

4. Line the excavated area with strips of landscape fabric cut 3 ft. longer than the planned height of the wall. Overlap the strips by at least 6".

Step B: Build a Base & Lay the First Row

1. Spread a 6" layer of compactible gravel into the trench. Compact the gravel, using a plate compactor.

2. Lay the first row of blocks into the trench, aligning the front edges with the string. If you're using flanged blocks, install the first row of blocks upside down and backward in the trench.

3. Check the blocks frequently with a level, and adjust them by adding or removing gravel.

Step C: Install Drain Tile & Add Rows

1. Lay the second row of blocks according to the manufacturer's instructions, making sure the joints are staggered with the course below. As you work, check to make sure the blocks are level.

2. Add 1" to 2" of gravel, as needed, to create a slight downward pitch as the drain tile runs toward the outlet.

3. Place perforated drain tile on top of the gravel, about 6" behind the blocks, with the perforations facing down. Make sure that at least one end of the pipe is unobstructed so runoff water can escape.

4. Lay the additional rows until the wall is about 18" high, offsetting vertical joints in successive rows.

TIP: CREATING HALF-BLOCKS

Half-blocks are often needed for making corners, and to ensure that vertical joints between blocks are staggered between rows. To make a half-block, score a full block with a circular saw outfitted with a masonry blade, then break the blocks along the scored line with a maul and chisel.

5. Fill behind the wall with coarse gravel, and pack it down with the hand tamp.

Step D: Lay the Remaining Rows & Backfill

1. Lay the remaining rows of block, except the cap row, backfilling with gravel and packing it down with a hand tamp as you work.

2. Fold the landscape fabric down over the gravel backfill. Add a thin layer of topsoil over the landscape fabric, then lightly pack down the soil, using the hand tamp.

3. Fold any excess landscape fabric back over the tamped soil.

Step E: Add the Capstones

1. Apply construction adhesive to the top blocks. Lay the capstones in place.

2. Use topsoil to fill in behind the wall and to fill in the trench at the base of the wall.

3. Add sod or other plants, as desired, above and below the wall.

C. *Lay a section of perforated drain tile behind the wall over the gravel, then lay the remaining rows of blocks.*

D. *Fold the excess landscape fabric over the gravel, then cover it with a layer of soil. Compress the soil with a hand tamp.*

E. *Apply adhesive along the top blocks, then lay the capstones so the joints are staggered with those below.*

Berm

Without imaginative treatment, flat yards can be short on privacy as well as style or character. Creating a *berm*, a built-up planting area with sloped sides, resolves several issues common to flat yards. A berm screens out undesirable views, adds interesting contours and even absorbs some of the noise from passing traffic.

Berms can be functional, but they can also serve strictly as ornamental features. An ornamental berm acts as a focal point, adding interest and color to your lawn. In colder climates, a berm planted

expressly for winter beauty is an especially welcomed addition to a snow-covered landscape. In warmer climates, they can be planted with specimen trees that change with the seasons. Berms for desert climates often showcase a variety of ground cover and cacti.

Whether you're creating a functional or an ornamental berm, keep in mind that the most attractive examples have gentle slopes and irregular shapes that accent the surrounding yard. If possible, avoid creating a steep or angular berm—these tend to look awkward, and may even erode over time. If you're planning to construct a particularly high or wide berm, carefully position it so that water drains efficiently. Avoid building a berm around an existing tree. Arborists caution that covering a tree's roots with more than 4" of topsoil can "smother" and eventually kill a tree.

Since building a berm involves creating an elevated area, you'll undoubtedly need to add soil. Before using soil from another area of the yard, collect samples and have a soil test conducted to make sure the soil is capable of supporting trees and plants. You may be better off purchasing high-grade topsoil from a soil contractor and having it delivered.

TOOLS & MATERIALS

- Basic tools (page 120)
- Flexible plastic edging
- Stakes
- Hand tamp
- Plantings
- Mulch

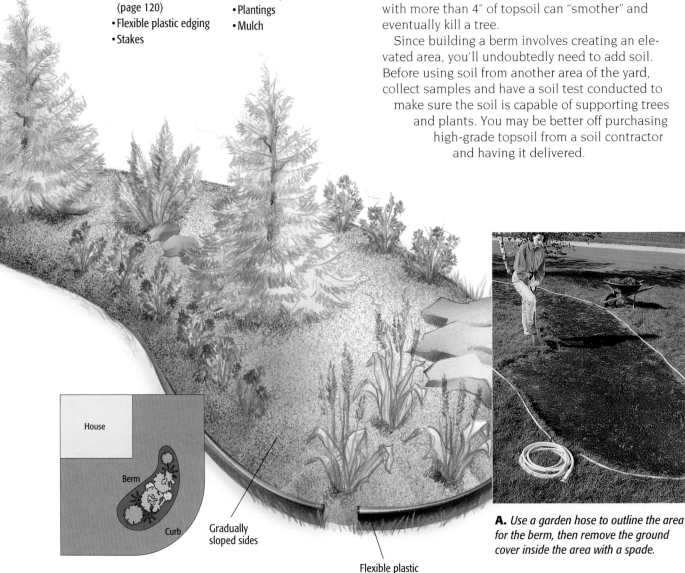

House

Berm

Curb

Gradually sloped sides

Flexible plastic edging

A. *Use a garden hose to outline the area for the berm, then remove the ground cover inside the area with a spade.*

HOW TO CREATE A BERM

Step A: Prepare the Site

Using a hose or rope, create an outline for the planned berm. Using a spade, remove all grass or ground cover growing inside the outline. If the berm is large, you may want to use a sod cutter.

Step B: Install Plastic Edging

With a trenching spade, dig a trench around the perimeter of the berm area, just wide enough to install the flexible plastic edging. To hold the edging in place, use a maul to drive stakes through the bottom rim of the edging.

Step C: Add the Soil & Shape the Berm

1. Fill the outlined area with topsoil. Using a garden rake, distribute the soil so that the berm is 18" to 24" tall at the highest point. When all the necessary soil is added, grade the sides into a gradual slope.

2. Using a hand tamp, compact the entire surface of the berm, then water the soil to further compress it.

Step D: Install Plants & Add Mulch

1. Plant trees, shrubs or other plants in the berm, using the planting techniques shown in "Trees" (page 172) and "Hedges" (page 170).

2. Apply a 2" to 3" layer of mulch over the surface of the berm to prevent weeds and retain moisture.

VARIATION: EDGING MATERIALS

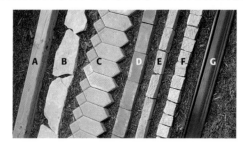

A variety of edging materials is available. Look for ways to repeat existing materials in your landscape. Here are a few commonly used options:

A. Cut timbers can be used as edging on straight garden beds.

B. Flagstones are relatively inexpensive. Their rough texture works well in informal, country or cottage-style landscapes.

C. Geometric pavers make an attractive, durable edging.

D. Bricks are a traditional material used in formal-looking landscapes. They can be arranged end to end, side by side, or even upright for a slightly raised edging.

E. Concrete rubble scavenged from demolition sites can be laid broken side up to make an inexpensive, textured edging.

F. Cut stones (called ashlars) are a premium building material that lends a unique, tailored look to berms.

G. Plastic landscape edging can be purchased at landscape and gardening centers.

B. *Place the edging in the trench along the perimeter of the berm, then drive edging stakes through the bottom lip.*

C. *Fill the area with soil, then grade it into a gradual slope with a garden rake. Use a hand tamp to compress the soil.*

D. *Arrange the plantings on the surface, then plant them in the berm. Apply 2" to 3" layer of mulch over the entire surface.*

Drainage Swale

If your yard has areas where rainwater collects and creates boggy spots or has slopes that send runoff water into unwanted places, you need to improve or re-direct its drainage. You can fill small low-lying areas by top-dressing them with black soil, but in large areas, the best solution is to create a swale.

A swale is a shallow ditch that carries water away from the yard to a designated collection area, usually a gutter, sewer catch bin, stream or lake. Some communities have restrictions regarding redirecting

runoff water, so contact your city or county inspector's office to discuss your plans before you begin. This is especially important if you're planning a swale that empties into a natural water source, such as a stream, pond or lake.

If you're building a swale between your house and a neighboring yard, talk to your neighbor about the project before you begin. If drainage is a problem in their yard as well, they may be willing to share the expense and the work of the project.

Building a swale is relatively simple, but it involves the labor of digging a trench. We'll show you how to construct the swale using a shovel, but there are rental tools that you might want to use instead. For larger yards or those with very dense soil, renting a trencher is an option worth considering. This machine, which can be adjusted to dig to an approximate depth, makes quick work of loosening the soil. If you decide to use a trencher, you'll still need to use a shovel to create the "V" shape and to smooth the sides of the trench, as pictured below.

Another machine you may want to rent is a sod cutter, which cuts the sod into even strips that can be replaced when the swale is complete. If you plan to

TOOLS & MATERIALS

- Basic tools (page 120)
- Stakes
- Trenching spade
- Sod cutter (optional)

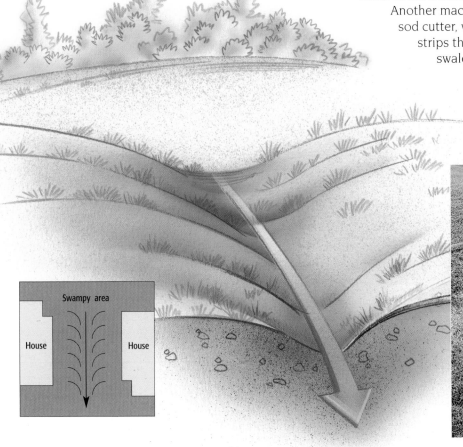

Swampy area

House   House

A. *Mark a route for the swale with stakes, making sure that the outlet for the water is at the lowest point.*

reuse the sod, store it in a shady area and keep it slightly moist until you replant it.

HOW TO MAKE A DRAINAGE SWALE

Step A: Mark the Route

After identifying the problem area, use stakes to mark a swale route that directs water toward an appropriate runoff area. To promote drainage, the outlet of the swale must be lower than any point in the problem area or along the planned route.

Step B: Remove the Sod

Carefully remove the sod from the outlined area. Set it aside and keep it moist, so that it can be replaced when the swale is complete.

Step C: Dig the Trench

Following the marked route, dig a 6"-deep "V"-shaped trench with wide, rounded sides. Shape the trench so it slopes gradually downward toward the outlet, making sure that the bottom and sides of the trench are smooth. Set the topsoil aside for other projects.

Step D: Replace the Sod

Lay the sod back into the trench. Compress it thoroughly, so the roots make contact with the soil and there are no air pockets beneath it. Water the sod and keep it moist for several weeks.

VARIATION: SWALE WITH DRAIN TILE

If you have very dense soil with a high clay content or severe drainage problems, you'll need to lay perforated drain pipe in the trench for the swale. Follow these steps to make a swale with drain tile:

Step A:

Dig a 1-ft.-deep trench, angled downward to the outlet point. Line the trench with landscape fabric. Spread a 2" layer of coarse gravel along the bottom of the swale, then lay perforated drain pipe over the gravel, with the perforations facing down. Cover the pipe with a 5" layer of gravel, then wrap landscape fabric over the top of the gravel.

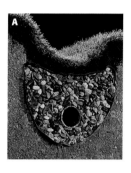

Step B:

Cover the swale with soil and the original or fresh sod. Set a splash block at the outlet under the exposed end of the drain pipe to distribute the runoff water and prevent erosion.

B. *Carefully remove the sod with a spade and set it aside, keeping it moist until you're ready to replace it.*

C. *Dig a 6"-deep trench that slopes to the center, creating a "V" shape. Use the shovel to smooth the sides as you work.*

D. *Replace the sod, compressing it against the soil. Water the sod and keep it moist for several weeks.*

141

Dry Well

A dry well is a simple but clever method for channeling excess water out of low-lying or water-laden areas, such as the ground beneath a gutter downspout. A dry well system typically consists of a buried drain tile running from a catch basin positioned at the problem spot to a collection container some distance away.

A dry well system is easy to install and surprisingly inexpensive. In the project shown here, a perforated plastic drain tile carries water from a catch basin to a dry well fashioned from a plastic trash can, which has been punctured, then filled with stone rubble. The runoff water percolates into the soil as it makes its way along the drain pipe and through the dry well.

HOW TO INSTALL A DRY WELL
Step A: Dig the Trench
1. Using stakes, mark a path running from the problem area to the location of the dry well. Carefully remove a 12" strip of sod and set it aside, keeping it moist so you can reuse it later. Dig a trench, 10" wide and 14" deep, along the staked path.

TOOLS & MATERIALS

- Basic tools (page 120)
- Line level
- Jig saw
- Stakes

- String
- Landscape fabric
- Gravel
- Plastic trash can

- Large stones
- Catch basin
- Perforated drain tile

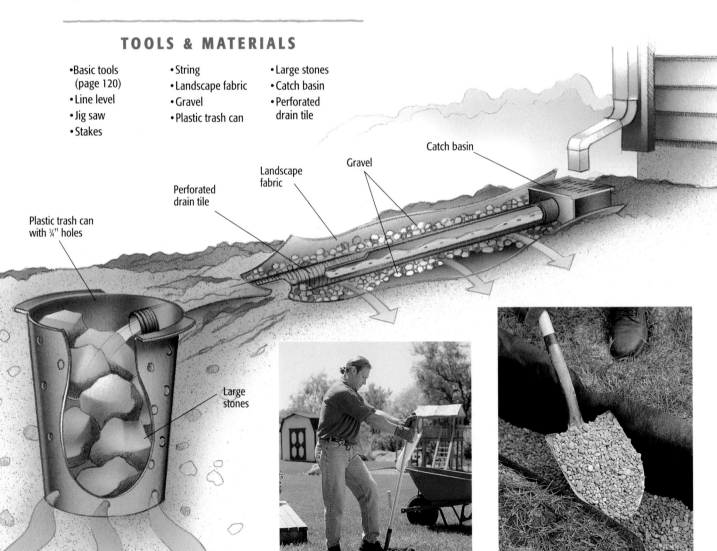

Catch basin

Gravel

Landscape fabric

Perforated drain tile

Plastic trash can with ¼" holes

Large stones

A. *Dig a 10"-wide, 14"-deep trench along the planned route from the catch basin to the dry well.*

B. *Line the trench with landscape fabric, then lay a 1" layer of gravel along the bottom of the trench.*

2. Slope the trench slightly toward the dry well, about 2" for every 8 ft., to ensure that water flows easily along the drain tile. To check the slope, place a stake at each end of the trench, then tie a string between the stakes. Use a line level to level the string, then measure down from it at 2-ft. intervals. Add or remove soil as needed to adjust the slope of the trench.

3. Remove the sod in a circle, 4" wider than the dry well container, then dig a hole at least 4" deeper than the container's height.

Step B: Lay the Drain Tile

1. Line the trench and hole with landscape fabric, folding the excess fabric back over each side of the trench and around the edges of the hole.

2. Lay a 1" layer of gravel along the bottom of the trench, then lay the drain tile in place, with the perforations facing down.

Step C: Create the Dry Well

1. About 3" from the top, trace the outline of the drain tile onto the side of the trash can, then use a jig saw to cut a hole. Using a power drill and a ¾" bit, drill drainage holes through the sides and bottom of the trash can, one hole every 4" to 6".

2. Place the trash can in the hole, positioning it so the large hole faces the trench. Insert the drain tile, perforated side down, with at least 2" of the tile

extending inside the trash can.

3. Fill the trash can with large stones. Arrange the top layer of stones so they are flat in the container.

4. Fold the landscape fabric over the rocks, then fill the hole with soil.

Step D: Connect the Catch Basin

At the other end of the trench, opposite the dry well, connect the catch basin to the drain tile. Position the catch basin so excess water will flow directly into it.

Step E: Refill the Trench

1. Fill the trench with gravel until the drain tile is covered by 1" of gravel. Fold the edges of the landscape cloth down over the gravel-covered drain tile.

2. Fill the trench with the soil you removed earlier.

3. Replace the sod, lightly tamp it with the back of a shovel, then water it thoroughly.

C. *Prepare the dry well container, then place it in the excavation, insert the drain tile and fill it with large rocks.*

D. *Attach a catch basin to the drain tile opening, and position the basin to collect the excess water in the problem area.*

E. *Cover the drain tile with 1" of gravel, then backfill the trench with soil and fold the landscape fabric over it.*

143

Utilities

Inside our homes, utilities make our lives easier and more comfortable. Similarly, plumbing and electricity can make outdoor rooms more functional and enjoyable. The idea of extending electricity and plumbing outdoors may seem daunting at first, but it's surprisingly simple.

Working with your existing electrical wiring, you can easily add a floodlight onto your house or garage and install an attractive low-voltage lighting system. Armed with a few basic wiring and plumbing techniques, you can go a step further and install new standard electrical or plumbing lines virtually anywhere in your yard.

With these new utility lines, you can create an outlet for powering electric appliances and tools, install a garden spigot for washing tools and even add an in-ground sprinkler system to simplify watering chores. Although adding a sprinkler system may sound difficult, there are a number of affordable do-it-yourself products available. If you install a system with an electric timer, you can program your sprinkler system to water your yard at any time of day, for any amount of time you wish.

In addition to being convenient, utilities also make your yard safer. Carefully placed GFCI receptacles eliminate the need to stretch extension cords across the lawn and protect against power surges and accidental shock. Garden spigots bring water within easy reach of planting beds and cleanup areas. Floodlights and landscape lighting increase security and help people navigate pathways and stairs at night.

The demonstrations in this chapter show you basic techniques for tapping into your home's plumbing and electrical systems and extending water and voltage lines into any area of your yard. If you aren't familiar with basic plumbing and wiring techniques, you may want to consult how-to books on these subjects, many of which are available at home centers, book stores and libraries.

One word of caution: always have underground utility lines marked before you begin projects that involve digging.

IN THIS CHAPTER

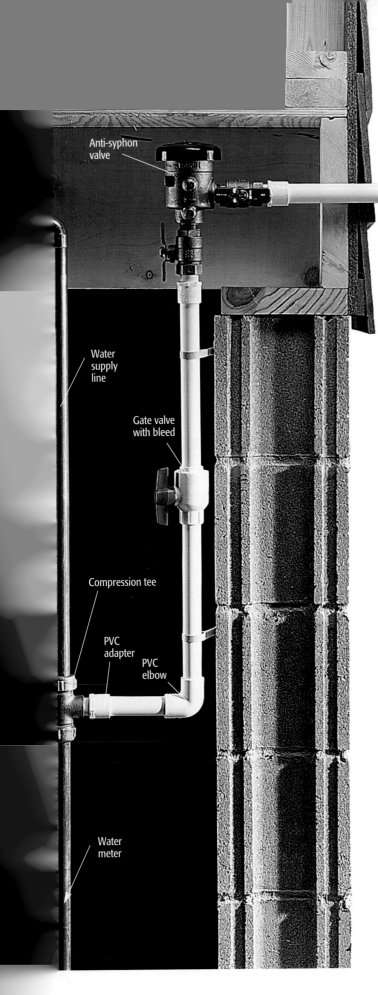

Anti-syphon valve

Water supply line

Gate valve with bleed

Compression tee

PVC adapter

PVC elbow

Water meter

Sprinkler System Basics

The most efficient way to water your yard is with an underground sprinkler system. Unlike hand watering or the hose-and-sprinkler method, sprinkler systems distribute water evenly and accurately, conserving water in the process.

Home supply centers and irrigation system catalogs sell affordable, high-quality kits and sprinkler system parts designed for do-it-yourself installation. Most of the DIY sprinkler systems now available have similar components and operate in much the same way. The following information will help you design and plan a customized sprinkler system for your yard.

A basic sprinkler system is connected to your home's water line by a *connecting line* that distributes water to a grouping of sprinkler control valves, called a *valve manifold*. The control valves are operated either manually or by a timer; each control valve supplies water to a grouping of *sprinkler heads*, called a circuit. The sprinkler heads are attached to the sprinkler line by flexible piping.

DETERMINING GPM

The first thing you'll need to do is determine your water system's GPM (gallons per minute) measurement. Your water system's GPM will determine the size pipe you'll need and the number of sprinkler heads that can be assigned to a single circuit.

To assess your water system's GPM, measure how long it takes to fill a one-gallon bucket from your outside faucet. Make sure there is no water running elsewhere, inside or outside the house, then turn the faucet on full force. To calculate the GPM, divide 60 seconds by the amount of time it takes to fill the bucket. For example, if it takes 6 seconds to fill the one-gallon bucket, the GPM is 60/6 seconds, or 10 GPM.

GALLONS-PER-MINUTE (GPM) TABLE

GPM Flow	Control Valve Size	PVC Pipe Size	Flexible PE Pipe Size
0-8	3/4"	3/4"	3/4"
9-12	3/4"	3/4"	1"
13-16	1"	1"	1 1/4"
17-28	1"	1 1/4"	1 1/2"

This cutaway photo illustrates a typical construction for a connecting line installed between the water supply line and the sprinkler system valve manifold.

SELECTING PIPES & CONTROL VALVES

Use the table on page 146 to determine what size valves and piping you'll need to buy, based on your GPM measurement. Select either semirigid PVC or schedule 40 pipe for the connecting line. You can choose either flexible polyethylene (PE) or PVC pipe for the sprinkler circuit piping—which includes the sprinkler line and the pipes to the sprinkler heads.

There are several other factors you'll need to consider when selecting the control valves. Automatic systems use a different style of control valve than manual systems. And Plumbing Code restrictions in your area may require that you use anti-syphon valves that prevent water backflow.

CHOOSING SPRINKLER HEADS

Manufacturers offer a variety of sprinkler heads, each with a different broadcast range and watering pattern. Some styles mount above the ground while others pop up from below the ground.

Each sprinkler head has a GPM measurement. For each circuit, select sprinkler heads with GPM ratings that add up to a total of no more that 75% of your water system's total GPM rating. This will ensure that no damage will occur to either the sprinkler system or your home's water system. So, for example, if your home's GPM measurement is 10, choose sprinkler heads so the total GPM assigned to the circuit does not exceed 7.5.

ASSIGNING THE SPRINKLER HEADS

Draw a map of your yard, and divide the areas that will need watering into squares or rectangles. Begin drawing the locations of the sprinkler heads that will water these areas. To ensure even coverage, position the sprinklers so that their range of coverage overlaps slightly.

MAPPING THE SPRINKLER CIRCUITS

Designate a spot for the control valve manifold, preferably close to an accessible plumbing line. Map the route from your home's water supply line to the control valve manifold.

Group the the sprinkler heads into circuits and draw the piping for each circuit. Draw a line extending from the control valve manifold to each circuit. Add lines branching out from the piping to each sprinkler head in the circuit (diagram, above right). Make sure the total GPM for all sprinkler heads in each circuit doesn't exceed 75% of your water system's GPM.

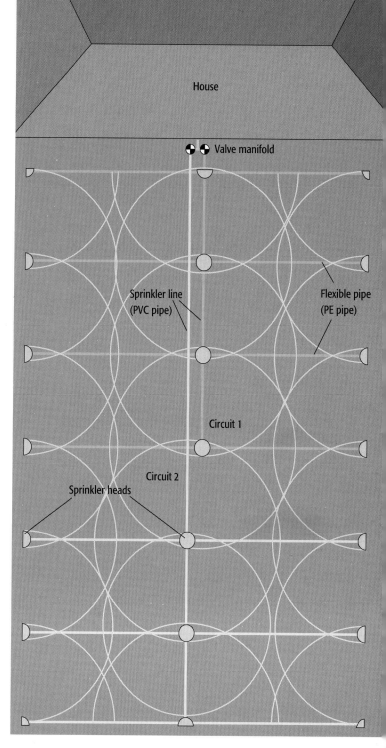

Sprinkler system components, such as these from Rain Bird™, are sold at home improvement centers and by mail order.

Sprinkler System

HOW TO INSTALL A SPRINKLER SYSTEM

Step A: Connect to the Water Supply System

1. Dig a 10"-deep hole for the valve manifold box, as indicated on the map you developed (page 147).
2. Drill a 1"-diameter hole through the wall where you'll be running the pipe from the water supply system to the valve manifold.
3. Turn off the water supply at the water meter, then cut into a cold water supply pipe and install a compression tee fitting.
4. Measure and cut the components to run a cold water line from the tee fitting through the hole you cut in the wall. The exact components will vary, depending on the configuration of your plumbing system, but you'll need several lengths of PVC pipe, PVC elbows, a PVC gate valve with a bleed fitting and a brass vacuum breaker. You'll also need three threaded PVC adapters for the points where plastic pipe is joined to metal.
5. Assemble the branch line by threading the PVC adapters onto the metal components, using solvent glue to join the PVC pipes to the adapters and to any elbows needed to extend the branch line through the hole leading outside the house. Once the branch line is in place, use pipe straps to anchor the new pipes to interior framing members or walls.
6. From outside, attach a PVC elbow and a length of PVC pipe to extend the supply line down the wall. Anchor the pipe to the wall, using pipe straps.
7. Connect a PVC elbow fitting and straight length of pipe to extend the water supply line horizontally into the center of the location for the valve manifold box.

Step B: Make the Manifold & Install the Valve Box

1. Use PVC elbows, tee fittings and pipes to split the water supply line into a manifold that includes one arm for each of the control valves.
2. Connect the sprinkler control valves, following manufacturer's instructions. Some valves use threaded fittings; others are solvent-glued.
3. Test the water line and connections

TOOLS & MATERIALS

- Basic tools, page 120
- Tubing cutter
- Copper compression tee
- Schedule 40 PVC pipe
- PVC elbows
- PVC gate valves with bleed (2)
- Brass vacuum breaker
- Threaded PVC adapters
- PVC solvent glue
- Pipe straps
- Valve boxes (2)
- PVC tee fitting and elbow
- Sprinkler control valves
- Stakes
- Spray paint
- Outdoor grade PE pipe
- Sprinkler heads

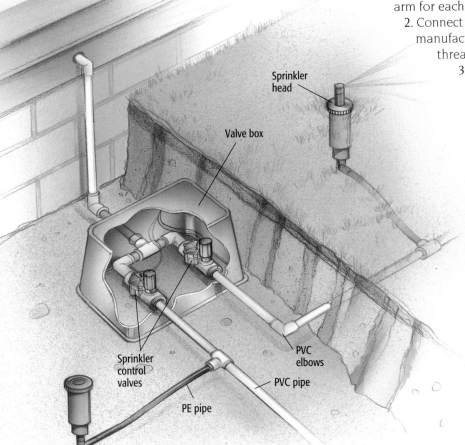

Sprinkler head

Valve box

Sprinkler control valves

PE pipe

PVC pipe

PVC elbows

A. *Tie into the water supply line with a compression tee, then assemble the connecting line that leads to the valves.*

for leaks by closing the control valves, then opening the gate valve and the main water supply valve inside your house. If you discover leaks, turn off the water, drain the system, and make any necessary repairs.

4. Place the valve box over the control valve manifold, pushing it firmly into the ground.

5. If you're installing an automatic system, mount the timer to a wall inside the house or garage, close to a 120-volt receptacle. Run a wire from the timer out to the control valves. Following manufacturer's instructions, connect each of the control valves to the timer.

6. Place the cover back on top of the valve box.

Step C: Lay Out the Circuits

1. Using your map as a reference, mark the locations of the sprinkler heads with stakes.

2. Mark the path for the circuit piping leading from the control valves into the yard, and for the piping leading from the circuit lines to the sprinkler heads.

3. Dig a hole for the second valve box, which will provide system drainage. Locate this box at the lowest point within the system.

4. Dig trenches for the circuit piping, making each trench 8" to 12" deep. The trenches should slope ⅛" per foot toward the house.

TIP:

If an area assigned to a single sprinkler head includes a tree, bush or other obstruction, add sprinkler heads to provide coverage behind it.

5. Dig trenches, 8" to 12" deep, extending between the sprinkler heads and the circuit piping. The trenches should slope ⅛" per foot as they run toward the circuit piping.

Step D: Install the Circuit Piping & Sprinkler Heads

1. Measure and cut the PVC piping for each circuit. Attach the pipe to the control valves and lay it in the trenches. At the trench with the second valve box, install a gate valve with a bleed on the end of the pipe.

2. Measure, cut and lay the flexible PE pipe running from the circuit pipes to each of the sprinkler heads.

3. Attach the flexible PE pipe to the PVC pipe with PVC tee fittings. Using a threaded PVC adapter, attach the PE pipe to the sprinkler head.

4. Assemble all the sprinkler heads for the first circuit. If you're using pop-up sprinklers, temporarily tie them to small stakes.

5. Turn the water supply back on and open the gate valve. Turn on the circuit control valve and check for any leaks. Adjust the sprinkler heads as necessary to provide even coverage.

6. Install and test the remaining circuits. When all of the adjustments are made, complete the installation according to the manufacturer's directions.

7. Refill the trenches, replace the sod, and water it.

B. *Assemble the control valve manifold and attach it to the connecting line. Attach the control valves.*

C. *Mark the route for the circuit piping. At the lowest circuit, dig a pit for a valve box, then finish digging the trench.*

D. *Install PVC tee fittings with adapters to the circuit piping. Attach the flexible PE pipe to the adapters and the sprinklers.*

Garden Spigot

You may already have a hose spigot or two attached to the foundation of your house, but adding one or two spigots to various areas of your outdoor home brings water right to the areas where you typically water plants or clean up garden equipment.

Our version of a garden spigot can be located almost anywhere in your yard. To install it, you'll need to run a branch line off your home's water supply system, through the foundation or exterior wall, and along an underground trench to a hose spigot anchored to a post, which is embedded in a bucket of concrete at the end of the plumbing run.

The project illustrated here uses copper pipe for the above-ground parts of the run, and PE pipe for the buried sections. Your local Plumbing Code may have requirements for the types of pipe you can use, so check it before you begin. Also, if local Plumbing Code requires it, be sure to apply for required permits and arrange for necessary inspections.

TOOLS & MATERIALS

- Basic tools (page 120)
- Spade bit
- Tubing cutter
- Soldering materials
- Copper tee fittings
- ¾" copper pipe
- Brass gate valve with bleed
- Copper elbows
- Brass vacuum breaker

- Stakes
- Valve boxes (2)
- Gravel
- ¾" PE pipe
- Insert couplings
- Stainless steel clamps
- 4-ft. 4 × 4 post
- Spigot
- Pipe straps•
- Concrete

- 2-gallon plastic bucket
- Barbed PVC tee fittings with threaded outlet and plug (2)
- Male-threaded copper adapters (2)
- Female-threaded PE adapters (2)

HOW TO INSTALL A GARDEN SPIGOT

Step A: Connect to the Water Supply System

1. Plan a convenient route from the water supply line to the location you've chosen for the spigot. Drill a 1" hole through the exterior wall, near where you'll be running the pipe from the water supply system to the valve box. Turn off the water at the main supply valve near the water meter.

2. Remove a small section of the cold water pipe and install a tee fitting. Install a straight length of copper pipe, then a gate valve with a bleed fitting.

3. Use straight lengths of pipe and elbow fittings to extend the branch line through the hole in the wall, installing a vacuum breaker at some convenient point along the way.

Step B: Lay Out the Branch Line & Install the Valve Box

1. Outside the house, stake a line marking the path

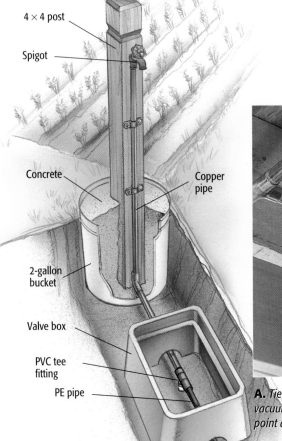

4 × 4 post

Spigot

Concrete

Copper pipe

2-gallon bucket

Valve box

PVC tee fitting

PE pipe

A. *Tie into your water supply, installing a vacuum breaker at some convenient point along the way.*

B. *Extend the branch line through the wall and down into the trench. Install the valve box.*

for the pipe run to the spigot location.

2. Use a trenching spade to remove sod for an 8"- to 12"-wide trench along the marked route. Dig a trench at least 10" deep and sloping toward the house at a rate of $\frac{1}{8}$" per foot.

3. Dig a hole for a valve box, directly below the point where the branch line exits the house.

4. Measure, cut and attach copper pipe and elbows, extending the branch line down to the bottom of the trench and out 12".

5. Install a valve box with the top flush to the ground. Lay a 4" layer of gravel in the bottom of the valve box.

Step C: Run the Supply Line to the Spigot Location

1. Dig a hole at the spigot location, sized to hold a valve box and the bucket. Install the other valve box.

2. Lay $\frac{3}{4}$" PE pipe in the trench, running from the valve box by the house to the valve box at the spigot location. Use couplings and stainless steel clamps when necessary to join two lengths of pipe.

Step D: Install the Spigot

1. Cut a 3-ft. piece of copper pipe and secure it to one side of the 4 × 4 post, using pipe straps. Mount the spigot on the top of the pipe, then attach an elbow to the bottom of the pipe.

2. Using a drill and spade bit, drill a 1" hole in the side of a 2-gallon bucket, 1" above the bottom.

3. Position the post in the bucket, with the pipe facing toward the hole. Measure, cut and attach a length of pipe to the elbow at the bottom of the post, ex-

TIP: WINTERIZING IN COLD CLIMATES

Close the valve for the outdoor supply pipe, then remove the cap on the drain nipple. With the faucet on the outdoor spigot open, attach an air compressor to the valve nipple, then blow water from the system, using no more than 50 psi of air pressure. Remove the plugs from the tee fittings in each valve box, and store them for the winter.

tending the pipe through the hole in the bucket and out into the valve box.

4. Place the bucket and post in the hole, with the pipe extending into the valve box. Fill the bucket with concrete. Use a level to make sure the post is plumb.

Step E: Connect the Supply Line to the Spigot

1. Install a barbed tee fitting with a threaded outlet, opening facing down, to the PE pipe inside the valve box. Cap the threaded opening with a plug.

2. Using male and female threaded adapters, join the copper pipe to the PE pipe.

3. Repeat steps 1 and 2 to join the pipes in the valve box located near the house. Restore the water and test the line for leaks. Make any necessary adjustments, then refill the trenches. Replace the sod, tamp it down with a shovel, and water it thoroughly.

C. *Lay a run of PE pipe along the bottom of the trench, joining sections with stainless steel clamps and insert couplings.*

D. *Attach the copper riser and spigot to the post. Place post in the bucket and fill it with concrete.*

E. *Inside the valve boxes, install a barbed PVC tee fitting with plug to the PE pipe. Join the copper and PE pipe with adapters.*

Garden GFCI Receptacle

Even if your home already has a few exterior electrical receptacles, you can benefit from running at least one more GFCI receptacle to a garden location. A GFCI can be added to any outdoor room to help with a variety of tasks, including operating power tools, recharging battery-operated yard tools, powering a fountain or operating low-voltage lighting.

The following sequence illustrates a basic method for creating a freestanding receptacle anchored to a wood post embedded in a bucket of concrete. The receptacle is wired with UF (underground feeder) cable running through a trench from a junction box inside your house or garage. Sections of conduit protect the outdoor cable where it's exposed.

If you'd like to attach the outlet to an existing landscape structure, such as a deck or fence, you can modify the project by attaching the receptacle box and conduit to that structure. Keep in mind that freestanding receptacles should be at least 12", but no more than 18", above ground level.

Before you begin this project, have your local inspector review your plans and issue a work permit. Inspectors rely on the National Electrical Code (NEC) as well as local Codes that address climate and soil conditions in your region. If local Code requires that your work be inspected, schedule these visits at the appropriate points during the project.

TOOLS & MATERIALS

- Basic tools (page 120)
- Wire cutters
- Utility knife
- Fish tape
- Wire strippers
- LB connector
- Metal sweeps

- 1" metal conduit (6 ft.)
- Compression fittings
- Plastic bushings
- Pipe straps
- 2-gallon bucket
- 4-ft. 4 × 4 post

- Metal outdoor receptacle box
- Concrete mix
- UF cable
- GFCI receptacle
- Wire connectors
- Cable staples
- Grounding pigtail

HOW TO INSTALL A GARDEN RECEPTACLE
Step A: Plan the Route & Dig the Trench

1. Plan a convenient route from an accessible indoor junction to the location you've chosen for the GFCI. Drill a 1"-diameter hole through the exterior wall, near the junction box.

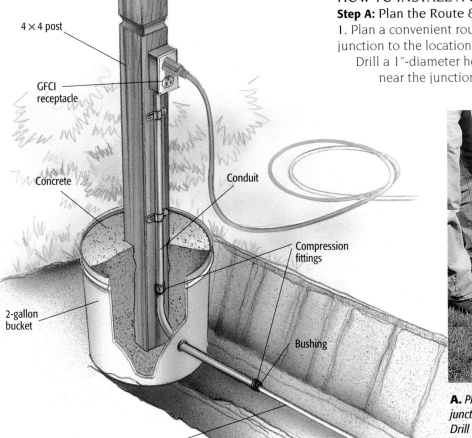

4 × 4 post

GFCI receptacle

Concrete

Conduit

2-gallon bucket

Compression fittings

Bushing

UF cable

A. *Plan and mark the route from the junction box to the receptacle location. Drill a hole through the exterior wall, then dig a trench along the marked path.*

2. Mark the underground cable run from the hole in the wall to the location for the receptacle.

3. Remove sod for an 8"- to 12"-wide trench along the marked route. Dig a trench that's at least 12" deep.

Step B: Install the LB Connector & Conduit

1. Install the LB connector on the outside of the hole.

2. Measure and cut a length of conduit about 4" shorter than the distance from the LB connector to the bottom of the trench. Attach the conduit to a sweep fitting, using a compression fitting. Attach a plastic bushing to the open end of the sweep to keep the sweep's metal edges from damaging the cable.

3. Attach the conduit assembly to the bottom of the LB connector, then anchor the conduit to the wall, using pipe straps.

4. Cut a short length of conduit to extend from the LB connector through the wall to the inside of the house. Attach the conduit to the LB connector from the inside of the house, then attach a plastic bushing to the open end of the conduit.

Step C: Assemble & Install the Receptacle Post

1. Drill or cut a 1½" hole through the side of a 2-gallon plastic bucket, near the bottom.

2. Mount the receptacle box to the post with galvanized screws. Position the post in the bucket.

3. Measure and cut a length of conduit to run from the receptacle box to a point 4" above the base of the

CHOOSING CABLE SIZES

This chart will help you determine what size UF cable you'll need to buy for this project.

Circuit Size	Circuit Length	Cable Gauge
15-amp	Less than 50 ft.	14
15-amp	More than 50 ft.	12
20-amp	Less than 50 ft.	12
20-amp	More than 50 ft.	10

bucket. Attach the conduit to the receptacle box and mount it to the post with pipe straps.

4. Insert a conduit sweep through the hole in the bucket and attach it to the end of the conduit, using a compression fitting. Thread a plastic bushing onto the open end of the sweep.

5. Dig a hole at the end of the trench. Place the bucket with the post into the hole, then fill the bucket with concrete and let it dry completely.

Step D: Lay the UF Cable

1. Measure the distance from the junction box in the house out to the receptacle box. Cut a length of UF cable 2 ft. longer than this measurement. At each end of the cable, use a utility knife to pare away 8" of the outer sheathing (page 155).

2. Lay the cable along the bottom of the trench from

B. *Mount the LB connector over the hole in the wall. Assemble a length of conduit and sweep fitting.*

C. *Assemble and attach the receptacle box and conduit to the post, then position the assembly at the end of the trench and fill the bucket with concrete.*

D. *Measure and cut UF cable and lay it in the trench. Use a fish tape to pull the cable up into the LB connector.*

Garden GFCI Receptacle (cont.)

the house to the receptacle location.

3. Open the cover on the LB connector and feed a fish tape down through the conduit and out of the sweep. Feed the wires at the end of the UF cable through the loop in the fish tape, then wrap electrical tape around the wires up to the sheathing.

4. Using the fish tape, carefully pull the end of the cable up through the conduit to the LB connector.

Step E: Fishing the UF Cable into the Receptacle Box

1. At the other end of the trench, feed the fish tape down through the conduit and out of the sweep.

2. Attach the exposed wires to the loop in the fish tape, and secure them with electrical tape.

3. Pull the cable through the conduit up into the receptacle box. About ½" of cable sheathing should extend into the box.

Step F: Connect the GFCI Receptacle

1. Using wire strippers, remove ¾" of the wire insulation around the two insulated wires extending into the receptacle box (opposite page).

2. Attach a bare copper pigtail to the grounding terminal on the back of the receptacle box. Join the two bare copper wires to the green grounding lead attached to the GFCI, using a wire connector.

3. Connect the black circuit wire to the brass screw terminal marked LINE on the GFCI. Connect the white wire to the silver terminal marked LINE.

4. Carefully tuck all the wires into the receptacle box, then mount the receptacle. Install the cover plate.

Step G: Connect the Cable at the Junction Box

1. From inside the house, extend the fish tape through the conduit and LB connector. Attach the cable wires to the fish tape, then pull the cable into the house.

2. Anchor the cable along framing members to the junction box, using wire staples.

3. **Turn off the power to the circuit serving the junction box.** Remove the junction box cover.

4. Use a screwdriver to open a knockout in the side of the junction box. Pull the end of the UF cable into the box through the knockout, and secure it with a cable clamp. About ½" of the outer sheathing should extend into the box, and the individual wires should be about 8" long. (Cut excess wire down to size.)

5. Using a wire stripper, remove ¾" of the wire insulation from the insulated wires (opposite page).

6. Unscrew the wire connector attached to the bare copper grounding wires inside the box. Position the new grounding wire alongside the existing wires and replace the wire connector.

7. Using the same technique, connect the new black wire to the existing black wires, and connect the new white wire to the existing white wires.

8. Replace the junction box cover and restore the power to the circuit. Fill the trench.

E. *Using the fish tape, pull the cable through the conduit and up into the receptacle box.*

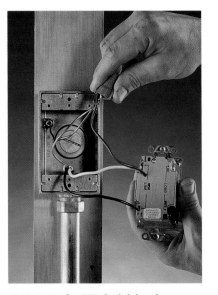

F. *Connect the GFCI by joining the grounding wires with a wire connector and connecting the black wire to the brass LINE terminal, the white wire to the silver LINE terminal.*

G. *Extend the UF cable into the juction box. Connect the new wires to the existing wires, using wire connectors.*

VARIATION: WIRING INTO AN EXISTING RECEPTACLE

Instead of wiring your garden GFCI into a junction box, you can wire it into an existing receptacle in your basement or garage. Before you begin, turn off the power to the existing receptacle.

1. Remove the cover plate and the receptacle. Loosen the mounting screws and remove the receptacle box.

2. Open a knockout in the side of the receptacle box with a screwdriver. Pull the end of the UF cable into the box through the knockout and secure it with a cable clamp.

3. Detach the circuit wires connected to the receptacle. Connect a bare copper pigtail to the ground screw terminal on the receptacle, a white pigtail to a silver screw terminal and a black pigtail to a brass screw terminal.

4. Using a wire connector for each set of wires, join the bare copper grounding wires, then the white neutral wires, then the black hot wires.

5. Carefully tuck the wires and receptacle back into the box. Replace the cover plate and restore the power.

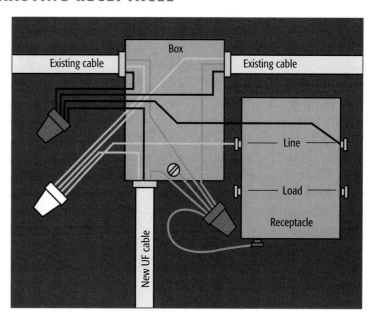

TIP: BASIC WIRING SKILLS AND TECHNIQUES

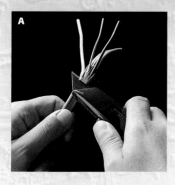

A. Stripping UF Cable Sheathing

Measure and cut a length of UF cable. At each end of the cable, use a utility knife to pare away 8" of the outer sheathing, using a technique similar to whittling a stick. Be careful not to nick or cut the wire insulation around the wires underneath.

B. Removing Wire Insulation

Strip 3/4" of the insulation from each wire in the cable, using the wire stripper openings on a combination tool. Choose the opening that matches the gauge of the wire, then clamp the wire in the tool. Pull the wire firmly to remove the insulation. Take care not to nick or scratch the ends of the wires.

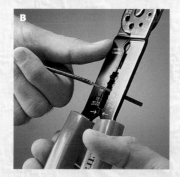

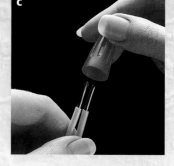

C. Connecting Two or More Wires

Hold the wires parallel, then screw a wire connector onto the wires. Tug gently on each wire to make sure it's secure. The wire connector cap should completely cover the bare wires.

155

Floodlight

Floodlights provide illumination for outdoor spaces frequently used at night, such as barbecue areas, basketball courts or garage entrances. In addition, floodlights improve your home's security.

In this project, we'll show you how to mount a motion-sensor floodlight on your garage. The light and its switch are wired into an existing GFCI receptacle located inside the garage.

Before you begin this project, draw a plan of your floodlight circuit and consult an inspector about local Code requirements. You'll also need to apply for a work permit with your local inspection office. If your Building Code requires inspections, make sure to have your work checked at the prescribed times.

TOOLS & MATERIALS

- Basic tools (page 120)
- Jig saw
- Cable ripper
- Wire combination tool
- Plastic light fixture box
- Plastic switch box
- 14-gauge NM cable
- Cable staples
- Floodlight with hardware
- Wire connectors
- Single pole switch

HOW TO INSTALL A FLOODLIGHT

Step A: Install the Light Fixture Box

1. Turn off the power to the circuit that operates the receptacle to which you'll be wiring the floodlight.
2. Position the light fixture box against the inside sheathing of the garage wall, adjacent to a stud. Outline the box on the sheathing, then drill a pilot hole and complete the cutout with a jig saw.
3. Position the box so its edges extend into the cutout, then attach it to the stud by hammering in the premounted nails.

Step B: Mount the Switch Box & Run the Cable

1. Position the switch box against the side of a stud inside the garage, located near a GFCI receptacle.
2. Attach the box to the stud by hammering in the premounted nails at the top and bottom of the box.
3. Cut one length of cable to run from the light fixture box to the switch box, with an extra 1 ft. at each end. Anchor the cable to framing members (within 8" of the boxes), using cable staples.

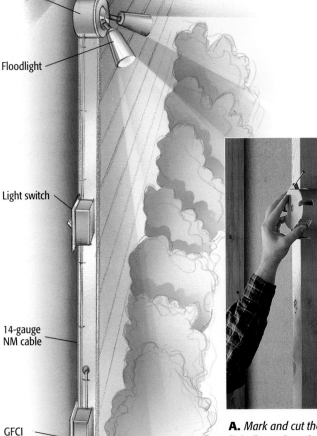

Light fixture box

Floodlight

Light switch

14-gauge NM cable

GFCI receptacle

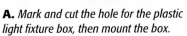

A. Mark and cut the hole for the plastic light fixture box, then mount the box.

B. Attach the switch box to the side of a stud near a source GFCI receptacle. Run NM cable between the boxes.

156

4. Cut another length of cable to run from the switch box to the receptacle box, allowing an extra 1 ft. at each end. Anchor it with cable staples.

5. Strip away 10" of outer sheathing from both ends of each new cable, using a cable ripper. Strip away ¾" of insulation from each of the insulated wires, using a combination tool (see page 155).

Step C: Wire the Floodlight

1. Open a knockout in the light fixture box, using a screwdriver. Insert the new cable into the box through the knockout opening, so that about ½" of the cable sheathing extends into the box.

2. Assemble the light fixture according to manufacturer's instructions. Attach a bare copper grounding wire to the grounding screw on the light fixture.

3. From outside the garage, join the circuit grounding wire and the light fixture grounding wire with a wire connector. Using the same technique, connect the white circuit wire to the white fixture wire. Then, connect the black circuit wire and black fixture wire.

4. Carefully tuck the wires into the box, and attach the light fixture faceplate to the fixture box.

Step D: Wire the Switch

1. Open a knockout in the top and bottom of the switch box, using a screwdriver. Insert the new cables into the box through the knockouts, so about ½" of the cable sheathing extends into the box.

2. Attach a bare copper grounding pigtail to the grounding screw on the switch, then connect the copper pigtail and the two bare copper circuit grounding wires, using a wire connector.

3. Attach the black wire leading from the GFCI to one of the screw terminals on the switch. Attach the black wire leading to the light fixture to the other screw terminal. Connect the two white neutral wires together, using a wire connector.

4. Tuck the wires inside the switch box. Secure the switch inside the box, then install the faceplate.

Step E: Connect to the GFCI Receptacle

1. Make sure the power to the GFCI is turned off. Remove the cover from the source GFCI, then gently pull the receptacle from the box and detach the wires.

2. Open a knockout in the box, using a screwdriver, and insert the new cable, so that about ½" of the cable sheathing extends into the receptacle box.

3. Join the grounding pigtail on the GFCI to both circuit grounding wires, using a wire connector.

4. Attach the white wire entering the box from the power source to the silver GFCI screw terminal marked LINE. Attach the black wire from the power source to the brass screw terminal marked LINE.

5. Attach the white wire running from the box to the switch to the silver GFCI screw terminal marked LOAD. Attach the black wire leading to the switch to the brass screw terminal marked LOAD.

6. Tuck all wires back inside the box and carefully force the receptacle into the box and secure it with mounting screws. Install the cover; restore the power.

C. *Attach the wires on the light fixture to the corresponding circuit wires, using wire connectors.*

D. *Attach the black wires to the screw terminals on the switch. Join the white wires and the grounding wires together.*

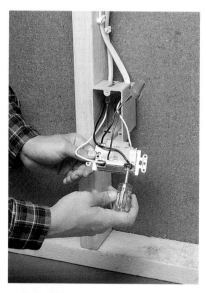

E. *Attach the wires from the power source to the LINE terminals and the circuit wires to the LOAD terminals.*

Landscape Lighting

Landscape lighting allows you to extend the use of your outdoor rooms well into the twilight hours, increases the security of your home and helps you safely navigate outdoor stairs and pathways at night. In addition, well-designed outdoor lighting transforms your landscape's appearance in the evening hours. The shapes, colors and textures of landscape elements are emphasized in new and striking ways.

The easiest way to add lighting to your outdoor rooms is with low-voltage lighting, available at home centers and garden supply stores. These outdoor lights are made of plastic or metal in a variety of styles that produce different effects. Several manufacturers have created modular kits that allow you to choose several styles of lights and the appropriate size power pack to operate them.

DESIGNING LOW-VOLTAGE LIGHTING

If possible, plan and install landscape lighting before you complete the planting areas. But if this isn't possible, carefully dig trenches and bury the lighting cable. When planning your lighting design, keep in mind that the most effective landscape lighting designs are created with a "less is more" philosophy. Overlighting, which is a common mistake, can make the landscape less inviting and disturb the neighbors. Good lighting designs focus on the glow of the lights and the illuminated objects, not the bulbs and fixtures. To achieve this effect, selectively position lights in unobtrusive places, such as garden beds, the eaves of a pergola, behind shrubs or even shining down from tree branches.

The illuminated objects and the glow of the lights, rather than the fixtures, are the focus of good landscape lighting designs.

Begin planning your lighting by touring your yard at night with a map of your landscape in hand. On your map, note the areas that need to be illuminated for safety or security reasons. Stairs, pathways, entrances, driveways and garages often require additional light. Also, consider which outdoor rooms you'd like to use at night and for what activities. For example, entertaining on a deck requires lighting for safety and convenience.

Next, note attractive garden features you'd like to highlight in the evening hours: interesting trees and shrubs, sculptures, flower beds or water gardens make a striking impression when lighted. In addition, look for architectural features, such as walls, arbors, trellises and gates, that will create interesting patterns of light and shadow.

Once you've noted the areas you'd like to highlight, determine the best way to illuminate each area. You may want to use some of the following methods suggested by professional landscape designers.

Backlighting: Highlights an object from behind, creating a silhouette that stands out from the background. This technique is especially effective with lacy shrubs and solitary objects.

Shadow lighting: Directs a single beam of light on a specific object that has a wall or fence behind it, creating a shadow of the featured object. This technique works best for objects with interesting shapes.

Moonlighting: Places several spotlights in a tree or large overhead structure and directs the light downward to simulate the effect of moonlight.

Spotlighting: Emphasizes an interesting architectural or landscape feature with one or more direct beams of light.

Uplighting: Highlights trees, shrubs or architectural features with well lights or floodlights hidden directly below the featured object, creating a dramatic effect with light and shadow.

Grazing: Focuses a broad beam of light on the high point of a wall or fence and indirectly lights the lower portion of the structure, emphasizing the texture of the surface and the low shadows.

Sidelighting: Lights a pathway, stairway or another surface with a series of small, horizontally mounted spotlights.

"Shadow lighting" casts the shadow of an interesting object onto a fence or wall that is directly behind the object.

"Uplighting" is achieved with floodlights or well lights, positioned to shine directly up at an object. Use uplighting to highlight trees, walls or outdoor sculpture.

"Sidelighting" uses a series of small, horizontally mounted spotlights to light a surface.

LIGHTING DESIGN TIP:

Place waterproof lights below the surface of the water to light water features, such as fountains and garden ponds. The lights shining up from the bottom make the water shimmer.

Low-voltage Lighting

Low-voltage lighting systems are a popular choice for landscape lighting because they're adaptable, easy to install and use little energy. Most outdoor lighting systems consist of the fixtures and bulbs, low-voltage connector cable, cable connector caps and a control box containing the power transformer, timer and light sensor. The control box for a low-voltage lighting system plugs into a standard outlet and uses standard 120-volt house current.

TOOLS & MATERIALS

- Basic tools (page 120)
- Trenching spade
- Ruler
- Low-voltage control box
- Low-voltage cable
- Outdoor-grade PVC conduit
- Pipe straps with screws
- Low-voltage lights
- Connector caps

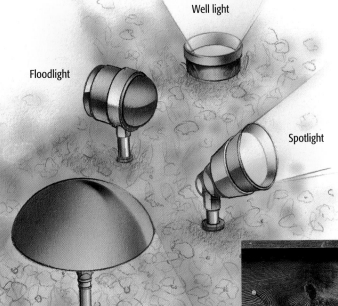

Well light

Floodlight

Spotlight

Garden light

HOW TO INSTALL LOW-VOLTAGE LIGHTING

Step A. Mount the Control Box

1. Mount the control box on an outside wall, close to a GFCI receptacle. Position the control box so that the sensor isn't covered by plants or other materials.
2. Slide the ends of the cables over the extended tabs on the base of the control box.
3. Dig a narrow trench for the light cable, about 6" to 8" deep. Start directly beneath the control box and extend the trench about 1 ft. out from the wall.
4. Measure the distance down from the base of the control box to the bottom of the trench. Cut a section of outdoor-grade PVC conduit to this length.
5. Feed the cable through the conduit, then position the conduit against the wall, with its bottom resting in the trench. Secure the conduit to the wall, using pipe straps.

Step B. Lay Out the Cable

Starting at the end of the conduit, lay out the cable along the ground. Since you'll need to bury the cable, select a path with few obstacles.

Step C. Attach the Light Fixtures

1. Beginning with the location closest to the control box, assemble the fixture you've picked for that spot.

A. *Mount the control box on an outside wall, close to a GFCI receptacle.*

B. *Lay out the cable following the path you planned in your lighting design plan.*

First, screw the bulb into the socket, then attach the lens and the hood to the fixture.

2. Carefully position the fixture, then firmly press its stake into the ground, in essence, planting the fixture.

3. Attach the fixture to the cable with a cable connector cap. Tighten the connector cap according to the manufacturer's directions, piercing the cable.

4. Repeat these steps to assemble, attach and position the remaining lights in your design.

Step D. Check & Adjust the Fixtures

Turn the lights on and survey your design. Look at the lights from several different directions and different areas of your yard, particularly from seating areas, to make sure that none of the lights produces a harsh glare or shines directly into your eyes. Adjust the fixtures as needed. If necessary, unfasten the connector cap, relocate a fixture, then reconnect it to the cable in its new location.

Step E. Dig a Trench & Bury the Cable

1. Beginning at the trench beneath the control box, dig a narrow trench, about 6" to 8" deep, along the cable path. At each fixture location, make a perpendicular slice with the spade to create a place to bury the section of cable leading to the fixture.

2. Gently push the cable into the bottom of the trench, using a wood or plastic ruler.

3. Replace the soil in the trenches and gently tamp it down with a spade.

VARIATION: LOW-VOLTAGE LIGHTING KIT

Home centers and garden supply stores carry a variety of low-voltage lighting products. Low-voltage outdoor light styles, like these from Toro®, include well lights (A), garden lights (B), adjustable spotlights (C) and adjustable floodlights (D). You'll also need low-voltage cable (E), halogen bulbs (F) and a control box (G), containing a transformer, timer and a light sensor to operate your light system.

C. Attach the fixture to the cable, using a cable connector cap.

D. Turn on the lights and survey the system from several areas, making adjustments as needed.

E. Cut a narrow trench along the cable path, then gently install the cable and close the trench.

Walls & Ceilings

Landscape walls and ceilings can increase privacy, improve home security, provide shade and diffuse strong winds. They also add interest by introducing new colors and textures, and by framing an attractive view or blocking an undesirable one. Walls often are installed along property lines, but can be used to define boundaries between rooms as well. Outdoor rooms also can be defined by ceilings, which offer the additional advantage of protecting a room and its contents from harsh sun or driving rain.

Walls and ceilings for an outdoor home can be created with nonliving materials, such as lumber and cut stone, or living materials, such as shrubs and trees.

Structures made from nonliving materials are generally easy to build and maintain, and provide attractive backdrops for decorative plantings and other landscape features. Wood, a relatively inexpensive material, is the most common choice for walls in today's outdoor homes. Wood fences are popular because they're attractive, easy to build and can be adapted to suit almost any landscape. Stone, another nonliving material, has a timeless appeal that blends well with almost any style of yard or garden. Building mortared walls may require more skill and experience than the average do-it-yourselfer possesses, but it's easy to create a beautiful, sturdy stone wall without mortar, using a technique known as dry laying.

Structures made of living materials contribute color, shape and texture to the landscape. For many people, the natural beauty of living materials more than offsets the routine care and maintenance they require. By using simple professional planting techniques, you can create anything from a tightly spaced, formal hedge to one that meanders gracefully across the contours of your yard.

IN THIS CHAPTER

Fence

Fences establish visual boundaries and define spaces. A wood fence is one of the easiest and least expensive landscape walls you can build. A board-and-stringer fence, such as the one described here, is ideal for flat or sloped yards.

A fence is as much a part of your neighbors' landscape as your own. That's why local Building Codes often include restrictions on building fences. To avoid problems and misunderstandings, check local Building Codes and talk with your neighbors as you begin planning your project.

Before laying out fence lines, determine the exact property boundaries. It's a good idea to position the fence at least 6" inside your property line, even if Building Codes don't specify setback rules. The finished side of the fence should face out, with the exposed posts and stringers on the inside.

A board-and-stringer fence is constructed from a basic frame with at least two rails, called *stringers*, that run parallel to the ground. Stringers are attached to posts secured in concrete footings. Vertical boards, called *pickets*, are attached to the stringers.

Our version of a board-and-stringer fence is built with cedar lumber. It includes a gate, which provides access to the yard without sacrificing privacy or security. For convenience, we've used a prefabricated gate, which you can find at most home centers.

To ensure sturdy construction, the bases of our fence posts are buried in concrete footings. Remember that footing depths are determined by your local Building Code and keep this in mind when determining the lengths of your posts.

TOOLS & MATERIALS

- Basic tools (page 120)
- Stakes & string
- Line level
- Masking tape
- Plumb bob

- Posthole digger
- Reciprocating saw
- Circular saw
- Paintbrush
- Gravel
- 4 × 4 posts
- Concrete mix
- 6-ft. 2 × 4 lumber

- Wood sealer/protectant
- Galvanized screws (2½", 2", 1")
- 2" fence brackets
- 6d galvanized nails
- 1 × 6 lumber
- Prefabricated gate & hardware

HOW TO BUILD A FENCE

Step A: Mark the Post Locations

1. Mark the fence line with stakes and mason's string. Attach a line level to the string, then adjust the string on the stakes until it's level.

2. Find the on-center spacing of

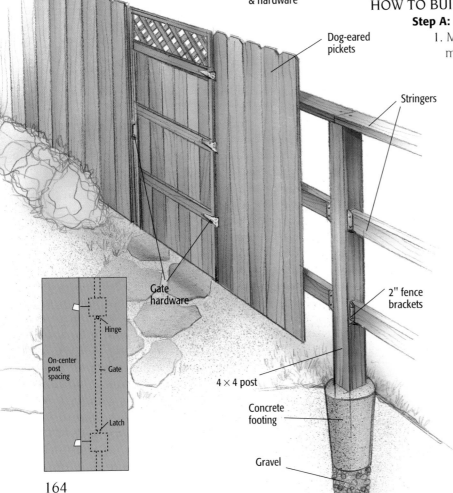

Dog-eared pickets

Stringers

2" fence brackets

Gate hardware

On-center post spacing

Hinge

Gate

Latch

4 × 4 post

Concrete footing

Gravel

A. *Mark the fence line with a pair of stakes and a leveled string, then mark the location of the gate and posts.*

the gate posts by measuring the gate width, including hinge and latch hardware, and adding 4". Place masking tape on the string to mark the location of the gate posts.

3. Use tape to mark the string with the remaining post locations, spacing them 6 ft. apart on center.

4. Pinpoint the post locations on the ground, using a plumb bob. Mark post locations with stakes, and remove the string from the fence line markers.

Step B: Set the Posts

1. Seal the portions of posts that will be buried and let them dry.

2. Dig the postholes, using a posthole digger or a power auger. Make the holes 6" deeper than the post footing depth specified by your local Building Code.

3. Pour a 6" layer of gravel into each hole.

4. Place each post in its hole, then use a level to plumb the post. Brace the post in place with scrap pieces of 2 × 4 driven into the ground and screwed to the sides of the post on adjoining faces.

5. When all of the posts are braced in position, use the mason's string to make sure they are in a straight line. Make adjustments as needed.

Step C: Pour the Footings

1. Mix concrete in a wheelbarrow, and fill the holes, slightly overfilling and tamping each one.

2. Check the posts with a level to be sure they're plumb, then shape the concrete to form a mound that will shed water away from the post.

VARIATION: FENCE PANELS

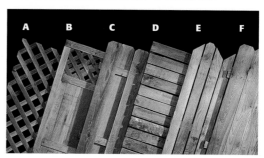

Preassembled fence panels are an attractive, timesaving option when building a fence. The entire panel is attached to the posts, eliminating the need to individually cut and attach stringers.

Some popular styles of prefabricated panels include:

A. Lattice panels   D. Horizontal board
B. Solid panels with lattice tops   E. Modified picket
C. Staggered board   F. Dog-eared board

3. Let the concrete dry for at least 24 hours before continuing with the fence installation.

Step D: Trim the Posts & Add the Top Stringers

1. On each end post, measure up from the ground to a point 1 ft. below the planned height of the fence. Snap a chalk line across all the posts at this height. Trim the posts to height with a reciprocating saw, making sure these cuts are square.

B. *Position each post in its hole. Adjust the post until it's plumb, then brace it with 2 × 4 cross braces driven into the ground.*

C. *Fill the holes with concrete. Recheck the posts for plumb, then shape the concrete into a raised cap.*

D. *Trim the posts, and place the cut stringers on top of the posts, with the joints centered. Attach with screws.*

165

Fence (cont.)

2. Cut 6-ft. 2 × 4 stringers and coat the ends with sealer. Let the sealer dry.

3. Place the stringers flat on top of the posts, centering a joint over each post. Attach the stringers to the posts with 2½" galvanized screws.

Step E: Install the Remaining Stringers

1. Measuring down from the top of each post, mark lines at 2-ft. intervals to mark the locations for the remaining stringers. At each mark, nail a 2" fence bracket to the side of the post, flush with the outside edge.

2. Position a 2 × 4 stringer between each pair of brackets. Hold or tack the board against the posts, and mark the back side, along the edges of the posts. (If the yard slopes, the stringers will be cut at an angle.)

3. Cut the stringers ¼" shorter than indicated, which will help them slide into the brackets easily. Coat the cut ends of the stringers with sealer/protectant.

4. If stringers are angled to accommodate a slope, bend the bottom flanges of the brackets to match the angles of the stringers. Position and nail the stringers into place, using 6d galvanized nails.

Step F: Attach the Pickets

1. Install the pickets, beginning at an end post. Measure from the ground to the top edge of the top

TIP:

Instead of digging the postholes with a post-hole digger, you can use a rented power auger to make the job faster and less strenuous.

stringer, then add 8½". Cut a picket to this length. Coat the bottom edge of the picket with sealer/protectant.

2. Position the picket so that the top extends 10½" above the top stringer, leaving a 2" gap at the bottom. Make sure the picket is plumb, then attach it to the post and rails with pairs of 2" galvanized screws.

3. Measure, cut and attach the remaining pickets to the stringers, using the same procedure. Leave a gap of at least ⅛" between boards, using a piece of scrap wood as a spacing guide. At the ends of the fence, you may need to rip-cut pickets to make them fit.

Step G: Hang the Gate

1. Attach three hinges, evenly spaced, to the gate frame. Make sure the hinges are parallel with the edge of the gate.

2. Position the gate upright between the gate posts, resting the hinge barrels against the face of the fence. Support the gate on wood blocks at the correct height, then attach the hinges to the fence.

3. On the opposite side, attach the latch hardware to the fence and to the gate. Open and close the gate to make sure the latch works correctly, then make any adjustments that are necessary.

4. Coat the fence completely with sealer/protectant.

E. *Attach the fence brackets to the inside faces of the posts. Position the stringers in the brackets, then nail them in place.*

F. *Measure and cut the pickets. Attach them to the posts and stringers, spacing the pickets at least ⅛" apart.*

G. *Attach the hinges according to the manufacturer's directions, then hang the gate and install latch hardware.*

VARIATION: FENCES

A. Combining materials modifies the total effect. The formality of these brick pillars is softened by the openness of the wood fence.

B. Chain-link fences are economical and sturdy. To help integrate them into the landscape, plant climbing vines, such as this clematis.

C. Brick fences lend an air of solidity and permanence to a landscape. Here, repeated materials result in a pleasing balance.

D. Details, such as the cutouts shown on the pickets above, can be used to create unique variations of standard fence styles.

E. A split-rail fence is an inexpensive, easy-to-build option that works best in rustic or informal landscapes.

Stone Wall

Stone walls are beautiful, long-lasting structures that add an elegant touch to any landscape. Surprisingly, they're simple to build. A low stone wall can be constructed without mortar, using a centuries-old method known as "dry laying." With this technique, the wall is actually formed by two separate stacks that lean together slightly. The position and weight of the two stacks support each other, forming a single, sturdy wall. A dry stone wall can be built to any length, but must be at least half as wide as it is tall.

The best place to purchase stone for this project is from a quarry or aggregate supply center. These centers sell different sizes, shapes and colors of stone, each type priced by the ton. For a dry stone wall,

you'll need to purchase stone in four sizes:
- Shaping: ½" the width of the wall
- Tie: the same width as the wall
- Filler: small shims that fit into cracks
- Cap: large, flat stones, wider than the wall

While dry walls are simple to construct, they do require a fair amount of patience. The stones must be carefully selected and sorted by size and shape. Some may also need to be shaped or split to maintain the spacing and structure of the wall.

To shape a stone, score its surface, using a circular saw outfitted with a masonry blade. Place a mason's chisel on the cut and strike it with a hand sledge until the stone breaks. Always wear safety glasses when cutting or shaping stone.

TOOLS & MATERIALS

- Basic tools (page 120)
- Stakes
- String
- Stone
- Circular saw with masonry blade
- Mason's chisel
- Mortar
- Masonry trowel

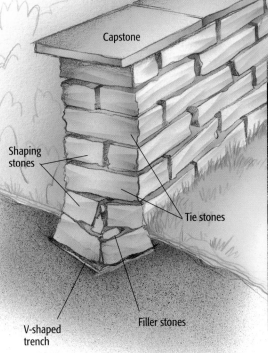

Capstone

Shaping stones

Tie stones

Filler stones

V-shaped trench

HOW TO BUILD A DRY STONE WALL

Step A: Dig the Trench

1. Sort the stones by size and purpose, placing them in piles near the building site.
2. Lay out the wall site, using stakes and string.
3. Dig a 2-ft.-wide trench, 4" to 6" deep, along the site, creating a slight "V" shape by sloping the sides toward the center. The center of the trench should be about 2" deeper than the sides.

Step B: Build the First Course

1. Select appropriate stones from the pile of shaping stones, and lay the first course along the bottom of the trench. Place pairs of stones side by side, flush

A. *After planning the wall location, dig a V-shaped trench for the wall. Sort the stones by size and purpose.*

B. *Lay the first course of shaping stones in the trench, adjusting them so that they slope toward each other.*

with the edges of the trench and sloping toward the center. As you position stones along the first course, use stones similar in height; if stones have uneven surfaces, position them with the uneven side facing down.

2. Fill any significant gaps between the shaping stones with filler stones.

Step C: Add the Second Course

1. Lay the second course of stones over the first, staggering the joints. If possible, use pairs of stones in varying lengths to offset the center joint.

2. Alternate the stones in a longer-shorter pattern. Keep the height of the second course even, stacking two thinner stones if necessary to maintain a consistent height.

3. Wedge filler stones into any large gaps.

Step D: Lay the Tie Stones

1. Following the same technique, lay the third course of shaping stones, placing a tie stone every 3 ft. To keep the tie stones uniform, you may need to cut them to length. Hold a level along the side of the wall periodically to check it for level.

2. Lay shaping stones between tie stones and continue placing filler stones into any cracks on the surface and sides of the wall.

Step E: Finish the Wall

1. Continue laying courses, maintaining a consistent height along the wall and adding tie stones to every third course.

TIP: MOVING STONES

To avoid injury, squat and lift heavy stones with the strength of your legs rather than your back.

Use a wheelbarrow for lifting and transporting heavy stones that are too large to carry. To load the stone, place the wheelbarrow on its side behind the stone, then roll the stone onto the edge. Stand behind the wheelbarrow and use the strength of your legs to pull the wheelbarrow toward you until it's resting upright.

2. When the wall is approximately 4 ft. high, check it for level. When you're satisfied with the placement of stones, blind-mortar the capstones to the top of the wall. Using a trowel, apply mortar to the center of the wall, keeping the mortar at least 6" from the edges. Center the capstones over the wall, and set them as close together as possible.

3. Carefully fill the cracks between the capstones with mortar. Let any excess mortar dry until crumbly, then brush it off. After two or three days, scrub off any residue, using water and a rough-textured rag.

filler stones

C. *Lay the second course of shaping stones over the first course, placing filler stones into the cracks as you work.*

tie stones

D. *Add the third course of stone over the second, using tie stones every 3 ft., checking periodically with a level.*

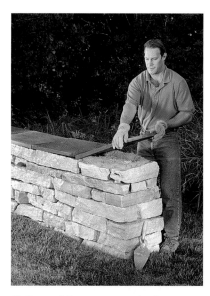

E. *Once all the courses are in place, mortar the capstones to the top course of stone, then seal the gaps between them.*

Hedges

Hedges are a natural choice for creating landscape walls. Because hedges are a living wall of individual shrubs, they easily blend into any landscape. Like fences and other nonliving walls, hedges can take many forms, depending on the purpose and style you have in mind. For instance, an informal hedge of flowering shrubs adds seasonal color, while a formal hedge of closely planted evergreens forms a dense screen that increases privacy.

Shrub choices generally fall into two groups: fast-growing or steady-growing. Carefully consider the pros and cons of each before selecting shrubs for a hedge. Fast-growing shrubs quickly form a solid hedge, but their rapid growth makes it necessary to prune them frequently in order to keep the hedge well shaped and healthy. Steady-growing shrubs require less frequent pruning, but take at least several years to grow into a solid wall.

Local nurseries will have a selection of bare-root, balled-and-burlapped and container-grown shrubs. Because planting a hedge involves many shrubs, container-grown plants are the best choice—they usually are more economical and easier to transport and plant. If you decide to plant either bare-root or balled-and-burlapped shrubs, refer to the information on transporting and planting these types in "Trees" (page 172).

To ensure that the shrubs grow into a dense hedge, determine their mature size and space them at about ¾ of this measurement. Check with a nursery before you begin planting—some shrubs require different spacing. The size of the excavation also has a tremendous influence on the success of your hedge. In most cases, you'll want to dig a hole twice as wide and just as deep as the container. However, if you have heavy soil, dig a hole that will position the top of the root ball slightly above ground, then

TOOLS & MATERIALS

- Basic tools (page 120)
- Stakes
- String
- Rope or hose
- Soil amendments
- Shrubs
- Mulch

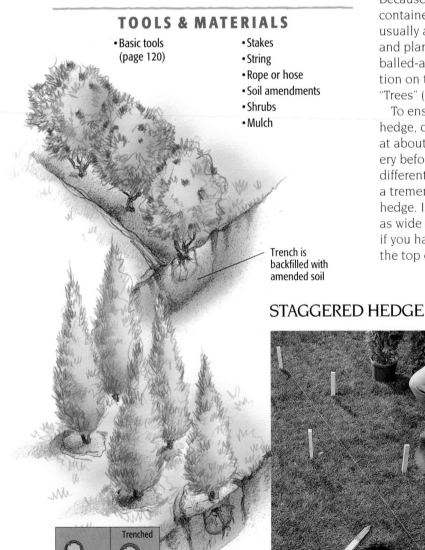

Trench is backfilled with amended soil

Planting hole is twice as wide and just as deep as the original container

Trenched

Staggered

STAGGERED HEDGE

A. *Dig holes twice as wide and just as deep as the shrub's container, staggering the rows along both sides of the line.*

B. *After partially backfilling soil around the plant, water the soil. Finish filling the hole and apply a thick layer of mulch.*

mound the soil up to cover the roots.

Begin training the shrubs into a hedge by pruning them the first year. Taper the shrub so the bottom of the plant is wider than the top. Don't overprune—in general, it's best to prune within 2" of the last pruning.

HOW TO PLANT A STAGGERED HEDGE

The staggered planting method is the best choice for quickly forming an informal, living wall. It's also the preferred method if you're using shrubs that can't be planted close together. Although the hedge demonstrated here is straight, you can use a rope to lay out a curved hedge.

Step A: Dig Planting Holes
1. Use stakes and string to lay out the hedge's path.
2. On one side of the string, mark the appropriate spacing for a row of planting holes, then dig them.
3. On the other side of the string, mark and dig another row of holes, staggered with the first row.

Step B: Install the Plants
1. Center a plant in the hole, positioning it so the root ball is at the desired depth.
2. Fill the hole ¾ full with amended soil.
3. When the hole is ¾ full, slowly add water, which will remove any air pockets. Finish filling the hole with soil and tamp it gently.
4. Apply 4" to 6" of mulch and water the shrubs.

HOW TO PLANT A TRENCHED HEDGE

Another option for planting a hedge involves digging a trench. This trench method works best if you want a formal or shaped hedge, and if you are willing to wait for the plants to grow into a solid screen.

Step A: Dig the Trench
Outline the path for a curved hedge, using a rope. If you're planting a straight hedge, use stakes and string to mark the path. Dig a trench, twice as wide and just as deep as the shrubs' containers.

Step B: Install the Shrubs
Plant the shrubs one at a time, spacing them appropriately for their mature size. Hold each plant so it's centered and straight in the trench. Use the same planting technique described in the "Staggered Hedge" instructions, then apply mulch and water the shrubs generously.

TIP: PREPARING CONTAINER-GROWN SHRUBS FOR PLANTING

Container-grown shrubs and plants often become "root bound" in their containers and need to be prepared for planting. To prepare a container-grown plant, remove it from the container just before planting. Using a trowel, make vertical slices into the sides of the root ball, slicing through roots as necessary. Use the hand trowel to slice an "X" in the bottom of the root ball. This allows the roots to spread naturally as the plant grows.

TRENCHED HEDGE

A. Lay out the hedge path with a rope, then dig a trench twice the width and the same depth as the container.

B. Plant the shrubs one at a time, spacing them ¾ of their mature size apart. Fill the trench with soil.

Trees

Trees help your landscape look more complete and add vertical interest to your yard. They also increase the value of the property and form natural landscape walls and ceilings. Planting trees in formation, similar to a hedge, creates a privacy screen, reduces noise and protects your house from strong winds. You can also plant a single tree that will, at mature height, form a graceful ceiling for one or more of your outdoor rooms.

SELECTING TREES

Nurseries and garden centers sell trees packaged in three different ways. Each packaging method has advantages and disadvantages. *Container-grown* are packed in pots of soil and are available in many sizes.

Bare-root trees are dug up during dormancy, so the branches and roots are bare. The roots are exposed and must be kept moist and protected from sun and wind damage during transport and before planting.

Balled-and-burlapped (B & B) trees are established trees with a large compact root ball that's tightly secured in burlap. Balled-and-burlapped trees are very heavy, and require special care when transporting. The soil and roots must not dry out before planting.

TRANSPORTING TREES

All trees need protection during transport. Because this can be a difficult process, many people opt to pay the nursery a delivery fee to handle the job. But, if you have access to a pickup or trailer, you can save money by transporting the tree yourself. Branches, foliage and roots must be protected from breakage, and wind and sun damage, during transport. To protect them, wrap them in burlap tied on with twine. Secure the tree inside the truck bed with straps or rope. Drive slowly and carefully, especially on corners, and unload the tree by lifting it only by the roots, not the trunk.

HOW TO PREPARE THE PLANTING HOLE

The planting hole is one of the greatest contributing factors to the health of a tree. To prepare the hole, start by digging a hole two to three times as

Protect a tree during transport by wrapping the roots, branches and leaves with burlap, then securing it with heavy twine.

wide as the root ball of the tree. If you're planting a bare-root tree, the hole should be two to three times wider than the spread of the branches. To help the roots develop horizontally, slope the sides of the hole toward the surface. When finished, the hole should resemble a wide, shallow basin.

Root ball

Basin-shaped hole

HOW TO PLANT BARE-ROOT TREES

The roots of bare-root trees should be planted at a depth that is slightly higher than that at which they were originally grown. Start by slightly backfilling the planting hole with the soil you removed. Hold the tree in the hole; if the tops of the roots are still below the top of the hole, backfill more soil into the hole. Position the tree so that the largest branches are facing southwest, then spread out the roots. Backfill into the hole, covering the roots. As you backfill, gently lift the tree up and down to prevent air pockets from forming. When the hole is ¾ full, tamp the soil and water it generously to remove any remaining air pockets. Completely fill the hole with soil, and lightly tamp it.

Position bare-root trees so that the largest branches face southwest. Then spread the roots out in the soil before backfilling the planting hole.

HOW TO PLANT B & B TREES

Carefully set the plant in the hole. Add or remove soil until the root ball rests slightly above ground level. Cut and remove the twine at the top of the ball. Cut the burlap away from top and sides of the root-ball and remove as much of it as possible. Set the tree back down and backfill until the hole is ¾ full. Lightly tamp the soil down, then water it slowly to remove the air pockets. Finish backfilling the hole, and tamp the soil.

(left) Cut and remove the twine from the top of balled-and-burlapped trees. Cut the burlap away, and remove it from around the tree.

(below) Trees are sold in several forms: bare root (A), container grown (B) and balled-and-burlapped (C).

CARING FOR NEW TREES

Trees require routine maintenance—especially during the first year. It takes almost a full year for a newly planted tree to establish a healthy root system. During the root development period, routine waterings are very important.

The best method for watering trees is to place a garden hose adjusted to release water in a slow trickle at the base of the tree for several hours. With this method, you can easily water the soil around the tree to a depth of 6" to 8". Use this method to water new trees any time the moisture depth in the soil is less than 6". In addition to watering, encourage root development by applying a fertilizer formulated for trees, every two to three years. Apply the fertilizer according to the directions on the label.

173

2 × 2 cross strip

2 × 6 tie beam

2 × 4 rafters

4 × 4 post

Cement

Gravel

Arbor

TOOLS & MATERIALS

- Basic tools (page 120)
- Stakes and string
- Line level
- Posthole digger
- Reciprocating saw
- Paintbrush
- Wood screw clamps

- Concrete mix
- Gravel
- Wood sealer
- 10-ft. 4 × 4 posts (4)
- 6-ft. 2 × 6 tie beams (2)
- Galvanized nails

- 7-ft. 2 × 2 cross strips (7)
- 7-ft. 2 × 4 rafters (4)
- Galvanized deck screws
- 3" lag screws (8)
- Rafter ties (8)

Arbors create a lightly shaded space and add vertical interest to your landscape. For increased shade, you can cover an arbor with meshlike outdoor fabric or climbing vines. You can even transform it into a private retreat by enclosing the sides with lattice.

Our version of a post-and-slat arbor is a 5-ft. × 5-ft., freestanding cedar structure with an extended overhead. You can easily adapt the design to different sizes, but don't space the posts more than 8 ft. apart. If you want to build a larger arbor, add additional posts between the corner posts. Before you begin construction, check your local Building Code for footing depth requirements and setback restrictions.

If you want to add climbing vines, such as clematis or wisteria, plant one vine beside the base of each post. Attach screw eyes to the outside of the posts, then string wire between the eyes. As the vines grow, train them along the wires.

A. *Lay out the location of the arbor posts, then check the diagonals for squareness.*

B. *Brace the posts into place, then use a level to make sure they are plumb.*

C. *Level and clamp the tie beam against the posts, then secure it with lag screws.*

HOW TO BUILD AN ARBOR

Step A: Dig Holes for the Footings

1. Lay out the location of the posts, 5 ft. apart, using stakes and string. Make sure the layout is square by measuring from corner to corner and adjusting the layout until these diagonal measurements are equal.
2. Dig postholes at the corners to the required depth, using a posthole digger.
3. Fill each hole with 6" of gravel.

Step B: Set the Posts

1. Position the posts in the holes. To brace them in a plumb position, tack support boards to the posts on adjoining faces. Adjust the posts as necessary until they're plumb.
2. Drive a stake into the ground, flush against the base of each 2 × 4. Drive galvanized deck screws through the stakes, into the 2 × 4s.
3. Mix one bag of dry concrete to anchor each post. Immediately check to make sure the posts are plumb, and adjust as necessary until the concrete begins to harden. Be sure to let the concrete dry at least 24 hours before continuing.

Step C: Install the First Tie Beam

1. Measure, mark and cut all the lumber for the arbor. Cut a 3" × 3" notch off the bottom corner of each tie beam, a 2" × 2" notch off the bottom corner of each 2 × 4 rafter, and a 1" × 1" notch off the bottom corner of each cross strip.

2. Position a tie beam against the outside edge of a pair of posts, 7 ft. above the ground. Position the beam to extend about 1 ft. past the post on each side.
3. Level the beam, then clamp it into place with wood screw clamps. Drill two ⅜" pilot holes through the tie beam and into each post. Attach the tie beam to the posts with 3" lag screws.

Step D: Add the Second Tie Beam

1. Use a line level to mark the opposite pair of posts at the same height as the installed tie beam.
2. Attach the remaining tie beam, repeating the process described in #2 and #3 of Step C.
3. Cut off the posts so they're level with the tops of the tie beams, using a reciprocating saw or hand saw.

Step E: Attach the Rafters

Attach the rafters to the tops of the tie beams, using rafter ties and galvanized nails. Beginning 6" from the ends of the tie beams, space the rafters 2 ft. apart, with the ends extending past each tie beam by 1 ft.

Step F: Install the Cross Strips

1. Position a cross strip across the top of the rafters, beginning 6" from the ends of the rafters. Center the strip so it extends past the outside rafters by about 6". Drill pilot holes through the cross strip and into the rafters. Attach the cross strip with galvanized screws. Add the remaining cross strips, spacing them 1 ft. apart.
2. Finish your arbor by applying wood sealer.

D. *Attach the other tie beam and trim the tops of the posts flush with the tie beams.*

E. *Attach the rafters to the tie beams with rafter ties and galvanized nails.*

F. *Space the cross strips 1 ft. apart and attach them to the rafters.*

Brick Pillars

Nothing gives a landscape a greater sense of permanence and substance than well-planned and well-executed masonry work. It makes the impression that the structures will be there for decades, not just a few summers. And masonry doesn't have to mean just simple projects like walking paths or borders around your plantings. If you're feeling ambitious, you can tackle a bit of bricklaying.

As masonry projects go, this one is fairly simple. Even if you're a beginner, you can build these elegant, professional-looking pillars if you proceed slowly and follow the instructions carefully. Of course, if you have a friend or relative who knows his (or her) way around brick and mortar, it can't hurt to have an experienced eye check out your progress. (See pages 314 to 316 for additional information on building with bricks.)

Your adventure in bricklaying begins with choosing a site for the pillars and pouring footings to support them. These below-grade columns of concrete provide a stable foundation that will protect your pillars when freezes and thaws cause the soil to shift.

The finished pillars can serve many functions. They can support a gate, frame a flower bed of which you're particularly proud, or support meandering vines. Whatever their primary purpose, you'll enjoy them for years, perhaps decades, as they weather and gain character. And you'll be proud to tell everyone that *you* built them.

TOOLS & MATERIALS

- Mason's string
- Shovel
- Wheelbarrow
- Pencil
- Masonry trowel
- Level
- Jointer
- Tape measure
- Circular saw
- Hand maul
- Rope
- Stakes
- 2 × 4s

- 2 × 2
- 1 × 2
- Concrete mix
- Standard modular bricks (4 × 2⅔ × 8")
- Type N mortar mix
- Small dowel
- Vegetable oil
- ½" wire mesh
- 2 capstones
- ⅜" plywood scraps
- 2½" deck or wallboard screws
- ⅜"-thick wood scraps

A. *Mark the site with stakes and mason's strings; then remove the sod and dig a hole for each footing.*

HOW TO BUILD BRICK PILLARS

Step A: Select & Prepare the Site

1. Select the area in the garden where the pillars are to stand, keeping in mind their rectangular shape and a preferred alignment—long sides or short sides facing out.

2. Make a rough outline of each footing, using a rope. Then lay out a 16 × 20" footing for each pillar, using stakes and mason's strings.

3. Strip away any sod or plant material up to 6" outside the mason's strings on all sides.

4. Dig a hole for each footing to the depth required by local building codes, using the mason's strings as guides. (The required depth depends on the depth of the frost line in your region.) A thin, narrow shovel works well for digging a square hole.

5. Following the layout of the stakes and strings, construct 16 × 20" forms (interior dimensions) for the concrete, using 2 × 4s and screws.

6. Sink the forms into the ground slightly just around the hole so the visible portions of the footings will look neat and provide a flat, even surface for laying bricks.

7. Drive stakes outside the 2 × 4s so the forms are firmly supported. Then adjust the forms until they're level and square.

Step B: Pour the Concrete

1. In a wheelbarrow, mix the dry concrete with water, following the manufacturer's instructions.

2. Pour the concrete into one footing hole, filling it to the top of the form.

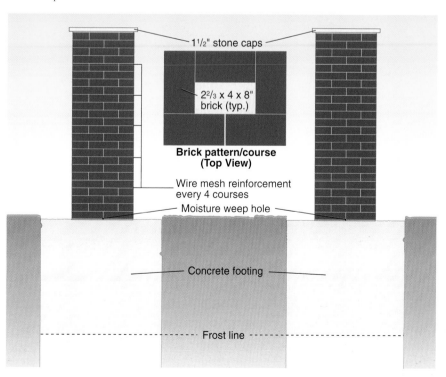

1½" stone caps

2⅔ x 4 x 8" brick (typ.)

Brick pattern/course (Top View)

Wire mesh reinforcement every 4 courses

Moisture weep hole

Concrete footing

Frost line

3. Drag a scrap 2 × 4 across the top of the form, "screeding" away any excess concrete. The surface of the footing should be smooth and even.

4. Repeat the process for the other footing, and then clean the wheelbarrow thoroughly with a hose.

5. Let the concrete cure for at least two days before removing the forms and building on top of the footings. Waiting a week is even better.

Step C: Build a Story Pole

1. As you build the pillars, a story pole allows you to check the positions of the courses of brick and the thickness of the mortar joints. To build a story pole, start by cutting a batch of spacers from ⅜" plywood.

2. On a wide, flat surface, lay out ten or more courses of brick. With the bricks lying on their sides, insert spacers between each pair, making sure the bricks are spaced ⅜" apart.

3. Place a straight 1 × 2 alongside the bricks; then mark the space between each pair of bricks, indicating the intended location and thickness of each layer

of mortar.

Step D: Dry-Lay the Bricks

1. After the footings have cured, arrange five of the bricks to form a rectangle on one of the footings.

2. Insert spacers between the bricks to establish the thickness of the vertical mortar joints. Take care that the bricks are correctly centered on each footing and square in relation to each other.

3. With a grease pencil or carpenter's pencil, draw reference lines on the footing around the bricks.

Step E: Lay the First Course

1. Prepare the mortar, according to the instructions on the bag.

2. Using a trowel, lay a bed of mortar within the reference lines to a thickness of about ⅜", forming the mortar into a rectangle.

3. Apply ⅜" of mortar to the sides of alternating bricks, so that mortar fills the spaces between them, and set the bricks on the mortar bed, tapping each one gently with the handle of the trowel.

B. *In order to create a smooth, level surface, drag a 2 × 4 across the top of the form, removing any excess concrete.*

C. *With the 1 × 2 lying beside the arranged bricks, mark the ⅜" spaces between the bricks to create a story pole.*

4. On the side of the pillar that's seen least often, use a small wooden dowel or pencil coated with vegetable oil to make a weep hole in the wet mortar between two bricks. (This weep hole helps ensure proper drainage of any moisture that accumulates inside the pillar.)

5. When all five bricks in the first course are laid, make sure they're square and level. If necessary, adjust bricks by gently tapping them with the handle of the trowel.

Step F: Lay the Second Course

1. Apply mortar to the top of the first course of bricks, again ⅜" thick.

2. Lay the second course of brick in the mortar, but rotate the pattern 180°. Gently remove the oiled dowel or pencil from the mortar of the first course.

3. Check the pillar with a level, making sure your work is both level and plumb. Gently adjust bricks as necessary. Then, use the story pole as a guide to make sure the two courses on all sides are correctly spaced. Small errors made low on the pillar will be exaggerated with each successive course. Check your work after every two courses of brick.

Step G: Add Wire Mesh

1. Proceed with the next two courses and apply mortar to the top of the fourth course. Then cut a piece of ¼" wire mesh slightly smaller than the dimensions of a course of bricks, and lay it into the mortar for lateral reinforcement. Apply more mortar to the top of the wire mesh, and lay the fifth course of brick.

2. Add wire-mesh reinforcement after every fourth course.

Step H: Tool the Joints & Complete the Pillar

1. After the fifth course, use a jointer to smooth and pack down (a step known as "tooling") the mortar joints below that have hardened enough to resist minimal finger pressure.

2. Continue to lay bricks until the next-to-last course. Remember to check your work with the story

D. *Dry-lay the first course by arranging the bricks as they will be mortared. Draw reference lines around the bricks.*

E. *Lay an oiled dowel into the wet mortar, creating a weep hole. Then fill in with mortar above the dowel.*

F. *When laying the second course of bricks, rotate the pattern 180° to add strength and create a more visually pleasing look.*

pole after every two courses, install wire mesh every four courses, and tool the joints as the mortar in each course becomes firm.

3. Apply mortar to the next-to-last course, and add a piece of wire mesh. Apply mortar to the entire surface of the wire mesh.

4. Lay the side of the last course formed by two bricks. Then add an extra brick in the center, over the mortar-covered wire mesh.

5. Lay the remaining bricks so they fit snugly around the center brick.

6. Tool any remaining joints, as soon as they become firm.

Step I: Build the Second Pillar

1. Lay the first course of brick, following the instructions in Steps D and E above. Measure the distance between the pillars with a tape measure.

2. Make a measuring rod by cutting a 2 × 2 or other straight board to match the distance between the bases of the two pillars. Use the rod every few courses to check that the second pillar is aligned with (parallel to) the first. Also, consult the story

G. *Lay a piece of wire mesh in the wet mortar after every four courses.*

H. *After the fifth course of bricks is laid, use a jointer to tool, or smooth, the mortar joints.*

pole after every two courses.

3. Complete the second pillar, following the instructions in Steps F through H.

Step J: Prepare & Install the Capstones

1. Have a stone supplier in your area cut two capstones so that each one is roughly 1½" longer and wider than the top of the pillars.

2. Draw diagonal reference lines from corner to corner on the bottoms of the capstones. Then, using the dimensions of the pillar and the diagonal lines, draw a rectangle centered on the bottom of each capstone.

3. Apply a ½"-thick bed of mortar to the top of the pillar, and center the capstone on the pillar, using the reference lines. Tool the mortar joint so it's flush with the brick. Note: If mortar begins to squeeze out of the joint, press ⅜"-thick wood scraps into the mortar on each side to support the cap. After 24 hours, use a hammer to tap out the wood scraps, and fill in the spaces with fresh mortar.

VARIATIONS: GARDEN PILLARS

Using these plans, it's possible to create garden pillars with different decorative or functional qualities.

• Build three or four pillars in graduated sizes to create a terraced effect.

• Use pillars as pedestals around the garden to highlight large pots full of cascading blooms or favorite outdoor statuary.

• Visit a masonry supply house or building center and gather ideas on how to use bricks of different colors and textures. You can lay bricks of different shades in alternating courses. For a more subtle effect, alternate same-colored bricks of different textures—smooth, rough, smooth, rough.

• Build short pillars that act as the base of an arbor or outdoor bench.

I. *Lay the first course of the second pillar. Measure and cut a 2 × 2 to match the distance between the pillars. As you build the second pillar, use this board to check its alignment.*

J. *Place mortar on top of the pillar, and set the capstone in position. Strike the mortar joint beneath the capstone flush with the pillar.*

Floors

Of all the elements in your landscape, floors are perhaps the most important. By serving as a background for the rest of your landscape, outdoor flooring visually sets the tone for the yard. Carefully chosen flooring transforms a yard into a series of living spaces by providing a suitable surface for each room's intended purpose and activities.

By their nature, outdoor floors must withstand heavy use and the seasonal stress of the weather. You'll need to carefully select your materials, keeping in mind the style and purpose of the area as well as the climate in your region.

Grass is the most common outdoor floor covering, but there are a variety of other materials you can use. Brick, stone, concrete, wood and gravel can be used alone or in combination to create attractive, durable outdoor floors. Look for ways of repeating materials used elsewhere in your landscape or house. For example, if you have an attractive wood fence, use the same type of wood in a deck. Or if your home has a distinctive brick facade, repeat this element in a patio or walkway.

The flooring projects in this section illustrate the basics of paving with gravel, stone, brick, concrete and wood. With an understanding of these techniques, you can easily complete projects as demonstrated or create variations. Many of the projects include suggestions for other materials, applications or techniques you can apply to the basic principles.

Because there are many situations where a traditional carpet of healthy green grass works best, we've also demonstrated professional methods for starting a new lawn or renovating an existing lawn.

IN THIS CHAPTER

Surface Preparation

A well-constructed base is crucial to the success of any paving project. The quality of the base, which protects the paving project from time- and weather-inflicted damage, determines the longevity of the project. Whether you're building a stepping-stone path, a concrete patio or a brick walkway, surface preparation is vital to the success of your project.

The best material for a paving base is compactible gravel. The gravel is applied and compressed over evenly excavated soil, creating a smooth surface to pave. In addition, gravel drains water easily, preventing erosion and frost heave.

For most paving projects, it's best to cover the base with a layer of landscape fabric. The fabric prevents grass and weeds from growing up through the paving. Cut the landscape fabric into sheets and arrange them so that the edges overlap by 6". For some projects, you'll need to add a layer of sand over the landscape fabric.

The most important part of surface preparation is excavating and creating a smooth base with the proper slope for drainage. Before you begin excavating, evaluate the grade of the area you're paving, as shown in "Grading" (page 128). If the area is uneven or has a severe slope, you'll probably need to excavate or fill the area, then level it before you begin paving.

TOOLS & MATERIALS

- Basic tools (page 120)
- Line level
- Stakes
- String
- Compactible gravel
- Sod cutter (optional)
- Rented plate compactor or hand tamp

HOW TO PREPARE SURFACES FOR PAVING

Step A: Outline the Excavation Area

1. If you're paving a straight design, outline the area with stakes and string. Place the stakes so that they're at least 1 ft. outside the site the intersecting strings will mark—the actual corners of the paved surface. Use a line

Compactible gravel

Excavated area

A. *Outline the paving area with stakes and string, then measure the diagonals to ensure the outline is square.*

level to level the strings. (For curves, use a rope or garden hose to lay out the design.)

2. Measure diagonally across the corners to make sure the outline is square. Adjust the stakes until these diagonal measurements are equal. For straight designs with rounded corners, as shown below, use a rope or garden hose to mark the curves.

Step B: Excavate the Area

1. Starting at the outside edge, use a shovel to evenly excavate the outlined area so it's about 5" deeper than the thickness of the planned paving.

2. Use a long 2 × 4 to check the surface for high and low spots, then redistribute soil as necessary to create a smooth, even surface across the entire area.

3. If you're building a paver patio or walkway, excavate 6" beyond the planned width and length of the project, which allows room for the edging.

Step C: Add Compactible Gravel

1. Pour compactible gravel over the excavated area, then rake it into a smooth layer at least 4" deep. The thickness of this base layer can vary to compensate for any unevenness in the excavation.

2. Use the 2 × 4 to check the surface once again for high and low spots, and add or remove gravel as needed to make the surface even.

Step D: Compact the Gravel

1. Use a rented plate compactor to pack the gravel

TIP: RENTING A SOD CUTTER

You may want to rent a sod cutter to strip grass from your pathway or patio site. Sod cutters, available at most rental centers, help you save time on big projects. These machines excavate at a very even depth, allowing you to roll up the removed sod. The cut sod can be replanted in other areas of your yard.

into a firm, even surface. For small areas, you can pack down the gravel with a hand tamp.

2. Check the evenness of the gravel base with a 2 × 4. Remove or add gravel as needed, then repack the base with the plate compactor.

B. *Remove soil from the outlined layer with a shovel until the excavation is 5" deeper than the height of the paving.*

C. *Pour compactible gravel over the excavated area, then rake it into a smooth 4" layer.*

D. *Use a rented plate compactor (pictured) or a hand tamp to pack the gravel into a firm, flat surface.*

Loose-fill Pathway

Walkways and paths serve as hallways between heavily used areas of your yard. In addition to directing traffic, paths create visual corridors that direct the eye to attractive features or areas.

A loose-fill pathway is a simple, inexpensive alternative to a concrete or paved path. Lightweight loose materials, such as gravel, crushed rock, bark or wood chips are used to "pave" a prepared pathway surface. Because the materials are not fixed within the path, edging is installed around the perimeter of the pathway to hold them in place. In addition to using standard preformed plastic edging, you can fashion edging from common hardscape building materials, such as wood, cut stone and brick pavers. For professional-looking re-

sults, repeat a material used in the exterior of the house or other landscape structures in the pathway edging. Select loose-fill materials that complement the color and texture of your edging.

Our loose-fill project uses brick edging set in soil, which works well for casual, lightly traveled pathways. However, this method should be used only in dense, well-drained soil. Bricks set in loose or swampy soil won't hold their position.

Loose-fill materials are available at most home and garden stores. Many stores sell these materials prebagged, which makes transporting and applying them easier. Aggregate supply companies also sell crushed rock and pea gravel in bulk, which is often a less expensive option. If you buy loose-fill material in bulk, it may be easier to have the supplier deliver it than to transport it yourself.

As you prepare to build a path, consider how it will normally be used, keeping in mind that loose-fill pathways are best suited to light-traffic areas. Also think about how the path will fit into the overall style and shape of your landscape. Curved pathways create a soft, relaxed look that complements traditional landscape designs, while straight or angular paths fit well in contemporary designs. You may want

TOOLS & MATERIALS

- Basic tools (page 120)
- Trenching spade
- Landscape fabric
- Rope
- Brick pavers
- Loose-fill material

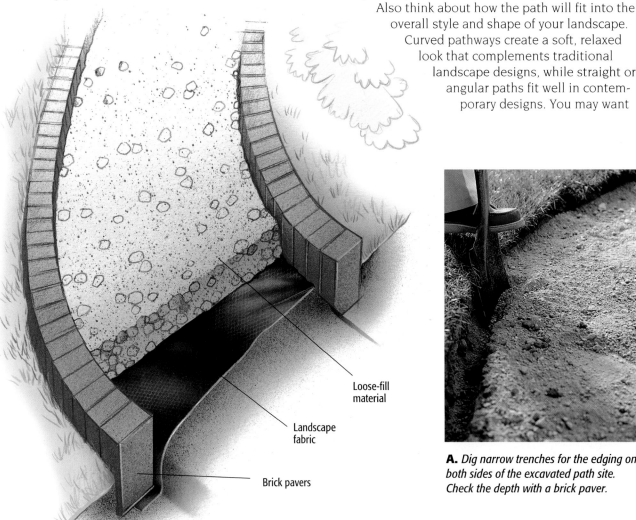

Loose-fill material

Landscape fabric

Brick pavers

A. *Dig narrow trenches for the edging on both sides of the excavated path site. Check the depth with a brick paver.*

to strategically place the path to lend depth to an area or highlight an interesting element.

HOW TO CREATE A LOOSE-FILL PATHWAY
Step A: Excavate the Path
1. Lay out the shape of the path with a rope or garden hose, then use a spade to excavate the area to a depth of 3". Rake the site smooth.
2. Dig narrow edging trenches along both edges of the path site, using a trenching spade or hoe. Make the trenches about 2" deeper than the path.
3. Test the trench depth with a brick paver placed on end in the trench—the top of the brick should stand several inches above ground. If necessary, adjust the trench to bring the bricks to the correct height.
Step B: Add Landscape Fabric
Line the trench with strips of landscape fabric, overlapping the strips by at least 6". Push the ends of the landscape fabric into the edging trenches.
Step C: Set the Bricks
1. Set the bricks into the edging trenches. Arrange them side by side, with no gaps between bricks.
2. Using a trowel, pack soil behind and beneath each brick. Adjust bricks as necessary to keep rows even.
Step D: Spread the Loose Fill
1. Spread the loose-fill material, adding material until it sits slightly above ground level. Level the

VARIATION: CHILDREN'S PLAY AREA

Using the same techniques shown here for building a path, you can pave the floor of an outdoor room with loose-fill material. Simply excavate and level the area, as shown in "Surface Preparation" (page 184).

Loose-fill paving, especially pea gravel or sand, works well in a children's play area.

surface, using a garden rake.
2. Tap the bricks lightly on the inside faces to help set them into the soil. Inspect and adjust the bricks yearly, adding new loose-fill material as necessary.

B. *Place strips of landscape fabric over the path and into the edging trenches, overlapping sections by 6".*

C. *Install bricks end to end and flush against each other in the trenches, then pack soil behind and beneath each brick.*

D. *Fill the pathways with loose-fill material. Tap the inside face of each brick paver with a mallet to help set them permanently in the ground.*

Stepping-stone Path

Whether you are paving a frequently traveled area, or introducing a sense of movement to your landscape, a stepping-stone path can be an ideal and inexpensive solution. A thoughtfully arranged stepping-stone design almost begs to be walked upon, and its open design complements, rather than overpowers, the landscape.

When designing your path, keep in mind that paths with gentle curves or bends are usually more attractive than straight ones. The distance between the stones is also an important consideration. Set the stones to accommodate a normal stride, so you can effortlessly step from one stone to the next.

There are a variety of materials available for constructing stepping-stone paths, from natural stone to prefabricated concrete. To ensure that your path blends with the rest or your landscape, select a material that suits your yard's style and existing materials. Natural stone indigenous to your area is often a good choice. Many stone yards sell 1" to 2½" sedimentary rock "steppers," which are ideal for stepping-stone paths. But you can also use cut stone, wood rounds or precast concrete pavers.

Even if you expect it to be more decorative than functional, keep safety in mind as you purchase materials and build your path. Select stones that are wide enough to stand on comfortably and have a flat, even, lightly textured surface.

Like other paved surfaces, stepping-stones can be adversely affected by the weather. Without a proper base, they can become unstable or settle unevenly. Prepare the base carefully and check the path each spring, adjusting stones as necessary for safety.

TOOLS & MATERIALS

- Basic tools (page 120)
- Sand or compactible gravel
- Stepping stones

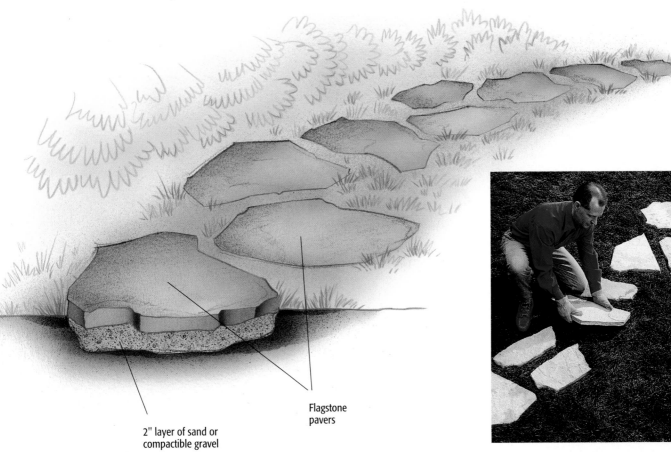

Flagstone pavers

2" layer of sand or compactible gravel

A. *Arrange the stepping stones on top of the grass, then test the layout by walking the path. Adjust the stones as necessary.*

HOW TO CREATE A STEPPING-STONE PATH

Step A: Arrange the Stones

Arrange the stones along the ground in your planned pattern. Walk the full course of the path, then adjust the spacing between the steppers so you can step smoothly from stone to stone.

Step B: Let the Ground Cover Die

If you're installing the path over grass or another living ground cover, leave the stones in place for three to five days. The ground cover beneath the stones will die, leaving a perfect outline of the stones.

Step C: Prepare the Base

1. Using a spade, cut around the outline, creating an excavation 2" deeper than the thickness of the stone.
2. Add a 2" layer of sand or compactible gravel and smooth it out with a garden rake.

Step D: Set & Adjust the Stones

1. Place the stones in the partially filled holes. Rock each stone back and forth several times to help it settle securely into the base.
2. Check to make sure the stones are stable and flush with the ground. Add or remove sand and readjust the stones as necessary.

VARIATION: PLANTING BETWEEN STEPPING-STONES

Consider planting a low-lying, spreading ground cover between the stones for added contrast and texture.

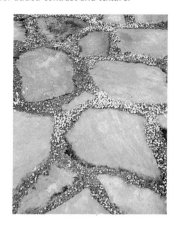

These plants are a few that work well with stepping-stone paths:

• Alyssum	• Candytuft	• Thymus
• Rock cress	• Lobelia	• Scotch moss
• Thrift	• Forget-me-not	• Irish moss
• Miniature dianthus	• Saxifrage	• Woolly thyme
	• Sedum	• Mock strawberry

B. *Leave the stones in place for several days to kill the grass beneath, leaving a visible outline for excavation.*

C. *Dig up the outlined areas, 2" deeper than the height of the stones. Spread a 2" layer of sand in each hole.*

D. *Reposition the stones, adding or removing sand as necessary until they're stable and flush with the ground.*

Flagstone Walkway

Natural flagstone is an ideal material for creating landscape floors. It's attractive and durable, and blends well with both formal and informal landscapes. Although flagstone structures are often mortared, they can also be constructed with the sand-set method. Sand-setting flagstones is much faster and easier than setting them with mortar.

There are a variety of flat, thin sedimentary rocks that can be used for this project. Home and garden stores often carry several types of flagstone, but stone supply yards usually have a greater variety. Some varieties of flagstone cost more than others, but there are many affordable options. When you buy the flagstone for your project, select pieces in a variety of sizes from large to small. Arranging the stones for your walkway is similar to putting together a

puzzle, and you'll need to see all the pieces. When you're ready to begin the project, sort the stones by size, and spread them out so that you can see each one.

The following example demonstrates how to build a straight flagstone walkway with wood edging. If you'd like to build a curved walkway, select another edging material, such as brick or cut stone. Instead of filling gaps between stones with sand, you might want to fill them with topsoil and plant grass or some other ground cover between the stones.

HOW TO BUILD A FLAGSTONE WALKWAY

Step A: Prepare the Site & Install the Edging

1. Lay out, excavate and prepare the base for the walkway (page 184). Remove the stakes and string when the base is complete.
2. Form edging by installing 2 × 6 pressure-treated lumber around the perimeter of the pathway.
3. Drive stakes on the outside of the edging, spaced 12" apart. The tops of the stakes should be below

TOOLS & MATERIALS

- Basic tools (page 120)
- Hand tamp
- Circular saw with masonry blade
- Landscape fabric
- Sand
- 2 × 6 pressure-treated lumber
- Flagstone pavers

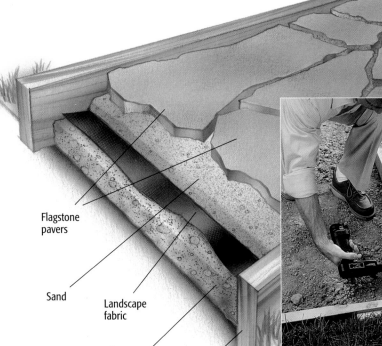

Flagstone pavers

Sand

Landscape fabric

Compactible gravel

2 × 6 wood edging

A. *Drive 12" stakes outside the 2 × 6 pressure-treated edging, then attach them together with galvanized screws.*

B. *Test-fit the flagstones inside the edging, mark them for cutting, then set them aside in the same arrangement.*

190

ground level. Drive galvanized screws through the edging and into the stakes.

Step B: Arrange the Stones

1. Test-fit the stones over the walkway base, finding an attractive arrangement that limits the number of cuts needed. The gaps between the stones should range between ⅜" and 2" wide.

2. Use a pencil to mark the stones for cutting, then remove the stones and place them beside the walkway in the same arrangement.

3. Score along the marked lines with a circular saw and masonry blade set to ⅛" blade depth. Set a piece of wood under the stone, just inside the scored line. Use a masonry chisel and hammer to strike along the scored line until the stone breaks.

Step C: Make a Sand Base

1. Lay strips of landscape fabric over the walkway base, overlapping the strips by 6". (If you plan to grow grass or another ground cover between the stones, skip this step.)

2. Spread a 2" layer of sand over the landscape fabric. Make a "screed" for smoothing the sand from a short 2 × 6, notched to fit inside the edging. (see inset photo) The depth of the notches should equal the thickness of the stones.

3. Pull the screed from one end of the walkway to the other, adding sand as needed to create a level base.

Step D: Lay the Flagstones

1. Beginning at one corner of the walkway, lay the

VARIATION: FLAGSTONE PATIO

Using the same technique for fitting and setting the stones, you can easily create a flagstone patio.

Follow the steps for preparing the patio base, as shown on pages 192 to 193. Then install the wood edging and flagstone as demonstrated below.

flagstones onto the sand base. Repeat the arrangement you created in Step A, with ⅜"- to 2"-wide gaps between stones.

2. If necessary, add or remove sand to level the stones, then set them by tapping them with a rubber mallet or a length of 2 × 4.

Step E: Add Sand Between the Stones

1. Fill the gaps between the stones with sand. (Use topsoil, if you're going to plant grass or ground cover between the stones.)

2. Pack sand into the gaps, then spray the entire walkway with water to help settle the sand.

3. Repeat #2 until the gaps are completely filled and tightly packed with sand.

C. *Spread a 2" layer of sand over the landscape fabric and smooth it out with a screed made from a notched 2 × 6.*

D. *Lay the flagstones in the sand base leaving a gap between stones. Use a rubber mallet to set them in place.*

E. *Pack the gaps between the stones and the edging with sand, then lightly spray the entire walkway with water.*

Brick Paver Patio

Brick pavers are versatile and durable, making them an excellent material for paving walkways and patios. They convey an impression of formality, quickly dressing up your landscape. Brick pavers are available in a variety of shapes, patterns and colors to complement your landscape. It's best to use concrete pavers rather than traditional clay bricks. Concrete pavers have self-spacing lugs that make them easy to install. To estimate the number of pavers you'll need, see

"Estimating Materials" (page 115).

The easiest way to build a patio or walkway with brick pavers is to set them in sand. With this method, the pavers rest on a 1" layer of sand spread over a prepared base. Pavers are then arranged over the sand, and the joints between them are densely packed with more sand. The sand keeps the pavers in place, but still allows them to shift if the ground contracts and expands with temperature changes.

TOOLS & MATERIALS

- Basic tools (page 120)
- Hand tamp
- Circular saw with masonry blade
- Landscape fabric
- Sand
- Rigid plastic edging
- 1"-thick pipe
- Brick pavers
- Rented plate compactor
- Broom
- 2 × 4

HOW TO BUILD A SAND-SET PAVER PATIO

After you've prepared the foundation for the patio (see "Surface Preparation," page 184), you're ready to begin installing the patio. Leave the stakes and strings in place to use as a reference.

Step A: Prepare the Surface

1. Cut strips of landscape fabric and lay them over the base, overlapping each strip by at least 6".

2. Install rigid plastic edging around the edges of the patio, below the reference strings. Anchor the edging by driving galvanized spikes through the predrilled holes and into the subbase. For curves and rounded patio corners, use rigid plastic edging

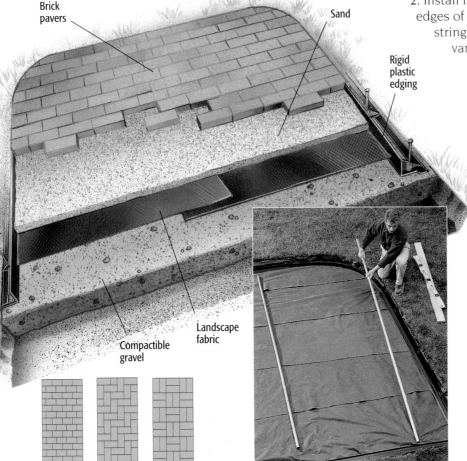

Brick pavers

Sand

Rigid plastic edging

Compactible gravel

Landscape fabric

Staggered **Herringbone** **Basket-weave**

A. *Cover the excavated area with landscape fabric, install the edging, and space 1" pipes every 6 ft. as spacers.*

B. *Remove the spacers from the 1" layer of sand, fill the depressions with sand and even the sand with a hand tamp.*

with notches on the outside flange.

3. Remove the reference strings, then place 1"-thick pipes or wood strips over the landscape fabric, spaced every 6 ft., to serve as depth spacers for laying the sand base.

Step B: Add the Sand Base

1. Spread a 1" layer of sand over the landscape fabric, using a garden rake to smooth it out. The sand should just cover the tops of the depth spacers.

2. Water the layer of sand thoroughly, then lightly pack it down with a hand tamp.

3. Screed the sand to an even layer by resting a long 2 × 4 on the spacers and drawing it across the sand, using a sawing motion. Fill footprints and low areas with sand, then water, tamp and screed again.

4. Remove the embedded spacers along the sides of the patio base, then fill the grooves with sand and pat them smooth with the hand tamp.

Step C: Set the First Section of Pavers

1. Lay the first border paver in one corner of the patio, making sure it rests firmly against the plastic edging. Lay the next paver snug against the first.

2. Set the pavers by tapping them into the sand with a mallet. Use the depth of the first paver as a guide for setting the remaining pavers in a 2-ft. section.

3. After each section is set, use a long level to make

sure the pavers are flat. Make adjustments by tapping high pavers deeper into the sand, or by removing low pavers and adding a thin layer of additional sand underneath them.

Step D: Complete the Patio

1. Continue installing 2-ft.-wide sections of the border and interior pavers.

2. At rounded corners, install border pavers in a fan pattern with even gaps between the pavers. Gentle curves may accommodate full-sized border pavers, but for sharper bends, you'll need to mark and cut wedge-shaped border pavers to fit. Use a circular saw with a masonry blade to cut the pavers.

3. Lay the remaining interior pavers. Use a 2 × 4 to check that the entire patio is level. Adjust any uneven pavers by tapping them with the mallet or by adding more sand beneath them.

Step E: Fill Joints & Compact the Surface

1. Spread a ½" layer of sand over the patio, then use the plate compactor to compress the entire patio and pack the sand into the joints.

2. Sweep up the loose sand, then soak the patio area thoroughly to settle the sand in the joints.

3. Let the surface dry completely. If necessary, spread and pack sand over the patio again, until all the joints are tightly packed.

C. *Lay the pavers tight against each other, setting them with the mallet. Check the height with a level.*

D. *Install border pavers in a fan pattern around the corners, and trim pavers as necessary to make them fit.*

E. *Spread a ½" layer of sand over the patio and pack it into the joints with the plate compactor. Sweep up the loose sand.*

Concrete Patio

Concrete is an inexpensive material for creating durable, low-maintenance outdoor floors. It can be formed into almost any shape or size, making it an ideal choice for walkways, driveways and patios.

The patio in our project is divided into four even quadrants separated by permanent forms. This construction method makes it possible to complete the project in four easy stages—you can pour, tool and seed each quadrant separately.

An isolation joint separates the patio from the foundation of the house, so footings aren't necessary. When calculating the depth of the base, remember to maintain adequate clearance between the top of the patio and the door threshold. The top of the patio should be at least 2" below the house sill or threshold, so the concrete has room to rise and fall without suffering damage from frost heave.

Concrete may be left as is or finished with a variety of techniques to give the surface an attractive texture or pattern. For this project, we added color and texture with a layer of seeding aggregate.

TOOLS & MATERIALS

- Basic tools (page 120)
- Masonry hoe
- Wood float
- Concrete edger
- Stiff-bristled brush
- Paint roller

- Pressure-treated 2 × 4s
- Stakes
- String
- 2½" deck screws
- Masking tape

- Wire mesh
- Bolsters
- Concrete mix
- Plastic
- Seeding aggregate
- Exposed aggregate sealer

HOW TO CONSTRUCT A CONCRETE PATIO
Step A: Prepare the Surface & Build the Forms
1. Lay out the patio, excavate the site and prepare the base (page 184). Leave the stakes and string in place as a reference.
2. Measure and cut pressure-treated 2 × 4s for the permanent form outlining the entire patio.
3. Lay the boards in place, using the strings as guides. Fasten the ends with 2½" deck screws.
4. Temporarily stake the forms at 2-ft. intervals, then use a 2 × 4 and a level to make sure the frame is level.
Step B: Divide the Form into Quadrants
1. Measure, mark and cut the 2 × 4s that divide the patio into quadrants. Attach these pieces to the frame with toenailed deck screws.
2. Drive deck screws halfway into the inside faces of

Cement

Bolster

Wire mesh

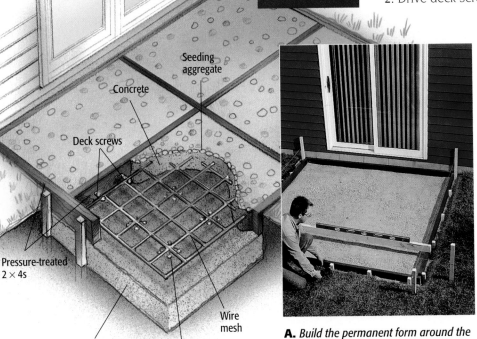

Seeding aggregate

Concrete

Deck screws

Pressure-treated 2 × 4s

Compactible gravel

Bolster

Wire mesh

A. *Build the permanent form around the patio perimeter and temporarily stake it into place, using a level as you work.*

B. *Install the 2 × 4s that divide the patio into four quadrants and attach them to the frame with deck screws.*

all the forms, spacing them every 12". These exposed screws will act as tie rods between the poured concrete and the forms.

3. Cover the tops of the forms with masking tape to protect them when you pour the concrete.

Step C: Pour the Concrete for the First Quadrant

1. Cut reinforcing wire mesh to fit inside each quadrant, leaving 1" clearance on all sides. Use bolsters to raise the mesh off the base, making sure it remains at least 2" below the top of the forms.

2. Mix the concrete in a wheelbarrow, then pour it into the first quadrant. Use a masonry hoe to spread the concrete evenly in the form.

3. Screed the concrete with a straight 2 × 4 that is long enough to reach across a quadrant.

4. Slide a spade along the inside edges of the form, then rap the outer edges with a hammer to settle the concrete into the quadrant.

Step D: Embed the Aggregate

1. Sprinkle handfuls of seeding aggregate evenly over the wet concrete.

2. Use a float to embed the aggregate. Make sure that the aggregate is firmly embedded, but still visible.

3. Tool the edges of the quadrant with a concrete edger, then use a wood float to smooth out any marks left by the tool. Cover the seeded concrete with plastic so it doesn't cure too quickly as you pour and finish the remaining quadrants.

4. Pour concrete into and finish the remaining quad-

VARIATION: WALKWAY

Using the same technique as used to finish the patio's surface, you can give a freshly poured concrete walkway an exposed aggregate finish. Apply the finish a section at a time for best results.

rants, one at a time, using the same technique.

Step E: Complete the Finish & Seal the Concrete

1. After the water has evaporated from the concrete surface, mist it with water, then scrub it with a stiff-bristled brush to expose the aggregate.

2. Remove the tape from the forms, then replace the plastic and let the concrete cure for one week. After the concrete has cured, rinse and scrub the aggregate again to remove any remaining residue.

3. Wait three weeks, then seal the patio surface with exposed-aggregate sealer. Apply the sealer according to the manufacturer's directions.

C. *Pour concrete into the first quadrant and screed the concrete smooth with a 2 × 4 that rests on top of the form.*

D. *Sprinkle handfuls of seeding aggregate evenly over the surface of the wet concrete and embed it with a float.*

E. *Mist the surface of the concrete with water and scrub it with a stiff-bristled brush to expose the aggregate.*

Platform Deck

A freestanding platform deck is a low-maintenance option for creating an outdoor floor. Because it can be constructed virtually anywhere, in almost any size, a platform deck works in nearly any landscape. The wood can be left natural, stained or painted to blend with your house and other landscape elements.

A deck built from weather-resistant materials will last for years. Galvanized hardware, which resists rust and corrosion, helps a deck remain strong and stable.

You'll be able to build this deck over a single weekend. It uses lumber in standard lengths, so you won't need to do a lot of cutting. In addition, this deck uses precast concrete footings, rather than poured footings. These precast footings are available at home improvement centers and lumberyards.

Our 12 × 12-ft. deck rests on a 10 × 10-ft. base formed by 18 concrete footings arranged in three rows of six footings each. Joists are secured in slots in the tops of the footings, simplifying the building process. If you're building your deck on sloped or uneven ground, you'll need to use 4 × 4 posts that fit in the center of the footings to level the joists (see page 86 for further information).

TOOLS & MATERIALS

- Basic tools (page 120)
- Paintbrush
- Circular saw
- Framing square
- Wood stakes
- Precast concrete footings (18)
- 12-ft. 2 × 6s (38)
- Wood sealer/protectant
- 2 lbs. galvanized 3" deck screws

HOW TO BUILD A PLATFORM DECK

Step A: Install & Level the Footings

1. Measure a 10 × 10-ft. area for the deck foundation, and mark the corners with stakes.
2. Position a footing at each corner, then measure from corner to corner, from the center of each footing. Adjust until the diagonal measurements are equal, which means the footings are square.
3. Place a 2 × 6 across the corner footings

2 × 6 hand rail

2 × 6 decking spaced ⅛" apart

2 × 2s spaced 4" apart

2 × 6 side joist

2 × 6 joist

Precast concrete footings

12" sleepers

2 × 6 rim joist

A. *Position the corner footings and the center footing for the back joist. Remove or add soil beneath the footings to level them.*

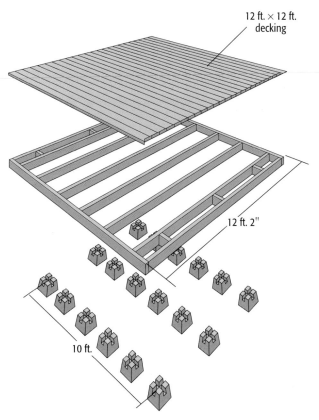

12 ft. × 12 ft. decking

12 ft. 2"

10 ft.

for the back row, setting it in the center slots. Check this joist with a level, then add or remove soil beneath footings as necessary to level it.

4. Center a footing between these corner footings. Use a level to recheck the joist, then add or remove soil beneath the center footing, if necessary. Remove the joist.

5. Repeat the process described in #3, #4 and #5 to set and level the footings for the front row.

6. Position the remaining 12 footings at equal intervals, aligned in three rows. Position a 2 × 6 from the front row of footings to the back, and adjust soil as necessary to bring the interior footings into alignment with, the front and back rows.

Step B: Install the Joists

1. Seal the ends of each 2 × 6 with wood sealer/protectant and let them dry completely.

2. Center a 12-ft. joist across each row of footings. Using a level, check the joists once again and carefully adjust the footings if necessary.

Step C: Add the Side Joists & Rim Joists

1. Line up a 2 × 6 flush against the ends of the joists along the left side of the deck, with the ends extending equally past the front and back joists.

2. Attach the side joist by driving a pair of deck screws into each joist.

3. Repeat this process to install the right side joist.

4. At the front of the deck, position a 2 × 6 rim joist flush between the ends of the side joists, forming a

butt joint on each end.

5. Attach the rim joist to the side joists by driving a pair of deck screws through the faces of the side joists, into the ends of the rim joist.

6. Repeat #1 and #2 to install the other rim joist.

Step D: Position the Sleepers

1. Measure and cut six 2 × 6 sleepers to fit between the front and back joists and the rim joists. Seal the cut ends with wood sealer/protectant and let them

B. *Position the remaining footings and insert the joists. Check to make sure the framework is level, and adjust as needed.*

C. *Install the front and back rim joists between the ends of the side joists, securing them with pairs of deck screws.*

D. *Position the sleepers in the slots of the footings, then attach them to the joists on both sides with pairs of deck screws.*

Platform Deck (cont.)

E. *After the framing is completed, measure the diagonals and adjust the frame until it's square.*

F. *Install the decking by driving a pair of screws into each joist. Use a framing square to leave a ⅛" space between boards.*

dry completely.

2. Position one sleeper in each row of footings, between the first joist and the rim joist. Attach each sleeper by driving a pair of galvanized deck screws through each of the joists and into the sleeper.

Step E: Square Up the Frame

1. Once the framing is complete, measure the diagonals from corner to corner. Compare the measurements to see if they are equal.

2. Adjust the framing as necessary by pushing it into alignment. You'll need a helper to hold one side of the framework while you push against the other.

Step F: Install the Decking

1. Seal the 2 × 6 decking boards with wood sealer/protectant and let them dry. Seal all exposed framing members as well.

2. Lay a 2 × 6 over the surface of the deck, perpendicular to the joists and flush with the rim joist. Secure this board with deck screws.

3. Repeat # 2 to install the rest of the decking. Use a framing square to set a ⅛" space between boards. You may need to rip cut the last decking board.

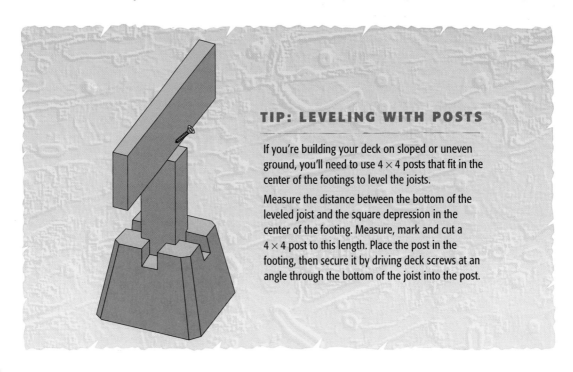

TIP: LEVELING WITH POSTS

If you're building your deck on sloped or uneven ground, you'll need to use 4 × 4 posts that fit in the center of the footings to level the joists.

Measure the distance between the bottom of the leveled joist and the square depression in the center of the footing. Measure, mark and cut a 4 × 4 post to this length. Place the post in the footing, then secure it by driving deck screws at an angle through the bottom of the joist into the post.

VARIATION: ADDING A RAILING

TOOLS & MATERIALS

- 12-ft. 2 × 6s (3)
- 42" 2 × 2s
  (one end beveled)
- Drill
- Level
- 2½" galvanized
  deck screws

Although this platform deck rests low to the ground, you may want to add a hand rail around two or three sides of the deck, especially if the deck will be used by young children or an elderly person. For each side of the deck to which you're adding railings, you'll need 25 2 × 2s, 42" long.

Step A:

1. Place the 2 × 2s flush together, adjust them so the ends are even, and draw a pair of straight lines, 3" apart, across each board, 1½" above the beveled end. Repeat the process and draw a single line 2¾" from the top of the other end. Using the lines as guides, drill pilot holes into the 2 × 2s.

2. Apply wood sealer/protectant to the ends of the 2 × 2s.

Step B:

1. Position a 2 × 2 flush with the bottom of the joist, then clamp it in place to use as a placement guide.

2. Position the corner 2 × 2s against the side joists, beveled end down, 4" in from the corner. Check for plumb, then drive deck screws through the pilot holes.

3. Attach the remaining 2 × 2s for each side, spacing them 4" apart.

Step C:

1. Hold a 12-ft. 2 × 6 that forms the top of the railing in place, behind the installed 2 × 2s.

2. Attach the 2 × 2s to the 2 × 6 top rails by driving deck screws through the pilot holes.

3. Connect the top rails at the corners, using pairs of deck screws.

4. Finish the railing by applying a coat of wood sealer, according to the manufacturer's directions.

A. *Gang together the 2 × 2s, then drill a pair of pilot holes into the beveled ends, and a single pilot hole in the opposite end.*

B. *Attach the 2 × 2s to the side joists, leaving a 4" gap between them.*

C. *Level the 2 × 6 railing behind the 2 × 2s, then attach it by driving screws through the pilot holes.*

Soil Preparation

Soil preparation is the most important step in establishing new lawns and other living ground covers. When you're starting from scratch, good soil preparation ensures that your lawn has the foundation it needs to develop a strong, healthy root system. Whether you're using grass seed, sod or planting another ground cover, the process of preparing the soil remains the same.

SIZING UP YOUR SOIL

The first step in soil preparation is finding out the condition of your existing soil. Start by getting a test done on the soil in the area where you plan to establish a lawn. For more information on collecting soil samples and getting a soil test report, see "Soil" (page 118). The soil test report will include information on the type of soil you have, the nutrient levels present and whether or not the soil is capable of supporting a healthy lawn. If the soil is within a desirable range, the report will also include detailed instructions for amending and fertilizing it.

AMENDING THE SOIL

If the test report indicates that you merely need to amend the soil, purchase the recommended amendments and rent a tiller to blend them into the soil.

Following manufacturer's instructions, set the tiller so that it digs to a depth between 4" and 6" (see photo, opposite page). Spread an even layer of the amendments over the surface of a small area and till them into the soil. Work your way across the yard in the same pattern you would use for mowing the grass. Once the entire lawn area is tilled, regrade and level the soil as necessary.

BRINGING IN NEW SOIL

If your soil fails the lawn compatibility test, don't despair. You can purchase high-quality topsoil to add to your existing soil. Topsoil, also called "black dirt," is sold by

Preparing the soil properly is one of the most important steps in establishing a thick, healthy lawn.

the cubic yard and can be delivered by soil contractors (below).

It's important not to create two distinct layers of soil, so you need to prepare the existing soil to mix with the new topsoil. Dig several small holes, then inspect and feel the texture of the existing soil. If it isn't severely compacted, you can simply loosen it with a tiller before adding topsoil. If, on the other hand, the existing soil is heavily compacted, hire a contractor to "slice" it before you add the topsoil. Slicing is performed by heavy machinery outfitted with a blade. The blade makes deep cuts into the soil, loosening it up and eliminating compaction.

When you order topsoil, give the contractor the dimensions of your lawn and order enough topsoil to spread a 4" layer over the entire area. If you're covering a large area, you may want to hire the contractor to distribute the soil as well as deliver it.

Even if the area you're covering seems manageable, consider asking friends or hiring someone to help you spread the soil. It's not difficult, but it takes some time and effort. Drop wheelbarrow loads of soil around the area, then use a rake to distribute the soil evenly over the entire surface. When all the soil is distributed, check and correct the grade of the yard (page 128).

SMOOTHING THE SURFACE

To create a smooth, even surface for seeding, sodding or planting ground cover, you'll need to slightly compress the soil. The goal is to lightly smooth the surface without compacting the soil. Fill a landscape drum ⅛ full with water, then roll it over the surface, walking in a row-by-row pattern (photo, right).

To amend the soil, begin by spreading an even layer of the prescribed amendments over the area. Then use a tiller to blend the amendments into the soil, working in a small area at a time.

(above) Order enough topsoil to spread a 4" to 6" layer over your existing soil. Before you spread new topsoil, loosen existing soil with a tiller or hire a contractor to "slice" the soil.

(left) Lightly compact the soil with a landscape drum. Roll it over the lawn, walking in a row-by-row pattern.

Seed Lawn

Seeding is the easiest and least expensive way to start a new lawn. But, there are a couple of factors you'll need to consider: The time of year, the type of grass seed used, the condition of the soil and the amount of water the seed receives all contribute to the success of a seeded lawn.

Timing is essential when seeding a new lawn. The best time to seed is during the growing season for grass shoots—the parts of a grass plant that spread and grow new leaves, forming a dense lawn. The timing of this window of opportunity varies, depending on where you live. In warmer climates, shoot growth primarily occurs in the spring. In cooler climates, there are two shoot-growth seasons—one in the early spring, and another in the early fall. Many experts feel that fall is the ideal time to seed lawns in colder climates, because fewer weeds are present and more frequent rains and cooler temperatures keep the grass seed moist.

When buying grass seed, choose a variety that's suited to your climate.(For more information on selecting seed, see the tip on page 203.) Grass seed is commonly sold in blends combining several different varieties of grasses. Purchase grass seed with a low percentage of crop, inert matter and weeds, and a high germination percentage for each of the desired grasses.

Soil condition is another factor that determines the success of seeding a lawn. The ideal soil for seeding has been properly prepared, as shown in "Soil Preparation" (page 200), and moistened to a depth of 4" to 6". Moisture not only nourishes the seeds, it protects them—seeds tend to blow away if the soil is too dry. Although the soil needs to be moist, try to avoid seeding just before a heavy rainfall, which could wash seeds away.

Once you've seeded a lawn, keep the soil moist during the germination period, a minimum of two weeks. After the germination period, water the grass as needed, making sure it receives a total of about 1" to 1½" of water a week in rainfall plus irrigation. If puddles

TOOLS & MATERIALS

- Broadcast spreader
- Leaf rake
- Landscape drum
- Grass seed

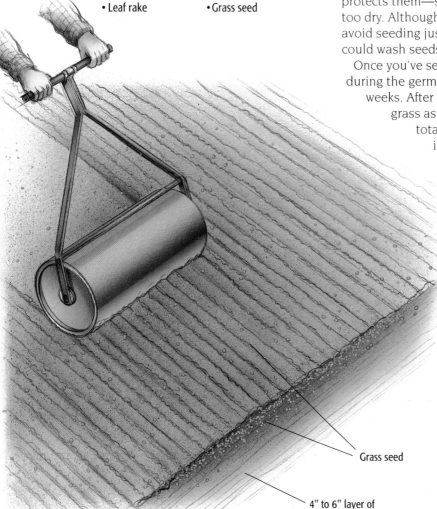

Grass seed

4" to 6" layer of topsoil

A. *Fill the broadcast spreader with grass seed in the amount listed on the package.*

form, stop watering until they recede. Don't overwater your new lawn—too much water encourages fungal problems and root disease.

HOW TO SEED A NEW LAWN
Step A: Prepare the Soil
1. Prepare the soil as shown on page 200. Water the soil until it's moist to a depth of 4" to 6".
2. Place a broadcast spreader on a paved surface, such as a driveway. Fill the spreader with the amount of grass recommended on the seed package.
Step B: Spread the Seed
1. Establish the desired rate of seed coverage by calibrating the spreader according to the recommendations on the seed package.
2. Apply the seed in two stages, following a grid pattern to ensure even coverage. First, push the spreader back and forth across the yard in straight passes. When you've covered the entire area, push the spreader up and down the yard, perpendicular to the first application.
Step C: Cover & Water the Seed
1. Use a rake to lightly rake the soil until only 10% to 15% of the seed is visible.
2. Lightly compact the raked soil by rolling over it with a half-filled landscape drum.
3. Water the yard until the soil is moist to a depth of 6", then keep the seed moist for several weeks.

TIP: READING GRASS SEED LABELS:

The type of grass you select will play a large part in the success of your lawn. But it can be difficult to tell exactly what you're buying. Whether it's a prepackaged blend or seed sold by the pound in bulk, there will always be a label that tells you exactly what type of seeds are included in that blend.

Lush Lawn Blend

Grass Seed & Supply Co., Fairtown, MN
Lot. No.: 5546-89 Test Date: 06/06/98

Pure Seed	Variety	Germination
42%	Colonel Kentucky Bluegrass	88%
33%	Fine Perennial Ryegrass	78%
21%	Red Tall Fescue	80%
0.4%	Inert Matter	
1.2%	Crop	
2.4%	Weed	

Pure Seed: the percentage of seeds for each variety that are capable of growing.

Germination: the portion of the pure seed that will germinate within a reasonable amount of time.

Inert Matter: materials present in the blend, such as broken seeds, hulls and chaff, that aren't capable of growing.

Crop: the percentage of agricultural grain and undesirable grass seed contained in the blend.

Weed: the portion of weed seeds present in the blend.

B. *Calibrate the spreader according to the seed package's instructions, then push the spreader across the lawn in two passes, following a grid pattern for even coverage.*

C. *Lightly rake the seed into the soil, then roll a landscape drum over the soil.*

Sod Lawn

Installing sod is the quickest way to create a new lawn. Within a few hours, you can transform bare dirt into a lushly carpeted lawn. It's simple to create a beautiful lawn from sod, but it does require a little planning, thorough preparation and some heavy work. To succeed, you need properly prepared soil, quality sod, careful installation and adequate water.

Sod can be installed at any time from the beginning of the spring through early fall, but it's best to avoid installing it during especially hot, dry weather. You can purchase sod from a sod farm, landscape supply store or landscape contractor. When you compare prices, make sure all the quotes include delivery; most suppliers charge a fee for delivering small orders. For the best results, request that your sod be cut within 24 hours of delivery. After the sod arrives, store it in a shaded area, and install it within one day of delivery. Keep the sod moist, but don't soak it. Sod that drys out won't establish roots, but overwatered sod is heavy and difficult to install.

Good soil preparation is vital: the soil should be properly amended, smooth and free from rocks or construction debris. Sod roots need to have contact with moist soil. If your soil is dry, water it the night before you plan to lay the sod.

Once the sod is laid, keep it constantly moist for three days. Following this period, water your lawn as often as needed to keep the first 4" of soil moist, as described on page 202. During extended hot, dry weather, you'll need to water the sod frequently.

HOW TO INSTALL SOD
Step A: Establish a Pattern
1. Following the guidelines on pages 200 to 201, prepare the soil.
2. Select a straight border, such as a walkway to use as a reference guide. If there isn't a straight surface in the immediate area, sprinkle flour on the ground

TOOLS & MATERIALS

- Basic tools (page 120)
- Sod knife
- Landscape drum
- Fresh sod
- Flour
- Topsoil
- Stakes

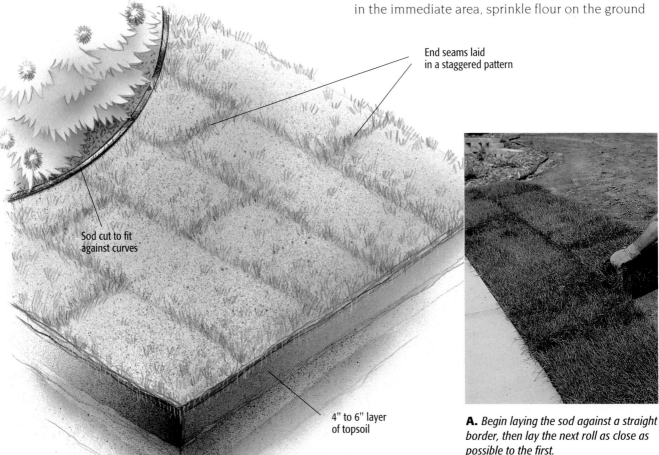

End seams laid in a staggered pattern

Sod cut to fit against curves

4" to 6" layer of topsoil

A. *Begin laying the sod against a straight border, then lay the next roll as close as possible to the first.*

as a reference line. Working parallel to your reference guide, install the first roll of sod. Firmly push the sod into the soil.

3. Continue placing rolls parallel to the guide, butting the seams as closely as possible. To help eliminate the appearance of seams, stagger the end seams.

Step B: Camouflage the Seams

1. Lift the edges of pieces that butt against each other, then press the edges down, knitting the two pieces together.

2. As each new piece is laid, cover the seams with ½" of topsoil to prevent the edges from drying out.

Step C: Stake the Slopes & Trim the Edges

1. Continue laying the sod, staggering the end seams. When sodding a slope, drive wooden stakes through the sod, 4" to 6" into the soil, to hold the sod in place.

2. Use a sod knife to trim excess sod around walkway curves, planting beds and trees.

Step D: Roll the Sod

1. Roll over the sod with a half-filled landscape drum, pressing the sod firmly into the soil.

2. Water the sod until it's thoroughly saturated.

TIP: GRASS SEED OR SOD— WHAT CHOICE IS BEST FOR YOU?

If you're starting a new lawn, you'll want to choose the method that works best for your situation. Seeding and sodding each have benefits, as well as drawbacks. Time, money, climate, maintenance requirements and the amount of stress the lawn will endure are all factors to take into account as you choose the best method for establishing a new lawn.

Sod	Seed
• Expensive	• Inexpensive
• Immediate results	• Takes longer to develop
• Limited variety of grasses	• Wide variety of grasses
• Establishes well on slopes	• Establishes strong root systems
• Fewer weeds	• Ideal planting times limited
• Heavy work	• Daily watering

B. *Lift up the edges of adjoining sod pieces, then press them down together, blending the seam between the pieces.*

C. *Use stakes to secure sod installed on sloped areas, then trim excess sod around curves with a sod cutter.*

D. *After installing all of the sod, use a half-filled landscape drum to seat it firmly.*

Lawn Renovation

Renovation can significantly improve the appearance of an established lawn. The process involves diagnosing and remedying lawn problems, then topseeding and fertilizing the lawn to grow a new crop of healthy grass. Typical conditions corrected during renovation include an abundance of weeds, large bare areas, excessive thatch buildup and soil compaction.

Before you begin planning your renovation, get your soil tested. For detailed information on requesting a soil report, see "Soil" (page 118). The soil test report will be available three to six weeks after you submit soil samples. This report will include detailed information on soil content and how it should be amended to support a healthy lawn.

Next, you need to determine what weeds currently are present in your lawn and evaluate the balance between weeds and grass. If you find weeds that you can't identify, take samples to a local nursery or extension service for more information. If over 40% of your lawn consists of weeds, simple renovation won't solve the problem—experts recommend demolishing the lawn and starting over again from scratch.

As a final step in the evaluation process, cut a small, 6"-deep pie-shaped wedge out of your lawn. Using this sample, measure the level of thatch, the layer of partially decomposed pieces of grass sitting on top of the soil (below, left). Healthy lawns include a moderate layer of thatch, but heavy layers can cause problems. If the thatch is more than ½" thick, add thatch removal to your renovation plan.

Finally, check the moisture content of the soil in the wedge. If the soil isn't moist all the way to the bottom, you need to add water. The soil should be moist to a depth of 6" before you begin work. Depending on the current conditions, it could take several days for the soil to reach adequate moisture levels, so plan accordingly.

HOW TO RENOVATE A LAWN
Step A: Eliminate the Weeds
Spot-kill the weeds in your lawn by applying weed killer, using a pressure sprayer. Wear gloves, safety goggles, a particle mask and protective clothing when using weed killer. Use a broadleaf herbicide to kill broadleaf weeds, such as dandelion and clover. For grassy weeds, such as crabgrass and quackgrass, use a nonselective herbicide containing glyphosate.

TOOLS & MATERIALS

- Basic tools (page 120)
- Pressure sprayer
- Vertical mower
- Leaf rake
- Aerator
- Broadcast spreader
- Gloves
- Goggles
- Particle mask
- Soil test report
- Fertilizer
- Grass seed

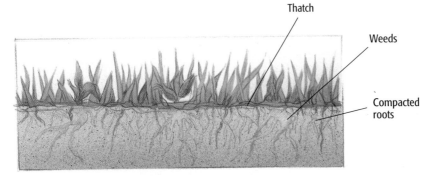

Thatch

Weeds

Compacted roots

Aerated soil

Grass seed

A. *Wearing protective clothing and gear, apply weed killer to the affected areas.*

Glyphosate kills all grass, plants, shrubs or trees it comes into contact with, so apply it carefully, and plan to replant affected areas, as shown in "Seed Lawn" (page 202), and "Sod Lawn" (page 204).

Step B: Remove Thatch Buildup

1. Remove thatch with a rented vertical mower, also called a power rake. Set the tines on the vertical mower to rake about ¼" below the surface of the soil.

2. Push the vertical mower over the entire lawn in a series of straight passes, then go over it again in perpendicular rows, covering the area in a grid pattern.

3. Rake up and discard the removed thatch.

Step C: Loosen the Soil

1. Relieve soil compaction and improve drainage by removing small cores of soil from your lawn with a rented aerator. Run the machine across the lawn, using the same grid pattern described in Step B.

2. Let the soil cores partially dry, then rake them up.

3. Using the vertical mower or a leaf rake, scratch the entire surface of the lawn to loosen the soil slightly.

Step D: Fertilize & Topseed the Lawn

1. Fill a broadcast spreader with the fertilizer blend recommended in the soil test report.

2. Calibrate the spreader according to the directions on the fertilizer package. Distribute the fertilizer, covering the lawn in perpendicular rows.

3. Fill the spreader with grass seed. Topseed the entire lawn (page 203).

TIP: REPAIRING BARE SPOTS

It's an all-too-familiar sight—an otherwise attractive lawn marred by bare spots. If your lawn is plagued with dying areas, you'll need to determine the cause and take preventive measures to keep the grass from dying again. Once the problem is solved, sprinkle grass seed over the bare area, lightly rake it into the soil, and gently tamp the soil down. Keep the area moist for at least two weeks while the seed germinates. Use the following guidelines to resolve common problems:

Cause	Solution
Dog damage	Immediately water areas where the dog urinates.
Compacted soil	Aerate the area, or till in an amendment, such as compost or peat moss.
Chemical burn	Remove several inches of topsoil from the bare area.
Disease	Consult your local extension service for diagnosis and treatment.
Foot traffic	Install a path or stepping stones to accommodate traffic.
Insects	Consult your local extension service for recommendations.

B. *Use a vertical mower to remove significant thatch buildup from the lawn.*

C. *Improve the lawn's soil structure by removing cores of soil with an aerator.*

D. *Apply the prescribed fertilizer blend to the lawn with a broadcast spreader.*

Garden Bed

Garden beds give your yard a finished look by adding color, shape and texture to the landscape. They also help define boundaries between outdoor rooms and soften transitions between architectural structures and the yard. Garden beds can be added almost anywhere, in both sunny and shady areas.

Mixing perennials and annuals is a popular choice for sunny or shady garden beds. Another option is to plant garden beds for year-round seasonal interest, using a combination of bulbs, shrubs, annuals and perennials. Many people also devote garden beds to growing vegetables and herbs.

Although you can create a garden bed in any shape, professional landscape designers recommend creating beds with curves. Curved beds are more visually appealing than straight ones and add variety to your landscape.

Before you create a planting bed, have a soil test conducted on the soil in the proposed location. Give the soil testing lab a list of the types of plants you plan to grow; the soil test report will include detailed instructions for amending your soil to support these plants. If your soil cannot be amended to support your garden, the best alternative is to build a raised bed (page 130).

HOW TO MAKE A GARDEN BED

Step A: Outline & Clear the Site

1. Using a rope or garden hose, outline the shape of the garden bed on the site you've chosen.
2. Remove all of the grass and other plants inside the outlined area with a garden spade. If the area has a lot of weeds, you might want to use a nonselective herbicide first, which will kill everything growing inside the outline.

Step B: Prepare the Bed

1. Apply an even layer of the recommended amendments and fertilizers over the soil.
2. Mix the amendments into the soil with a shovel or rented tiller. For flower beds, blend amendments to a depth of 6". For vegetable beds, till to a depth of 10".

TOOLS & MATERIALS

- Basic tools (page 120)
- Motorized tiller
- Rope or garden hose
- Soil test report
- Soil amendments
- Flexible plastic edging
- Plants
- Mulch

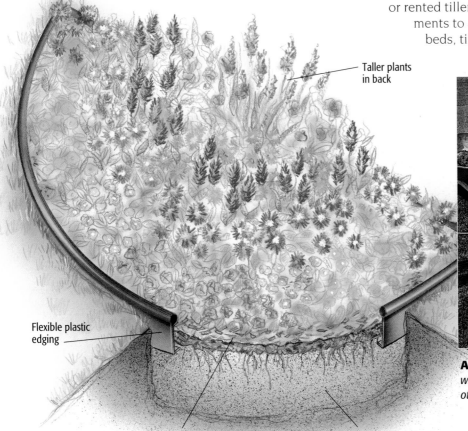

Taller plants in back

Flexible plastic edging

2" to 3" layer of mulch

6" to 10" layer of tilled, amended soil

A. *Outline the shape of the garden bed with a hose, then remove any grass or other plants growing inside the outline.*

3. Dig a narrow edging trench along the perimeter of the bed. Make the depth of the trench equal to the height of the edging.

4. Insert flexible plastic edging in the trench so that the beaded edge is flush with the ground. Join the ends of the edging with union connectors. Anchor the edging by driving spikes every foot, using a hand sledge. Pack the soil around the edging.

5. Lay out your garden design with the plants still in their containers. As you arrange them, consider the mature sizes, bloom times and foliage textures of the plants as well as their colors.

Step C: Insert the Plants

Working with one plant at a time, use a spade or hand trowel to dig a hole twice as wide and the same depth as the plant's container. Remove the plant from the container and loosen the root ball. For large container-grown plants, use the technique for slicing through the root ball demonstrated on page 171. Place the plant in the hole and fill around it, gently patting the soil until it's compacted just enough to support the plant. Repeat with remaining plants.

Step D: Add the Mulch

Apply a 2" to 3" layer of organic mulch, such as shredded bark, shredded cypress or cocoa bean hulls, around your plants to inhibit weed growth and keep the soil moist. Water the plants thoroughly.

VARIATION: BRICK EDGING

Brick edging adds an attractive touch to garden beds, especially if you have other brick structures in your landscape. Here's an easy way to install brick edging:

1. Dig a flat-bottomed trench around the perimeter of the bed, using a flat spade. Make the trench about ½" deeper than the height of the edging material.

2. Place a ½" layer of sand in the trench and smooth it out. Place a strip of landscape fabric over the sand.

3. Lay the bricks side by side in the trench, as pictured above. Place a 2 × 4 over the bricks and tap it with a rubber mallet.

4. Spread sand over the bricks and use a broom to work the sand into the cracks.

5. Lightly mist the bricks with water to set the sand.

B. *Till amendments into the soil, then install the flexible plastic edging. Design and test the layout of the plants.*

C. *Working with one plant at a time, dig a hole twice as wide and the same depth as the container. Loosen the roots and insert each plant.*

D. *Apply a 2" to 3" layer of organic mulch over the entire bed, then water the plants thoroughly.*

Decorating Your Outdoor Home

Part 3, Decorating Your Outdoor Home, was on our minds for almost a year before it finally reached the drawing board. During that time, we were so interested in designing and building garden ornaments that they jumped out at us from every direction. Friends contributed suggestions, colleagues brought us photographs, and our families supported the growing amount of time we spent puttering with materials, testing designs, and playing with ideas.

Those months of experimentation provided a base of material that a talented team of designers, photographers, technicians, and artists brought to life in ways that exceeded our imaginings. Developing these projects was a true labor of love, and it gives us both great pleasure to introduce you to the delight of building garden ornaments.

Some of the projects in Part 3 require carpentry skills, and others require a little dexterity, but they're all well within the capabilities of any motivated gardener with access to a few power tools. And whenever possible, we've included variations to help you adapt our ideas. You may want to enlarge a project or use materials that better suit the style, theme, or colors in your garden. In fact, before you purchase materials or begin building, envision the project in place and consider possible modifications.

The best advice we can give you is this: Let your imagination run wild. Follow your instincts and trust your own sense of style. If you build and buy only ornaments that you truly love, they will come together to create a garden that speaks to your heart.

We'd love to hear from you and see photographs of the ornaments you build. Drop us a line at 5900 Green Oak Drive, Minnetonka, MN 55343, or e-mail us at diy@creativepub.com.

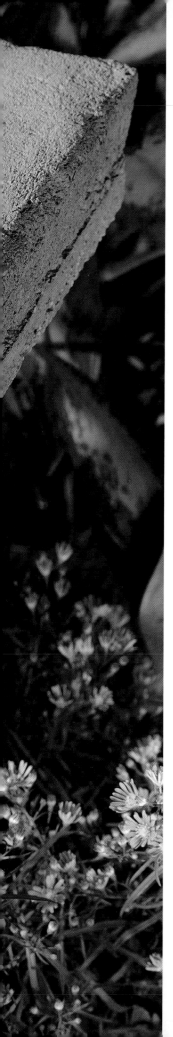

Water Features

Many people find the sound of running water soothing and refreshing. Although water features are everywhere these days—from garden centers to Buddhist boutiques—most of them carry fairly hefty price tags. With any of the projects in this chapter, it's possible to bring the delights of water into your garden at a very reasonable cost. You can have a great deal of fun in the process, too: Every one of these projects is a joy to build.

Water features offer tremendous opportunities to express creativity. For example, you can easily build an attractive terra cotta fountain (page 214) by following the instructions to the letter. Or, by selecting other types of vessels, stones, and plants, you can create a fountain that reflects your own personal style and taste. Similarly, the stone, spray pattern and plantings you choose for a cobblestone fountain (page 226) will make it unique.

If you want to attract attention to your yard and garden, there are few better ways than building a copper sprinkler (page 222) to throw graceful sprays across the garden. And despite being remarkably easy to put together, the water garden variation (at right on page 221) draws a good deal of attention as well. A small, relatively inexpensive device sends mist rolling from behind the decorations, creating a mysterious effect.

Terra Cotta Fountains

Small fountains are quite popular, but the prices put them out of reach for many gardeners. But with these designs, you can bring the soothing sounds of trickling water to your garden easily and inexpensively. Assembling these terra cotta fountains is amazingly quick—you can shop for the materials and complete a fountain in just one day.

Purchase a small submersible pump with a flow rate of about 60 gallons per hour; then select a base container that's deep enough to submerge the water intake portion of the pump. Also, make sure the flexible tubing you purchase fits the pump's discharge outlet.

Choose smooth, uniform terra cotta pieces for these fountains. As you purchase pots, assemble them approximately as they'll be positioned in the completed fountain to make sure they stack evenly.

You can buy stones to place in the fountain, but if you live near a river or lake shore, it might be more fun to gather them. Smooth river stones will look more natural and appropriate in the fountain than sharp or jagged stones.

Check the water level in the fountain frequently. When a fountain, especially a small one, is operated in dry weather, rapid evaporation makes it necessary to replenish the water every two or three days. If possible, purchase a pump that shuts itself off when the water level falls below a set point. This feature keeps the pump from burning out if you can't refill the fountain for some reason.

In time, the clay pots in your fountain may develop a white residue caused by mineral deposits. To remove the stains, take the fountain apart and scrub each pot, using a nylon or natural-bristle brush. You can also rinse the pots with bleach to discourage the growth of mold, mildew, or algae.

TOOLS & MATERIALS

- Drill with ⅜" masonry bit and conical rasp bit
- 8" round bastard file
- Masking tape
- Clear aerosol acrylic sealer
- Ruler
- Permanent marker

- 5-gallon bucket
- Terra cotta saucers, one 18", one 8", one 6", and three 4"
- Terra cotta pots, one 6" and one 5"
- Submersible pump
- 12" length of flexible tubing

- Marine-grade sealant
- Embellishments, such as clean river rocks, gravel, coral or shells
- Small potted plants, candle, or small statue

HOW TO MAKE A TERRA COTTA FOUNTAIN
Step A: Prepare the Pottery

1. Put masking tape around the outside of the upper edge of the 18" saucer to protect the edges from overspray. Spray a coat of acrylic sealer on the inside of the saucer and let it dry. Apply two more coats of sealer to the interior of the saucer and let them dry.

2. Center and mark an X on the bottom of the 8" saucer, using a ruler and permanent marker. Place this saucer and the 6" pot, the 6" saucer, and two 4" saucers in a bucket of water; let them soak for at

least an hour.

3. Position the 8" saucer over a scrap of wood and drill a hole at the X, using a ⅜" masonry drill bit. Test-fit the flexible plastic tubing and enlarge the hole, if necessary, using a conical rasp bit. Drill slowly while applying light pressure, and check the fit at frequent intervals. The flexible plastic tubing should fit snugly through the hole in the saucer.

4. Use the drill to adjust the hole in the bottom of the 6" pot until the flexible plastic tubing fits snugly through it as well. Using a round bastard file, cut four notches in the lip of the pot, sizing one notch to accommodate the electrical cord of the pump.

5. File one notch for a water spout in the edge of the 8" saucer, using a round bastard file. To create the best water flow, angle the notch toward the inside edge of the saucer, leaving the outer lip of the notch higher than the inner edge.

6. File an angled notch in the 6" saucer and in one 4" saucer.

7. File four notches equally spaced around the upper edge of another 4" saucer.

Step B: Attach the Pump

1. Connect the flexible plastic tubing to the discharge outlet of the pump. If it's difficult to slide the

A. *File four notches in the lip of the 6" pot. Make one of the notches large enough to accommodate the pump's cord.*

B. *Connect one end of the tubing to the discharge outlet of the pump; then insert the other through the inverted pot and saucer.*

tubing over the outlet, place the end of the tubing in hot water for a minute or two; then try again.

2. Turn the 6" pot upside down and insert the free end of the tubing through the pot, then through the 8" saucer to create the tallest column of the fountain.

Step C: Position the First Column

1. Pull the flexible plastic tubing up through the saucer until it's taut, and then trim it, leaving about ½" of tubing above the saucer. Use marine-grade sealant to seal gaps between the tubing and the saucer. Let the sealant cure, following manufacturer's instructions.

2. Place the pump and column in the 18" base saucer. Adjust the pump's electrical cord to fit through the notch you cut for it in the lip of the pot. Find the 4" saucer with four notches; place it upside down in the center of the 8" saucer, concealing the tubing.

Step D: Arrange Remaining Columns

1. Turn the 5" pot upside down and position it in the base saucer, next to the first column.

2. Place the notched 6" saucer on top of the pot, forming the middle column.

3. Turn the unnotched 4" saucer upside down and place it in the base saucer; place the notched 4" saucer on top, creating the short column.

Step E: Add Water & Embellish the Fountain

1. Fill the base with water, adding more water until it's about ⅜" from the rim of the saucer. Turn on the pump and check the flow of the water.

2. Adjust the position of the notched saucers until water pours smoothly from one column of the fountain to the next.

3. Adjust the flow rate of the pump, if necessary, to achieve a smooth, even flow of water.

4. Add clean rocks, gravel, coral, or shells to the saucers as desired.

5. Place a potted plant, candle, or small statue on top of the tallest column to weight down the inverted saucer and add the finishing touch to your terra cotta fountain. Position a second potted plant in the base saucer, if desired.

C. *Pull the flexible plastic tubing up through the saucer until it's taut, trim it, and seal any gaps with marine sealant.*

D. *Stack the middle column and place it in the base saucer. Top an inverted, unnotched 4" saucer with a notched saucer, creating a short column.*

E. *Fill the fountain with water and run the pump. Adjust the position of the columns and the pump's flow rate until the water flows smoothly from one level to another.*

VARIATION: STRAWBERRY POT FOUNTAIN

You can make another simple, attractive fountain by topping a stack of standard pots with a strawberry pot. Again, you use a small pump to recirculate water through the stack, sending a graceful flow out of the openings of the strawberry pot and down the stack.

For this fountain, you'll need the same general supplies as for the Terra Cotta Fountain. You'll also need:

• 15" base container or saucer

• 10" pot

• 8" saucer

• 10" strawberry pot

• Duct tape

• Plaster of Paris.

If there's a drainage hole in the base container, fill it with plaster of Paris. Working from the bottom of the container, put duct tape across the hole. Mix a small amount of plaster of Paris, following manufacturer's instructions. Fill about half of the hole with plaster and let it harden. Repeat to fill the remainder of the hole. When the plaster is dry, seal the interior of the bowl (page 215).

Mark the center of the strawberry pot and the 8" saucer; soak both of them and the 10" pot in water for at least an hour. Drill a hole in the saucer (page 215); then drill or enlarge the hole in the strawberry pot to fit the discharge tube of the water pump.

File four equally spaced notches in the upper edge of the 10" pot, using a round bastard file. Size one of the notches to accommodate the electrical cord of the pump.

Connect the flexible plastic tubing to the pump (page 215). Turn the 10" pot upside down and insert the free end of the tubing through the pot and the saucer, and then through the bottom of the strawberry pot.

Position the pump and stacked pottery in the base container and fit the pump's electrical cord through the appropriate notch. Pull the flexible plastic tubing taut and use marine sealant to seal any gaps between the tubing and the strawberry pot. Allow the sealant to cure, following the manufacturer's instructions.

Fill the strawberry pot with about 3" of gravel; keep the flexible plastic tubing centered in the pot. Trim the tubing, leaving about ½" above the surface of the gravel.

Add water to the base container until it reaches within about ⅜" of the container's rim. Plug in the pump and adjust the flow rate as necessary. Place gravel, rocks, or shells in the rim of the saucer and base, if desired. Add a potted plant to the top of the strawberry pot.

File notches in the base pot, and drill holes in the pottery. Stack the pieces and position the water pump and its tube.

Position the stacked pots in the base saucer; then add gravel, water, and plants.

217

Water Gardens

Water gardens add a dreamy, peaceful feeling to quiet spaces. If you don't have the space or time to maintain a formal pond, you might have the perfect spot on a deck or patio or in a boring corner of the yard for this simple, easy-to-build water garden.

Almost any vessel that holds water can be turned into a water garden, but some materials work better than others. One of the easiest ways is to start with a vinyl all-purpose tub, and then build a cedar surround to give it a finished appearance.

All-purpose tubs are available at most building supply stores, farm supply stores, and pet supply stores. Measure the tub you select; then purchase cedar lumber that's at least as wide as the depth of the tub, probably 1 × 12s or 1 × 10s.

Although it's not required, a small spray is a nice addition. Buy a small submersible pump with a fountain

head attachment. A pump with a flow rate of 80 gallons per hour will create a fountain spray about 10" high, which suits a water garden of this size quite nicely.

Many nurseries stock a large variety of aquatic plants, but they're also available from mail-order sources. Aquatic plants include those that grow in containers of soil submerged beneath the surface of the water as well as floating plants, whose roots dangle in the water. The chart on page 220 lists several commonly available aquatic plants.

Many traditional potted plants and flowering plants can be placed in water gardens if the pots are only partially submerged. Floating pond plants block the sunlight from the water, which helps reduce algae growth. To further reduce the growth of algae, periodically replace the water in the garden.

To create a more interesting arrangement, select plants in a variety of textures and heights. Keep in mind, though, that plants should cover no more than three-fourths of the water's surface.

TOOLS & MATERIALS

- Circular saw or jig saw
- Drill with countersink bit
- Paintbrush
- Tape measure
- Large vinyl tub
- 1 × 12 or 1 × 10 cedar lumber
- 1 × 2 cedar lumber
- #6 × 2" galvanized deck screws
- Wood sealer
- Submersible pump
- Aquatic plants
- Pea gravel
- Bricks or clay saucers

A. *Align the front and one side; then drill three counterbored pilot holes. Drive screws to fasten the pieces.*

HOW TO BUILD A WATER GARDEN

Step A: Assemble the Frame

1. Measure the width of the vinyl tub from the outside edges. Add ½", then measure, mark, and cut two 1 × 12s or 1 × 10s to this adjusted measurement. These pieces will form the sides of the surround.

2. Measure the outer length of the tub and add 2". Cut two pieces to this length to form the front and back of the frame.

3. Lightly sand the edges and ends of the cut boards as necessary. Drill a notch at one end of the back piece, placed near the lower edge, to accommodate the pump's electrical cord.

4. Apply wood sealer to both faces and to the edges of the boards. Allow them to dry completely.

5. Align the front piece with a side piece. Drill three pilot holes, using a countersink bit. Drive screws into the pilot holes, fastening the front to the side. Repeat for the remaining side, then for the back.

Step B: Add the Casings

1. Measure the length of the box. Add ½", then measure, mark, and cut two pieces of 1 × 2 to this length. These pieces will form the front and back casings.

2. Set the front and back casings in place, centering each over the frame and extending ¼" beyond the ends of the frame. Measure the frame between the front and back casings, and cut two pieces of 1 × 2 to this length for the side casings.

3. Apply wood sealer to all the edges and cut ends of the casing pieces. Allow them to dry.

4. Realign the front casing, making sure it's centered on the frame. Drill three counterbored pilot holes; then secure the casing to the frame, using deck screws. Repeat with the back casing.

B. *Center the casing on top of the frame, extending it ½" beyond the inside edge. Drill counterbored pilot holes; then fasten the casing with screws.*

C. *Place the tub in the surround. If necessary, use boards or bricks to bring the tub up to within ½" of the top of the surround.*

5. Center one side casing between the front and back casings. Drill counterbored pilot holes; then drive screws to fasten the casing to the frame. Repeat on the opposite side.

Step C: Install the Tub and Surround

Place the tub inside the surround. If necessary, use boards or bricks to elevate the tub to within ½" of the top of the surround.

Step D: Install the Pump & Fountain Head

Position a submersible pump in the tub. Run the electrical cord over the edge of the tub, under the surround, and through the notch you drilled for it. Fill the tub with water, turn on the pump, and adjust the flow rate of the pump to create an effect that appeals to you.

Step E: Embellish the Garden

1. Place pea gravel on top of the soil in potted plants; then position them in the tub. Use inverted terra cotta pots, saucers, or bricks to adjust each plant to its recommended water depth, as indicated on the nursery tag. Set taller plants in position to camouflage the spot where the electrical cord is draped over the tub.

2. Arrange floating plants to balance the appearance of the water garden.

TYPES OF AQUATIC PLANTS

CONTAINER PLANTS		FLOATING PLANTS
Arrowhead	Spike rush	Parrot feather
Canna	Variegated	Water hyacinth
Cattail	sweet flag	Water lettuce
Dwarf papyrus	Water iris	
Lizard tail	Water lilies	
umbrella palm		

D. *Place the pump in the tub. Add water; then adjust the flow rate to create a pleasing effect.*

E. *Arrange potted and floating plants in the water garden.*

VARIATION: FOUNTAIN GARDENS

BARREL WATER GARDEN

You can create simple, attractive water gardens in purchased containers. For the water garden (below, left), you need:

- Oak whiskey barrel
- Marine-grade sealant
- Rubber spatula
- 4d finish nails
- Submersible pump with fountain head attachment
- Floating and potted aquatic plants.

Scrub and rinse the interior of the barrel to remove any acids or alcohol residue. Let it dry.

Using a hammer, tap along the inside of the barrel to make sure the base is snug against the sides. Drive nails through the base, angling them into, but not through, the sides of the barrel.

Spread marine-grade sealant liberally around the inside of the barrel, particularly the side seams and any nail holes. Let the sealant dry; then apply a second coat and let it dry thoroughly.

Put the barrel in place and fill it with water. Use clean bricks, blocks, or clay pots to elevate the pump and plants.

MIST WATER GARDEN

Although it's amazingly easy to put together, this water garden (below, right), simply commands attention. The fog maker device, which works much like an ultrasonic humidifier, creates a mist that's almost mesmerizing (source listed on page 320). To create this water garden, you need:

- Ceramic container
- Mist maker fountain head
- Decorative accents.

Fill the base with water and place the mist maker about 1½" under the surface of the water. The mist effect changes with the amount of water covering the device, so adjust its position until the mist rises in a way that appeals to you. Note: *With containers larger than 20" in diameter, it may be necessary to use more than one fog maker to create the desired effect.*

Arrange stones, a small statue, or a miniature plant in the water garden.

Place the transformer portion of the fog maker in a sheltered area to protect it from the weather.

Check the water level often and refill as necessary. Do not leave the pump running if you'll be away from home for an extended period.

Left. *A whiskey barrel can become an inexpensive, attractive water garden.* **Above.** *A mist maker and a few accessories transform a piece of pottery into a unique water garden.*

Copper Sprinkler

Even when standing still, this sprinkler is an artistic addition to any yard or garden. In motion, it's utterly fascinating. As the hoop spins, it throws shimmering spirals that water an area as large as 15 ft. in diameter.

Despite the impressive results, this is an inexpensive project. Some of the parts come from unexpected sources, but they're all widely available. You can find copper pipe and fittings at virtually any home center. Round brass tubing (made by K&S Engineering) is available at hobby and crafts stores, and the bushings are distributed by auto parts stores. Hinge pin bushings made by Motormite work well and fit nearly perfectly. They're GM replacement parts, so they should be easy to find.

Flexible copper bends more easily when it's new, and building a bending jig helps you create a uniform circle, which distributes the weight evenly and allows the hoop to spin smoothly.

Spacing the holes is mildly tricky, but not complicated if you understand the concept. To create the directional force that makes the head spin, the holes must gradually move from the front side of the hoop to the back side. As water is pushed out the holes, the pressure rotates the hoop.

This sprinkler has a simple motif, but the project lends itself to adaptation. You're sure to come up with a dozen variations you'd like to try. Go ahead—copper sprinklers are fun to build, they make wonderful gifts, and the materials are inexpensive.

TOOLS & MATERIALS

- Tubing cutter
- Wire brush or emery cloth
- Bench grinder or rotary tool
- Flux brush
- Propane torch
- Circular saw
- Jig saw
- Drill
- $^{11}/_{32}$" round brass tubing
- $^{5}/_{16}$" round brass tubing
- Brass hinge pin bushings (GM #38375) (4)
- Flux
- Solder
- $^{1}/_{2}$" flexible copper tubing, about 3 ft.

- $^{1}/_{2}$" Type L copper pipe, about 4 ft.
- $^{1}/_{4}$" flexible copper tubing, 2 ft.
- $^{1}/_{2}$" copper tee
- Two scraps of plywood (16" square)
- 1" deck screws (8)
- Cotton twine
- Permanent marker
- 6" galvanized wicket
- $^{1}/_{2}$" brass shower ell
- $^{1}/_{2}$" copper threaded adapter
- Teflon tape
- Machine screws & nuts (2)
- Metallic copper spray paint
- Brass hose connector

HOW TO BUILD A COPPER SPRINKLER
Step A: Make Assemblies for the Swivel Joint

1. Cut one 5" piece and one 36" piece of $^{1}/_{2}$" Type L copper pipe, using a tubing cutter. Also cut one 2" and one 4" piece of $^{11}/_{32}$" brass tubing, and one 6" piece of $^{5}/_{16}$" brass tubing. Deburr the pieces, being careful not to flare the ends; use a wire brush or emery cloth to polish the ends.

2. Test-fit the hinge pin bushings inside the 5" piece of copper. If necessary, use a bench grinder or a

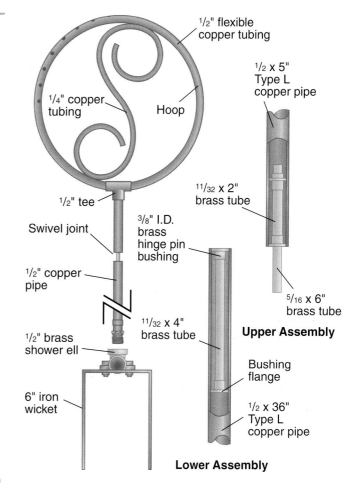

SWIVEL JOINT DETAILS

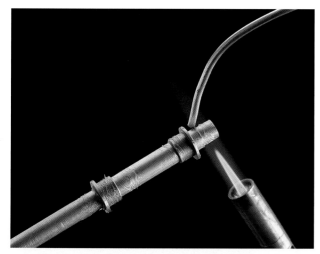

A. *Solder upper assembly, connecting the $^{5}/_{16}$" tube, the $^{11}/_{32}$" tube, and the bushing. Heat all three pieces; first feed solder into the joint between the brass tubes, then into the bushing joint.*

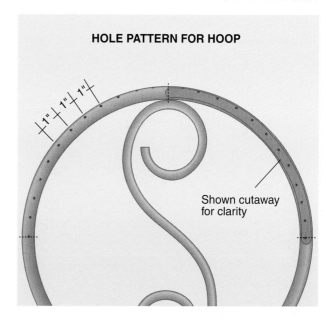

HOLE PATTERN FOR HOOP

Shown cutaway for clarity

rotary tool to slightly shape the flanges of the hinge pin bushings so they fit snugly within the pipe. Note: *Using a scrap of the ¹¹⁄₃₂" tubing as a spindle helps you get a uniform edge.*

3. To form the upper assembly, slide a bushing onto each end of the 2" length of ¹¹⁄₃₂" brass tubing, with the flanges facing the ends of the tube. Set the flange of one bushing back ⅛" from the end of the tube; position the other bushing flush with the opposite end. Slide the 6" length of ⁵⁄₁₆" brass tubing inside the ¹¹⁄₃₂" tube, positioning the inner tube to protrude ⅜" beyond the top (setback) bushing.

4. To form the lower assembly, slide a bushing onto

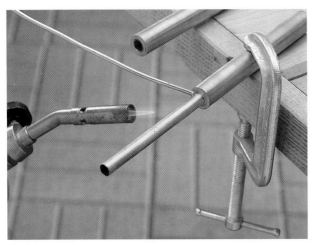

B. *Place the upper and lower assemblies of the swivel joint at the edge of a work surface, and solder the joints. To avoid letting solder run into the brass tubes, feed the solder from the bottom.*

each end of the 4" piece of ¹¹⁄₃₂" brass tubing, flanges facing outward, flush with the ends of the tube.

5. Begin soldering at the top of the upper assembly (see page 310 for soldering techniques). Heat all three pieces—the ⁵⁄₁₆" tube, the ¹¹⁄₃₂" tube, and the bushing. Feed solder into the joint between the two brass tubes first; feed solder into the bushing joint, approaching that joint from the side opposite the flange.

6. Solder the three remaining bushing joints, each time feeding the solder into the joint from the side opposite the flange.

Step B: Construct the Swivel Joint

1. Flux the inside of the 5" piece of ½" copper and the flange of the bushing on the upper assembly. Slide the assembly inside the copper pipe, positioning the lower bushing to be flush with the end of the copper pipe.

2. Flux the inside of the 36" piece of copper and the shoulder of one bushing on the lower assembly. Slide the assembly inside the pipe, positioning the bushing flange to be flush with the top of the pipe.

3. Place the assembled pieces at the edge of a protected work surface, and solder each one, being careful not to displace the bushings. Concentrate the flame on the copper pipe as you heat the joints, and feed the solder from the bottom; don't let the solder run into the brass tube.

Step C: Form the Hoop

1. To create a bending jig, cut two 16" squares from scrap plywood. Centered on one of the squares, mark concentric circles, one 13" and one 14⅛" in diameter. Using a jig saw, cut out the inner circle, and then cut

C. *Build a plywood bending jig; then shape flexible copper tubing into a circle for the hoop.*

D. *Mark the placement of the holes and drill them along the hoop. (Be sure to drill through only one wall of the hoop.)*

along the line marking the outer circle.

2. Secure the 13" circle to the other plywood square, using 1" deck screws. Next, attach the outer edge of the cutout, centering it around the circle to form a channel that will guide the flexible tubing as you bend it into a hoop. Measure and mark lines dividing the circles into exact quarters.

3. Cut a generous length of ½" flexible copper tubing. Place one end in the channel, and then push the tubing into the jig, bending it down into the channel and around the inner circle as smoothly as possible. Mark and cut the tubing at the point where the ends meet. With the joint exactly lined up at the lower quarter mark on the jig, mark the other quarters on the tubing.

4. Remove the hoop from the jig, and add a ½" copper tee to one end. Bring the other end of the hoop around to the center of the tee, mark a cutting line, then cut the tubing.

5. Clean the cut ends and the tee, using a wire brush or emery cloth, and then flux the mating surfaces. Solder the tee in place.

Step D: Drill the Holes

1. Use a piece of twine to mark the curving pattern for the holes (diagram, page 223). Hold one end of the twine on the quarter mark on one side of the hoop. Pull the twine around the top of the hoop and down to the quarter mark on the opposite side.

2. Stretch the twine taut to create a smooth, curving line, and then transfer the quarter marks to the twine. Remove the twine and mark it at 1" intervals between the two quarter marks.

3. Wrap the string around the hoop, as before, aligning the quarter marks on the twine with those on the hoop to create a smooth curve. Tape the twine in place, and then use it as a pattern to mark the 1" intervals on the tubing. Drill a hole through one wall of the hoop at each mark.

Step E: Add the Swivel Joint & the Design Motif

1. Dry-fit the upper assembly of the swivel joint to the tee at the bottom of the hoop (be sure the brass tube is extending down). Flux mating surfaces and solder the joint.

2. Measure the inside diameter of the hoop, and then bend ¼" flexible copper tubing into an S shape to fit within the hoop (see page 223). You can alter the design if you wish, but keep in mind that its weight must be evenly distributed in order for the hoop to spin smoothly. Flux the appropriate spots and solder the design motif in place.

Step F: Build the Stand & Assemble the Sprinkler

1. Center a ½" brass shower ell on top of a 6" galvanized wicket, and mark the holes. Drill holes in the wicket, and then secure the ell to it, using machine screws and nuts. Spray paint these pieces to match the copper color of the sprinkler. Let the paint dry.

2. Solder a ½" threaded copper adapter to the open end of the stand pipe. When the piece is cool, wrap the threads of the adapter with Teflon tape. Screw the adapter into one end of the shower ell and a hose connector to the other.

3. Set the hoop into the stand pipe, mating the upper and lower portions of the swivel joint. Attach a garden hose to the hose connector.

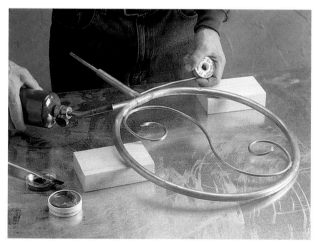

E. *Solder the swivel joint to the tee at the base of the hoop, and then form and solder the design motif to the interior of the hoop.*

F. *Assemble the stand. Connect the stand pipe to one end of the shower ell and a garden hose connector to the other.*

Cobblestone Fountain

A cobblestone fountain typically is set flush with a paved garden path or surrounding grass. The cobblestone surface could be cut stone or smooth river rock, depending on your taste and what's available in your area.

In one afternoon, with one wheelbarrow-load of ordinary materials, you can transform a boring corner into a special place in the garden—the construction of this fountain is simple and the materials are inexpensive.

You can use something as simple as a five-gallon bucket for the basin. In fact, any watertight plastic vessel at least 12" in diameter and 15" deep will work. To protect children and animals, you need to cover the opening of the basin with a sturdy grate, such as 9-gauge ¾" expanded metal mesh, which is available at some building centers or at any steel yard.

To eliminate weeds and help keep debris out of the basin, cover the excavated area with landscape fabric.

Set the pump on a brick to keep it above the floor of the basin and out of the residue that will collect there. For extra protection, you could put the pump in a clay pot, and then fill the pot with lava rocks that will filter debris.

The illustration at right shows suitable dimensions for the fountain in this project, but you can adapt them as necessary to suit your location.

If you want to build a cobblestone fountain in an area not currently served by a GFCI outlet, install one near the proposed location (page 152).

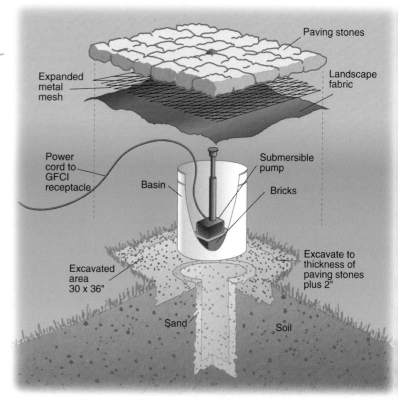

TOOLS & MATERIALS

- Shovel
- Tape measure
- Level
- Bolt cutters
- Metal file
- Hand tamp
- Plastic bucket or tub
- Sand
- Gravel
- Bricks (2)

- Submersible pump with telescoping delivery pipe
- Landscape fabric
- 9-gauge ¾" expanded metal mesh, 30" × 36"
- 6" paving stones, (approximately 35)
- Plants and decorative stones, as desired

HOW TO BUILD A COBBLESTONE FOUNTAIN

Step A: Dig the Hole & Test Fit the Basin

1. Begin digging a hole 2" to 3" wider than the diameter of the bucket or tub you selected for the basin of the fountain. Keep the edges of the hole fairly straight, and the bottom fairly level.

2. Measure the height of the basin, add the height of the paving stones you've chosen, and then add 4" to this total. When the hole is approximately as deep as this combined measurement, test fit the basin and check it with a level. Remove dirt from the hole until the basin is as close as possible to level.

Step B: Dig the Paving Area

1. Cut out the grass or soil in a 30" × 36" rectangle surrounding the hole. To bring the surface of the fountain to ground level, dig this area 2" deeper than the height of the paving stones.

A. *Dig a hole approximately as deep as the combined height of the basin and the paving stones plus 4".*

B. *Cut out a 30" × 36" rectangle surrounding the hole, digging 2" deeper than the height of the paving stones.*

C. *Add a layer of gravel and then sand, tamping and adding sand until the top of the basin is level with the paving area.*

D. *Place the pump in the bucket, centered on the bricks. Position the electrical cord to run up and out of the hole.*

2. Spread sand over the paving area, and then dampen and tamp the sand. Continue adding and tamping the sand until you've created a level 2" layer over the entire area.

Step C: Position the Basin

1. Add about 3" of gravel to the hole, and then add a 3" layer of sand. Dampen and tamp the sand; then test fit the basin again. Adjust until the top of the basin is level with the prepared paving area.

2. Fill the edges of the hole with gravel and/or sand to hold the basin firmly in place.

Step D: Install the Pump & the Grate

1. Clean out any sand or dirt, and then put two clean bricks on the bottom of the basin. Center the pump on top of the bricks; then extend the electrical cord up over the edge of the basin and out to the nearest GFCI receptacle.

2. Lay landscape fabric over the paving area. Extend the fabric over the edges of the basin by 5" or 6", and then trim it to shape.

Step E: Fill the Basin & Adjust the Flow Valve

Fill the basin with water. Turn on the pump and adjust the flow valve, following manufacturer's instructions. Adjust and test until the bubbling effect or spray appeals to you. (Keep in mind that the fountain's basic dimensions will be somewhat different when the paving stones are in place.)

Step F: Add the Paving Stones

1. Place the grate over the paving area, making sure the water delivery tube fits cleanly through an opening in the grate. If necessary, use bolt cutters and a metal file to enlarge the opening.

E. *Fill the basin with water and adjust the flow valve on the pump to create a pleasing effect.*

F. *Position the grate, and then set the paving stones in place. Be sure to leave space for water to recirculate between stones.*

2. Put the paving stones in place, setting them in evenly-spaced rows. Be sure to leave an area open around the water delivery pipe so the water has room to bubble up around the stones and then return to the basin.

Step G: Camouflage the Pump's Electrical Cord

Place plants and stones at the edge of the fountain to disguise the electrical cord as it exits the basin and runs toward the nearest GFCI receptacle.

VARIATION: PAVER OPTIONS

You can pave the fountain area with river stones, overlapping them in a fish-scale pattern.

You can even pave the fountain floor with a collection of colorful pebbles if you cover the grate with a second layer of landscape fabric to keep the pebbles from falling into the basin.

G. *Arrange plants and stones to disguise the electrical cord as it runs to the nearest GFCI receptacle.*

Hypertufa Birdbath

Birds add color, movement, and music to a garden. As if that's not enough to make them welcome guests, some species eat their weight in mosquitoes, grubs, and insects daily. The single most important thing you can do to attract birds is to provide a source of water, a fact that puts a birdbath near the top of any list of appealing garden ornaments.

This birdbath is sturdy, inexpensive, and easy to build. Best of all, its classic lines only improve with age. If you place it in a shady spot and encourage patches of moss to develop (page 263), it will blend into the landscape as if it's been part of your garden for decades.

It's made from hypertufa—a mixture of portland cement, peat moss, and sand or perlite. Work-

ing with hypertufa is like making mud pies, except that it dries into an attractive substance that holds its shape and stands up to years of use. For general instructions on working with hypertufa, see page 312. For this birdbath, use Recipe #2, which creates a watertight formula.

Since birdbaths need to be cleaned frequently, this one is designed in sections that are easy to take apart. When it's assembled, the sections are held in place by interlocking pieces of PVC pipe that keep it from being toppled by strong winds or aggressive creatures.

To help attract birds to your birdbath, keep it clean, refill it with fresh water regularly, and place stones or branches in it to provide footing for your guests.

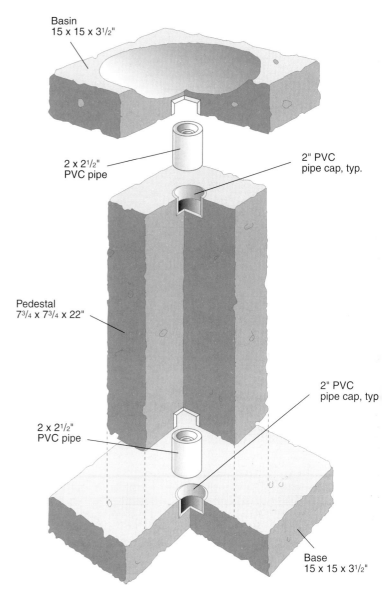

Basin
15 x 15 x 3½"

2 x 2½"
PVC pipe

2" PVC
pipe cap, typ.

Pedestal
7¾ x 7¾ x 22"

2" PVC
pipe cap, typ

2 x 2½"
PVC pipe

Base
15 x 15 x 3½"

TOOLS & MATERIALS

- Tape measure
- Straightedge
- Jig saw
- Drill
- Hacksaw
- Hoe
- Trowel
- 2" polystyrene insulation board
- Gaffer's tape
- 3" deck screws
- Gloves
- Scrap of 2" PVC pipe, at least 6"
- 2" PVC pipe caps (4)
- Portland cement
- Peat moss
- Sand
- Scrap 2 × 4
- Shallow plastic bowl
- Vegetable oil

HOW TO BUILD A HYPERTUFA BIRDBATH
Step A: Build the Forms

1. Following the cutting list (below, right) measure and mark dimensions for the forms onto polystyrene insulation. Cut out the pieces, using a jig saw.

2. Construct the forms, supporting the joints with gaffer's tape (see page 313), then securing them with deck screws. The goal is to create forms for a 15" × 15" × 3½" base, a 15" × 15" × 3½" basin, and a 7¾" × 7¾" × 22" pedestal.

The mass of the pedestal piece creates quite a bit

A. *Build forms, using polystyrene insulation board, gaffer's tape, and deck screws.*

CUTTING LIST

Pedestal form	Basin & Base forms
7¾" × 22" (2)	15" × 5½" (4)
11¾" × 22" (2)	19" × 5½" (4)
11¾" × 11¾" (1)	15" × 15" (2)

231

of pressure against the walls of the form when the hypertufa is wet, so you may want to screw together a 1 × 2 collar to support the form, as shown in Photo C. Or, you could use strap clamps to reinforce the forms, if necessary .

Step B: Pour the Base

1. Mix the hypertufa, using Recipe #2 (see page 312 for recipe and instructions).

2. Mark the center of the form, and then center a pipe cap exactly over the mark, open side down. Pack hypertufa into the form, and tamp it down, using a short piece of 2 × 4. Continue packing and tamping until the hypertufa is level with the top of the form.

3. Rap the surface with the 2 × 4 to eliminate air bubbles. Smooth the surface, using a trowel. Cover the piece with plastic and allow it to cure.

Step C: Pour the Pedestal

1. Mark the exact center of the bottom of the pedestal form, and then place the open end of a PVC pipe cap on the form, centered over the mark.

2. Pack hypertufa into the form until it's nearly level with the top. Insert a PVC pipe cap at the center of the form, open side up, so its top edge is flush with the top of the form. Tamp and smooth as directed in

#3 of Step B. Cover the piece with plastic and allow it to cure.

Step D: Pour the Basin

1. Mark the center on the bottom of the form, and press the open end of a PVC pipe cap into the form, centered over that mark.

2. Pack the hypertufa into the form in a layer about 2" thick.

3. Coat a shallow, gently sloped plastic bowl with vegetable oil, and then press it into the hypertufa, forming the depression of the basin. Continue packing and tamping the hypertufa around the bowl until you've created a smooth, even surface that's level with the top of the form. When the hypertufa is set, remove the bowl, cover the basin with plastic, and let it cure.

Step E: Construct the Birdbath

1. After the pieces have dried for 48 hours, disassemble the forms and remove the pieces of the birdbath. If you like a weathered look, now's the time to distress the pieces. Using a hammer and chisel, knock off corners and remove any sharp edges (see page 313).

2. Set the pieces outside, cover them with a tarp,

B. *Place the open end of a PVC pipe cap over the exact center of the base form. Pack and tamp hypertufa into the form, making sure the end cap stays in place. Add hypertufa until it reaches the top of the form.*

C. *Place a PVC pipe cap over the center of the bottom of the pedestal form, and then pack hypertufa into the form. Embed a PVC pipe cap at the top of the pedestal, centered within the form.*

TIP: ATTRACTING BIRDS TO YOUR GARDEN

If you want to attract birds to your garden, remember that they have much the same physical needs as humans: water, shelter, and food. Include garden features that will satisfy these needs—a birdbath, water garden, or fountain for water; trees, shrubs, and birdhouses for shelter; feeders or edible plants for food.

You can encourage birds to make a home in your garden by choosing plants that appeal to them. Hummingbirds are drawn to bright flowers, especially red and violet annuals. Other birds are attracted by sunflowers, marigolds, asters, and other flowers that produce lots of seeds, especially if you let the plants go to seed rather than deadheading them.

Birds are attracted to water at ground level, but that puts them in a vulnerable position when predators approach. Place water basins two to three feet above ground and close enough to shrubs or trees that birds have a place to flee if necessary—but not so close that predators can hide in them.

Clean your birdbath thoroughly every few days: Remove algae and bird droppings, and wash the basin with a solution of vinegar and water.

---

and let them cure for several weeks. Every few days, rinse the pieces with water to remove some of the alkaline residue from the hypertufa.

3. After several weeks, move the pieces back indoors and protect them from moisture. When you're sure the hypertufa is completely dry, paint a coat of good quality masonry sealer onto the depression of the basin.

4. Cut two 2½" pieces of 2" PVC pipe, using a hacksaw. Make sure the cuts are square.

5. Position the base, and then insert one 2½" piece of pipe into the pipe cap at the center of the base. Align the pieces and connect the PVC pipe to the cap embedded in the pedestal.

6. Insert the other 2½" piece of pipe in the cap at the bottom of the basin. Align this pipe with the cap on the top of the pedestal, joining the pieces.

D. *Place a PVC pipe cap at the exact center of the basin form, and then pack a layer of hypertufa into the form. Use an oiled plastic bowl to create a depression in the basin.*

E. *Insert a 2½" piece of PVC pipe into the cap at the center of the base and connect it to the pipe cap in the bottom of the pedestal. Insert another 2½" piece of PVC pipe into the cap in the basin and connect it to the cap in the pedestal.*

Accent Pieces

Accent pieces are the details—the grace notes—of a garden. These little flourishes transform your garden from a collection of random elements into a cohesive atmosphere of your own choosing. They also reinforce the impression that the person who tends this garden loves his or her work, down to the smallest detail.

Attractive plant markers (page 238) won't make your flowers bloom more abundantly, and innovative hose guards (page 239) won't protect your borders more vigilantly than plain ones, but they will make you and your visitors smile. And you'll surely take special pleasure in strolling along a path of stepping stones you created yourself (page 240) or in watching a delighted child hopscotch from one to the next. Brightly painted birdhouses (page 246) may not attract more birds, but they will attract more attention.

Most of the projects in this chapter include variations and suggestions for ways to adapt the basic ideas to suit your own tastes and style. By virtue of their small scale, accent pieces offer inexpensive, low-risk opportunities to experiment with unusual materials and new ideas. Accent pieces also make terrific gifts for other gardeners.

Stakes, Markers & Hose Guards

Marking and supporting plants are similar to housekeeping—not particularly thrilling, but necessary. However, even maintenance tasks can be fun if you take a lighthearted approach. With a handful of inexpensive materials and a couple of hours, you can build special stakes, markers, and hose guards that add splashes of color or touches of whimsy as they help you maintain your garden. The plant stakes shown here are easy to make, but the soldering may take a bit of practice. You have to work quickly to avoid reheating, and thereby softening, the previous joints.

Plant markers are traditionally used to identify plants; the generous size of these markers also gives you a handy place to keep notes about a plant's care requirements. You can use permanent markers to add color-coded symbols to the back of each marker, identifying plants that require staking, indicating the best pruning time, and noting any special fertilization needs.

TOOLS & MATERIALS

- Tape measure
- Tubing cutter
- Diagonal pliers
- Propane torch
- Pliers
- Drill
- Hacksaw
- Hand maul
- 1/4" flexible copper tubing
- 6-gauge copper wire

- 12-gauge copper wire
- 1/2" copper pipe (4")
- Flux
- Solder
- 1 1/2" glass marble
- 1" glass marble
- 1/2" glass marble
- 10-gauge plastic-coated wire (3 ft.)
- #3 rebar (30")

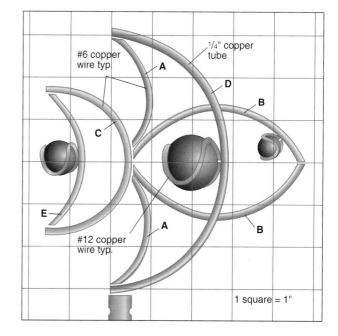

#6 copper wire typ.

1/4" copper tube

A

C

D

B

E

A

B

#12 copper wire typ.

1 square = 1"

HOW TO MAKE GARDEN STAKES

Step A: Create the Outline

1. Using the grid system or a photocopier, enlarge the pattern at right, and tack it to a work surface.

2. Use a tubing cutter to cut a piece of 1/4" copper tubing to the approximate length of the front arc of the fish's fin. Use diagonal pliers to cut a piece of 6-gauge copper wire to the approximate length of each remaining piece of the fish. Place the copper over the pattern, bend each piece to match the pattern line it represents, and then cut the pieces to fit.

3. Layer the pieces together to form the design. Start with the body of the fish. Add the two arcs that form the back of the fin, and then the front arc of the fin. Finally, position the tail pieces.

4. On a heat-resistant surface, solder the joints (see page 310). Begin by joining the back arcs of the fin (A) and the main pieces of the body (B). Add the first piece of the tail (C). Let these joints cool until they're rigid and have lost their shine.

5. Add the front arc of the fin (D), soldering it only to the fish body and the top fin joint. Solder the remaining piece of the tail (E) in place. Let the joints cool completely.

Step B: Add the Embellishments & the Stem

1. Cut a 4" piece of 1/2" copper pipe. About 1" from one end, drill a hole through each side of the pipe. Position the pipe at the lower fin joint of the fish. Solder the joint closed, connecting the fish to the pipe in the process.

2. Cut three pieces of #12 copper wire: 6 3/4", 5 1/2",

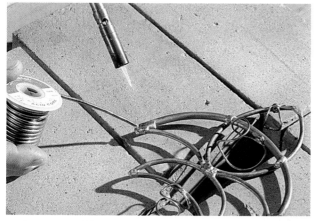

A. *Cut copper tubing and shape it to match the pattern. Layer the pieces together, and then solder the joints.*

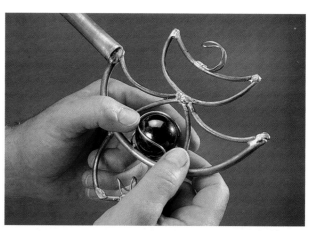

B. *Form wire circles and solder them into position. Bend the circles into loops to support the marbles.*

and 3¾". Form each piece into a circle, and then solder the circles in place, following the diagram on page 31. Let the solder cool completely.

3. Fold each wire circle into a loop, put a marble in its center, and shape the wire to hold the marble in place.

Step C: Install the Stake

1. Cut a 30" piece of rebar, using a hacksaw. With a hand maul, drive the rebar into the garden soil about 12". Set the fish ornament over the rebar.

2. Thread a 3-ft. piece of plastic coated wire through the holes at the top of the copper pipe. Bend each half of the wire back around the pipe, and then use pliers to make a 1" hook at each end. Surround the plant with the wires, and hook them together to support heavy stems.

C. *Thread plastic-coated wire through the stem of the ornament, and wrap it back around the stem. Form a hook at each end; loop the hooks together to support the plant.*

TOOLS & MATERIALS

- Straightedge
- Awl
- Mallet
- Aviation snips
- Drill
- Kitchen tongs
- Sheet of thin copper
- 100-grit sandpaper
- Fine steel wool
- Spray acrylic sealer
- ¾" copper pipe (10")
- 8-gauge galvanized wire
- Raffia or natural twine
- Permanent marker
- Wood backer

HOW TO MAKE GARDEN MARKERS

Step A: Create the Designs

1. Draw the outline for the tags on a sheet of copper, using a pencil. Draw a second line, repeating the shape, ¼" to ½" inside the outline.

2. Mark a hanging hole about ⅛" from the top edge of each tag and centered within the design. Place the copper over a smooth piece of wood, and then use an awl and a mallet to punch the hanging hole.

3. Punch decorative holes about ⅛" apart around the inside line of each tag.

4. Cut out the design along the traced outline, using aviation snips. Trim off sharp points, if necessary. Remove any rough edges by lightly sanding the edges of the tags with 100-grit sandpaper.

5. Hold each tag over a flame, such as the burner of a gas range, using tongs. Move the tag randomly

A. *Mark outlines onto copper sheet; mark hanging holes, and use an awl and a mallet to punch a design.*

B. *Sand the edges of the tags, oxidize the surface of each, then spray with acrylic sealer. Thread raffia through the hanging hole and loop it onto a stake made from 8-gauge galvanized wire.*

through the flame to produce color changes, checking it occasionally. Let the tags cool.

6. Lightly rub the tags with fine steel wool to remove any fingerprints; wipe clean. Spray each tag with acrylic sealer and let it dry.

7. Use a permanent marker to write a plant name on each tag.

Step B: Make the Stakes & Hang the Tags

1. To create a bending jig, drill a hole through a piece of ¾" copper pipe, and clamp the pipe in a vise. For each stake, cut a 21" piece of 8-gauge galvanized wire, using aviation snips. Insert one end of the wire into the hole in the pipe, and wrap the wire twice around the pipe. Snip off the wire at the hole and remove the stake.

2. Push the stake about 6" into the garden soil. Thread a 3" piece of raffia through the tag, and then through the loop of the stake, and tie it securely.

TOOLS & MATERIALS

- Paintbrush
- Hand maul
- Drill
- Wood deck post finials
- Exterior paint or stain or wood sealer
- Garden stakes

HOW TO MAKE HOSE GUARDS
Install Stakes & Add Finials

1. Stain and seal deck post finials, or paint them with two coats of exterior paint, depending on the finish you prefer. Let them dry thoroughly.

2. Position the finials to guide the hose around your planting beds rather than through them. Mark their locations, and drive a garden stake flush with the soil at each marked spot, using a hand maul. Drill a pilot hole and screw a finial into each stake.

Drive garden stakes flush with the soil, and then screw one finial into each stake.

VARIATION: DRAIN TILE HOSE GUARDS

You can make simple but attractive hose guards from ordinary drain tile. Place the tiles around the edges of a border, positioning them to keep the hose from being dragged across the planting area. Mark these positions.

At each mark, dig a hole the same diameter as the drain tile and approximately 6" deep. Set a drain tile into each hole and adjust until the tile's level.

Add a 2½" layer of pea gravel, and then fill the drain tile with potting soil and add plants.

Dig a 6"-deep hole for each drain tile. Set the drain tile in place and adjust until it's level. Add pea gravel and potting soil; plant as desired.

Stepping Stones

In some gardens, stepping stone paths beckon, virtually begging to be followed. Handmade stones add a unique, personal touch to a garden—you can even inscribe them to commemorate special days, such as birthdays or anniversaries.

This is a great project to share with children—there's almost no way to go wrong and you can use a nearly infinite variety of materials, depending on the ages and interests of the children. There are many stepping-stone kits on the market, but you don't need one—the materials are readily available.

To form stepping stones, use quick-setting concrete mix—about one 40-lb. bag of mix for each 18"-square stone. This mix is caustic: Wear a dust mask and gloves when using it.

Experiment with textures, patterns, and shapes. If you don't like a pattern, smooth the surface and start again. Remember, though, that you must work fairly quickly—quick-setting concrete sets up within 30 minutes. To slow the process, you can lightly mist the surface with water after "erasing" a pattern.

In addition to the decorative techniques described on the next page, you can make gorgeous accent stones from pieces of broken china or pottery. You can buy broken bits of china at craft stores, but it's less expensive to buy old dishes at garage sales or flea markets and break them yourself. Place the dishes in a heavy paper bag and then tap the bag with a rubber mallet. Wear safety goggles and heavy gloves when handling broken pieces, and file any sharp edges with a masonry file.

A. *Select molds; coat them with petroleum jelly. Mix quick-setting concrete and fill the molds. Skim off excess water.*

TOOLS & MATERIALS

- Shovel
- Hand tamp
- Containers to be used as molds
- Petroleum jelly
- Gloves
- Dust mask
- Quick-setting concrete mix
- Bucket
- Mason's trowel
- Embellishments, as desired
- Compactible gravel

HOW TO BUILD STEPPING STONES

Step A: Prepare the Molds & Pour the Concrete

1. Select molds for the stepping stones. Use aluminum pie plates, plastic plant saucers or large plastic lids, plywood forms or shallow boxes. Select molds deep enough (1½" to 2") and large enough (12" to 18") to make stones that can bear weight and comfortably accommodate an adult's foot.

2. Fill the molds with dry concrete mix to estimate the amount necessary. Following manufacturer's instructions, mix water, concrete dye if desired, and the concrete mix. Check a handful—it should hold its shape when squeezed, something like cookie dough. If necessary, add water and mix again.

3. Coat the molds with petroleum jelly, covering all the corners and edges.

4. Fill the forms with concrete. Smooth the surface with a mason's trowel, and then use a scrap 2 × 4 to skim off any excess water.

Step B: Embellish the Surface

1. Decorate the stones as desired.

Stamping Technique: Let the concrete dry for 10 to 15 minutes. While it's still damp, press ornaments firmly onto the surface, and then remove them. You can use a variety of natural ornaments such as leaves, twigs, small evergreen branches, shells, or stones. Or, you can use rubber stamps, available at craft stores.

Embedding Technique: Let the concrete dry for 10 minutes. Press ornaments into the surface, partially submerging them. Make sure the ornaments are firmly settled into the cement.

2. Let the stones cure several hours or overnight. Remove them from the molds.

Step C: Install the Stepping Stones

1. Cut out the turf and dig out 3½" to 4" of soil, following the shape of the stones.

2. Add a 2" layer of compactible gravel and tamp it thoroughly. Test-fit each stone, adjusting the gravel layer until the stone is level and stable.

B. *Decorate the stones with stamped designs or embedded ornaments. Let the stepping stones harden thoroughly.*

C. *Cut out the turf and remove 3½" to 4" of soil. Add a layer of compactible gravel, and then set each stone in place. Adjust until each stone is level and stable.*

241

Garden Lantern

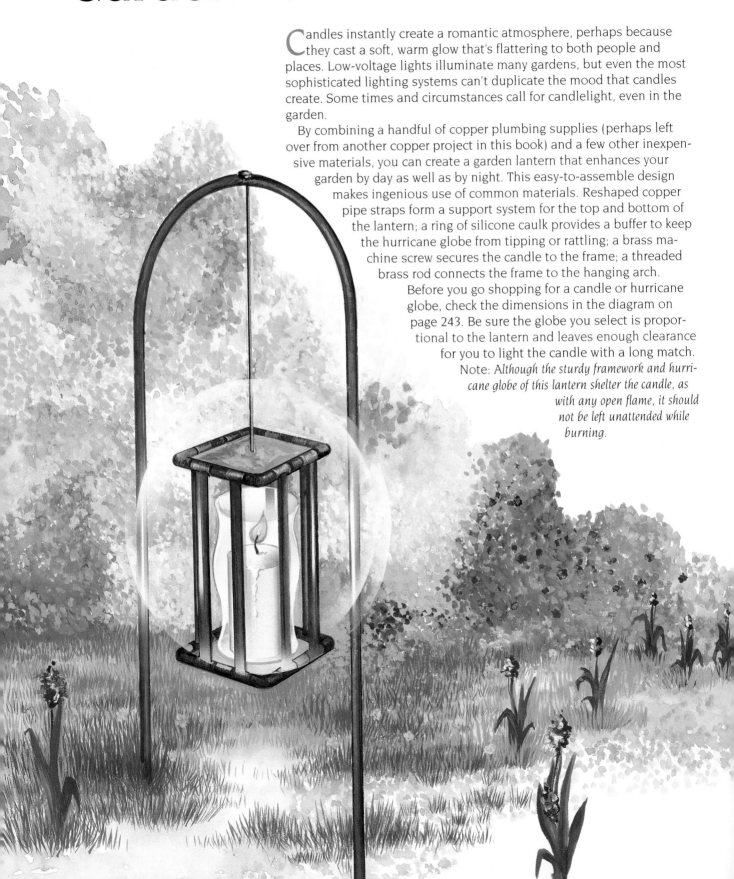

Candles instantly create a romantic atmosphere, perhaps because they cast a soft, warm glow that's flattering to both people and places. Low-voltage lights illuminate many gardens, but even the most sophisticated lighting systems can't duplicate the mood that candles create. Some times and circumstances call for candlelight, even in the garden.

By combining a handful of copper plumbing supplies (perhaps left over from another copper project in this book) and a few other inexpensive materials, you can create a garden lantern that enhances your garden by day as well as by night. This easy-to-assemble design makes ingenious use of common materials. Reshaped copper pipe straps form a support system for the top and bottom of the lantern; a ring of silicone caulk provides a buffer to keep the hurricane globe from tipping or rattling; a brass machine screw secures the candle to the frame; a threaded brass rod connects the frame to the hanging arch.

Before you go shopping for a candle or hurricane globe, check the dimensions in the diagram on page 243. Be sure the globe you select is proportional to the lantern and leaves enough clearance for you to light the candle with a long match.

Note: *Although the sturdy framework and hurricane globe of this lantern shelter the candle, as with any open flame, it should not be left unattended while burning.*

TOOLS & MATERIALS

- Tape measure
- Tubing cutter
- Propane torch
- Flux brush
- Aviation snips
- Drill
- Hand maul
- ½" copper pipe (10 ft.)
- ½" copper 90° elbows (8)
- ½" copper tees (16)
- Gaffer's tape
- Emery cloth
- Flux
- Sheet of thin copper, at least 16" square
- ½" copper pipe straps (8)

- #6-32 × ⅜" brass machine screws (8)
- #6-32 brass machine screw nuts (9)
- #6-32 × 2½" machine screw
- Silicone caulk
- Petroleum jelly
- ⅛" threaded brass rod, 11" long
- Nuts to fit threaded rod (3)
- Acorn nut to fit threaded rod
- ⅝" flexible copper tubing, 100" long
- Plywood, 20" × 20"
- #4 rebar, 30" long (2)
- Candle
- Hurricane globe

HOW TO BUILD A GARDEN LANTERN

Step A: Cut the Pipe & Construct the Frame

1. Measure and mark the copper pipe, following the cutting list shown below.

2. Cut the copper pipe, using a tubing cutter. Place the cutter over the pipe and tighten the handle until the pipe rests on both rollers and the cutting wheel is positioned over the the marked line. Turn the tubing cutter one rotation, so that the cutting wheel

A. *Connect copper pipes, elbows, and tees to form the base of the frame, and then add the legs and top.*

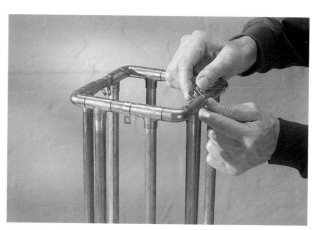

B. *Bend pipe straps around the sides of the frame, positioning them to support the covers on the base and top of the lantern.*

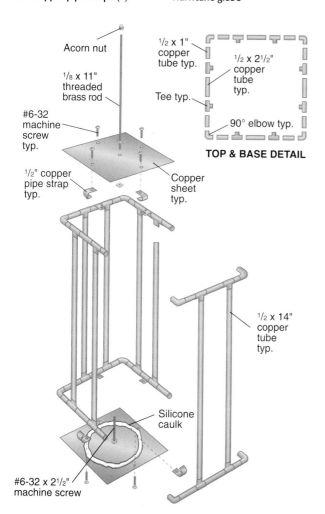

Acorn nut

⅛ x 11" threaded brass rod

#6-32 machine screw typ.

½" copper pipe strap typ.

½ x 1" copper tube typ.

Tee typ.

½ x 2½" copper tube typ.

90° elbow typ.

TOP & BASE DETAIL

Copper sheet typ.

½ x 14" copper tube typ.

Silicone caulk

#6-32 x 2½" machine screw

CUTTING LIST

½" Copper Pipe

Quantity	Length
8	14"
8	2½"
16	1"

scores a continuous straight line around the pipe. Rotate the cutter in the opposite direction, tightening the handle slightly after every two rotations until the cut is complete. Remove any sharp metal burrs from the inside edges of the cut pipe, using the reaming point on the tubing cutter or a round file.

3. Clean and flux the pipes, tees, and elbows (see page 310). Dry fit the pieces of the frame, top, and base, following the diagram on page 243. If you have

C. *Cut a piece of sheet copper for the base cover and secure it to the pipe straps, using machine screws and nuts. Add a circle of silicone caulk to buffer the lantern's globe.*

trouble getting the pieces to stay in place as you work, tape down each tee, which will hold the base steady. When all the connections fit properly, disassemble the frame and rebuild it, soldering the joints as you go (see page 310).

Step B: Install Supports for the Covers

1. Center one ½" copper pipe strap along each side of the top and each side of the bottom of the frame. Wrap one side of each strap around the pipe and extend the other end toward the center of the frame. Later, these extensions will support the base and top.

Step C: Add the Base Cover

1. Measure the inside dimensions of the base of the frame, and then mark and cut a sheet of copper to match, using aviation snips. Position the base so the straps support the edges, and mark the locations of the pipe strap holes. Drill a hole through the cover at each of these marks, as well as at the exact center of the cover.

2. Center the globe over the hole in the middle of the base, draw a pencil line just outside the lip, then remove the globe. To form a buffer for the globe, run a bead of silicone caulk around this circle, just inside the line. While the caulk sets up, apply petroleum jelly to the lip of the globe and use it to make an impression in the bead of caulk.

3. Working up from the bottom, attach the base cover to the frame, threading #6-32 × ⅜" machine screws through the pipe straps and the sheet of copper and securing them with machine screw nuts.

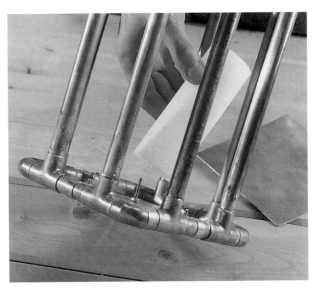

D. *Run a 2½" machine screw through the center of the base cover and secure it with a nut. Thread a candle onto the screw, and then settle the hurricane globe into place.*

E. *Run a piece of threaded brass rod through the center of the top and secure it with one nut above and one below the sheet of copper.*

Step D: Position the Candle & Hurricane Globe

Run a #6-32 × 2½" machine screw through the hole in the center of the base cover and secure it with a nut. Thread the candle onto the screw, and then position the hurricane globe over the candle.

Step E: Install the Top Cover & Hanging Rod

1. Measure the inside dimensions of the top of the frame, and then mark a sheet of copper to match. Cut the sheet, using aviation snips. Position the top cover and mark the locations of the pipe strap holes. Drill a hole at each mark as well as at the exact center of the cover.

2. Working from the top down, secure the top cover to the frame, again using #6-32 × ⅜" machine screws and machine screw nuts.

3. Insert the threaded rod through the hole in the center of the top, and secure it with one nut below and one above.

Step F: Create the Arch & Hang the Lantern

1. Cut a 100" piece of ⅝" flexible copper tubing. Mark the center, and drill a ⅛" hole all the way through the tubing.

2. Cut a plywood circle 20" in diameter, mark it into quadrants, and clamp or screw it to a workbench. Line up the hole in the tubing with the marked top of the plywood circle, and bend the sides of the tubing down around the circle, forming a smooth arch.

3. Select a location and press the arch into the

F. *Add a nut to the top of the hanging rod; slide it through the hole in the supporting arch. Secure the rod with an acorn nut.*

ground to mark the leg positions. At each mark, drive a 30" piece of #4 rebar about 18" into the ground.

4. Slide the legs of the arch over the rebar and press down to seat the copper firmly into the ground.

5. Screw a nut onto the hanging rod, and then insert the rod into the hole at the center of the arch. Thread an acorn nut onto the rod and tighten it.

VARIATION: ICE LUMINARIES

Gardens sometimes look forlorn in winter. When temperatures consistently remain below freezing, brighten and warm your garden with ice luminaries.

For each ice luminary, you need a plastic jar such as a mayonnaise or peanut butter jar, a handful of rocks, and a one-gallon bucket. Fill the jar with rocks, and place it in the center of the bucket. Add water to the bucket until it reaches the rim of the jar.

Set the bucket outside or in a freezer until the water freezes. Remove the rocks, and pour warm water into the jar. When the ice releases the jar, remove it.

Wrap the outside of the bucket with a warm, wet towel until it releases the ice. Remove the ice from the bucket. Place a candle in the center well and put the luminary in the garden.

These luminaries last for quite a while if temperatures stay below freezing. If the ice gets cloudy, spraying it with water will clear it.

Ice luminaries warm and brighten dark winter nights.

Birdhouse

Birds, like humans, go where they feel most welcome. They prefer gardens that offer fresh water, plentiful food, and comfortable shelter. In addition to birdbaths and feeders, birdhouses are an essential part of attracting birds to your garden.

Many cavity-nesting birds are drawn to birdhouses about 4" square and about 8" tall. If you build the house so that one side pivots open, you can clean the house after nesting season or remove nests built by birds you don't want to encourage.

To build comfortable, long-lasting birdhouses, use 1 × 6 cedar or redwood lumber. The thickness of the lumber provides some insulation against both heat and cold, and the cedar or redwood, which is weather resistant, helps the house withstand the elements for several years. You can paint the outside of a birdhouse, but never the interior. Subdued colors such as brown, tan, and gray are good choices because they're pleasing to many types of birds.

Before you start building birdhouses, decide what species of birds you want to invite to your garden. The recommended diameter of the entrance hole and the height for mounting the birdhouse (see chart on page 248) depends on the species you're trying to attract.

Although the birdhouse shown below is designed to be hung, you can easily adapt the plans to build a birdhouse that can be mounted vertically or on a garden post (page 249).

TOOLS & MATERIALS

- Drill and 1/16" bit
- Spade bit sized for desired entrance hole
- Jig saw or circular saw
- Carpenter's square
- Cordless screwdriver

- 1 × 6 redwood or cedar
- 4d galvanized finish nails
- Exterior wood glue
- Shoulder hook
- Screw eyes (2)

HOW TO BUILD A HANGING BIRDHOUSE

Note: *Cut all pieces from 1 × 6 cedar lumber. The actual measurements of dimensional lumber vary: Make sure the lumber you select measures 5 1/2" in width.*

Step A: Cut the Bottom & Sides of the House

1. Cut a 4" square for the bottom of the house. Trim diagonally across each corner, 1/2" from the corner, to allow for drainage.

2. Cut two 4" × 5 1/2" pieces for the sides of the house.

Step B: Cut the Front, Back, & Roof

1. Cut two 5 1/2" × 8 3/4" pieces, one for the front and one for the back of the house.

2. On each piece, mark a point 2 3/4" down from the top on each adjacent side. Draw lines from the center point down to these side points, then cut along these lines.

3. Cut one 5 1/2"× 6 1/2" piece and one 4 3/4" × 6 1/2" piece for the roof.

Step C: Drill the Entrance Hole & Score Grip Lines

1. Mark a point on the front piece, 6 3/4" from the lower edge, centering the mark from side to side. Place the tip of a spade bit on the marked point and drill an entrance hole. Begin at low speed, and gradually increase the speed as the bit enters the wood.

2. Use a wood screw or an awl to make several deep horizontal scratches on the inside of the front piece, starting 1" below the entrance hole. These grip lines help young birds hold on as they climb up to the entrance hole.

A. *Trim diagonally across each corner, 1/2" from the corners.*

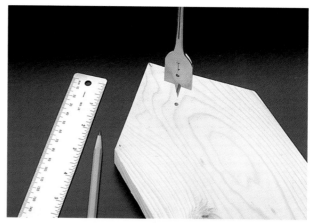

B. *Mark the center of the front, and then use a carpenter's square to mark the pitch of the roof. Cut along marked lines. Repeat for the back of the house.*

C. *Center a mark 6 3/4" from the lower edge. Drill the entrance hole, using a spade bit.*

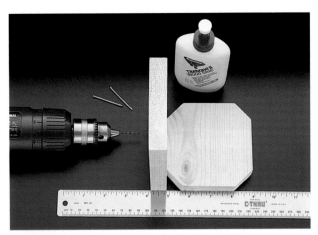

D. *Glue a side piece to the bottom piece. Drill pilot holes and nail the pieces together, using 4d galvanized finish nails.*

E. *Align the remaining side wall, then drive one nail through each side, about ⅝" from the upper edge of the front and back.*

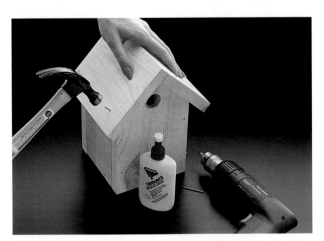

F. *Glue the shorter roof piece to the front and back, aligning the top of the roof with the peak of the house. Position the remaining roof piece, drill pilot holes, and nail the roof in place.*

Step D: Attach the Bottom

1. Apply wood glue to one edge of the bottom piece. Set a side piece in place, so the bottoms of the two pieces are flush. Drill pilot holes and secure the pieces with 4d galvanized finish nails.

2. Apply wood glue to the edges of the side and bottom. Align the front piece and adjust until its edge is flush with the face of the side. Drill pilot holes and secure the front to the side, using 4d finish nails. Repeat this process to attach the back.

Step E: Install the Pivoting Side Wall

Put the remaining side piece in place, but do not glue it. To secure this piece to the front wall and back pieces, drive a nail through the front and another through the back wall, each positioned about ⅝" from the upper edge. This arrangement allows the piece to pivot.

Step F: Add the Roof

1. Apply glue to the upper edges of one side of the front and back. Set the 4¾" × 6½" roof piece on the house with its upper edge aligned with the peak of the house.

2. Apply glue to the 5½" × 6½" roof piece and set it in position. Drill pilot holes and drive nails through the roof and into the front. Repeat to secure the roof to the back of the house.

Step G: Add the Finishing Touches

1. Drill a pilot hole in the edge of the front piece, placed about 1" from the lower edge of the house.

Bird	Diameter of Hole
Carolina Wren	1½"
Chickadee	1⅛"
Downy Woodpecker	1¼"
House Wren & Winter Wren	1" to ½"
Nuthatch	1¼"
Titmouse	1¼"

Screw in a shoulder hook, positioning it to hold the side closed.

2. Sand the birdhouse smooth, and then paint or stain it as desired.

You can embellish this basic birdhouse many ways. There are, however, a few important things to keep in mind: Don't paint or apply preservatives to the inside of the house, the inside edge of the entrance hole, or within ¼" of the face of the entrance hole. And remember, some birds are wary of bright colors, so stay within medium tones as you choose paint and ornaments. If you live in a warm climate, avoid using black or other very dark colors—they absorb heat and can make the house too hot for birds to inhabit.

3. Attach screw eyes through the roof, near the peak. Attach chains to the screw eyes and hang the birdhouse.

G. *Drill a pilot hole about 1" from the lower edge of the front, and then insert a shoulder hook to secure the pivoting side.*

VARIATION: VERTICALLY-MOUNTED BIRDHOUSE

Cut a piece of 1 × 6 for the back, 5½" × 11¾". Mark a line, 3" from the lower edge, and then drill three pilot holes. Trim diagonally across the lower corners, removing 1" from each.

Nail two narrow wood strips on the back side of this piece. This creates space between the house and the mounting surface, which keeps water from collecting behind the back of the birdhouse.

Continue as in Steps A through G on pages 247 to 248. Align the lower edge of the bottom with the line drawn on the back piece and omit the screw eyes in Step G. To mount the birdhouse, drive screws through the back and into a post, tree, or other structure.

Cut the back piece, drill pilot holes, and trim the lower corners.

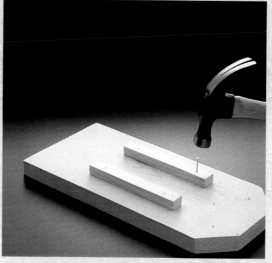

Nail two wood strips to the back of the birdhouse. Complete construction as for the hanging birdhouse.

Deck Rail Planter

If the number and variety of containers offered through garden centers and catalogs is any indication, container gardening is more popular now than ever. And no wonder—containers allow you to control soil conditions, move plants as necessary to meet their sun requirements, and brighten otherwise plain areas of your yard or garden. This deck rail planter offers an easy, inexpensive way to turn your deck into an extension of your garden.

The planter, which is designed to hold potted plants, is basically a four-sided bottomless box with spacers that hold the planter in place. The open construction makes it easy to rotate the plants with the seasons. Pots of early pansies can make way for the geraniums, petunias, and marigolds of summer, which in time can yield to chrysanthemums, extending the season long into fall.

This planter is 10" wide and 42¾" long, but you can build it to any length you want. If you're building a planter that's more than 32" long, add a center support to keep the boards from warping as they weather.

Before deciding on a specific length for a planter box, determine the size of the pots and saucers you plan to use; then calculate a length that will accommodate an even number of pots with a bit of space in between. Keep in mind that the inside length of a planter without a center support will be 2¼" less than the outside length; in one with a center support, it's 3⅛" less. It might be helpful to draw a diagram (such as the one on page 251), including the pots you plan to use.

When buying lumber, select the straightest, most knot-free boards you can find, and add 10% to the length you need, to allow for trimming. Mark cuts carefully to avoid having knots at cut ends—they're unreliable anchoring points and it's difficult to screw into them.

TOOLS & MATERIALS

- Straightedge
- Tape measure
- Utility knife
- Jig saw or circular saw
- Drill and $^3/_{32}$" bit
- Cordless screwdriver
- 1 × 8 cedar lumber

- 3" galvanized drywall or deck screws
- 1$^5/_8$" galvanized drywall or deck screws
- Exterior wood glue
- Wood preservatives, stain, or paint

A. *Mark the desired lengths and score along the marked lines. Cut the pieces, using a jig saw or circular saw.*

HOW TO BUILD A DECK RAIL PLANTER

Step A: Cut the Front and Back Pieces

Mark a 1 × 8 board at 42$^3/_4$". To keep the wood from splintering when you cut it, lightly score along the marked line, using a utility knife. Cut this front piece, using a jig saw or circular saw. Use this piece as a template to mark and cut the back.

Step B: Cut the End Pieces & Support Pieces

1. Mark an end piece 8$^1/_2$" long. Score along the marked line and cut the piece. Use this piece as a template to mark the other end piece and the center support (if your planter is more than 32" long).

2. Trim 1" off the bottom of each end piece (and center support, if necessary), so each measures 6$^1/_4$" × 8$^1/_2$". Set the scraps aside for spacers in Step D.

Step C: Assemble the Main Pieces

1. Mark the placement for three screws, $^3/_4$" from one end of the front piece. Place one mark 1" from

B. *On end pieces and center support, trim 1" from the lower edge, creating 6$^1/_4$" × 8$^1/_2$" pieces.*

CUTTING LIST

42$^3/_4$" 1 x 8	(1, for front)	
42$^3/_4$" 1 x 8	(1, for back)	
8$^1/_2$" 1 x 8	(2, for ends)	
8$^1/_2$" 1 x 8	(1, for support)	

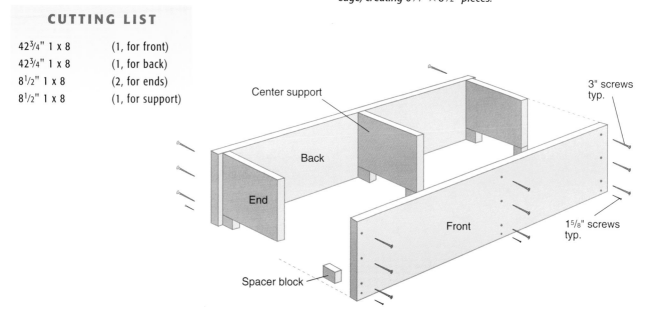

Center support
Back
End
3" screws typ.
Front
1$^5/_8$" screws typ.
Spacer block

the upper edge, one mark 2" from the lower edge, and one centered between the first two marks. Repeat at the center of the front piece and at the opposite end.

2. Repeat the process for the back piece.

3. Stand one end piece upright and position the front piece against it, extending the front piece $1/4$" beyond the end piece. At each mark, drill a pilot hole, using a $3/32$" bit. To secure the pieces, drive 3" drywall or deck screws through the front and into the end piece. Repeat the process for the other end piece and the center support.

Step D: Add the Spacers

1. Measure the width of your deck rail and add $1/8$" to that measurement. Subtract the total from the inside width of the box. From the scraps set aside in Step B, cut spacers equal to one half this measurement. Cut six spacer blocks—two for each end piece and two for the center support.

2. Glue one spacer block to each side of the end pieces and the center support, offsetting the blocks $1/8$" from the front and end pieces. Drill pilot holes and drive a $15/8$" drywall or deck screw into each.

Step E: Apply a Finish

Apply two coats of primer and then paint the boards. Make sure you let the primer dry thoroughly between coats. Or, if you want the planters to have a more natural appearance, apply wood preservative or exterior wood stain to the inside, outside, and all edges of the boards.

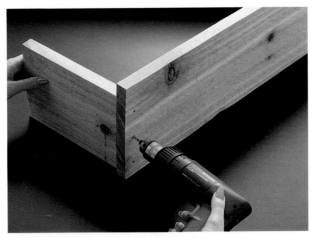

C. *Mark the placement of three screws, and then drill pilot holes at the marked locations. Drive screws through pilot holes, securing both end pieces and the center support.*

PLANTER WIDTH FORMULA

5½" (width of deck rail)	8½" inside width
+⅛"	-5⅝" of box
----------	----------
5⅝"	2⅞"

2⅞" divided by 2 = 1⁷⁄₁₆" spacer blocks

D. *Attach spacer blocks to each side of the end pieces and the center support, offsetting them ⅛" from the edges of the front and end pieces.*

E. *Apply wood preservative, stain, or paint to all faces and edges of the planter.*

TIP: MAINTAINING A CONTAINER GARDEN

Container gardens are so portable and versatile that they can be located virtually anywhere, even in unexpected areas. An ordinary deck rail can become an herb garden, a stairway can become a flower patch, or a basic privacy fence can come alive with foliage in hanging baskets. You can create an almost instant garden anywhere you can place a planter or hang a basket.

Although container gardens often are filled with well-known annuals, hundreds of plant varieties can be grown in containers. Just remember that the containers must hold enough soil to support the plants, provide adequate drainage, and be placed in locations with appropriate lighting conditions.

Container gardens have a few other requirements. The most important is an increased need for water. It makes sense when you think about it—plants in open ground can extend their roots in search of moisture, but container-grown plants don't have that option. They rely on you to provide consistent moisture.

In warm weather, you may have to water a container garden more than once a day. The general rule is to keep soil moist but not soggy. Damp soil often is darker than dry, and a pot filled with dry soil typically weighs less than one filled with moist soil. Wilting leaves are signs of stress, too, but it's best not to let your plants dry out to the point that they're suffering that much stress.

Water during the early to mid-morning hours to reduce the amount of moisture lost to evaporation and give plants extra strength to withstand the afternoon heat. On hot or windy days, water again at dusk.

In cooler weather, you'll probably only have to water once a week, preferably in the late morning. Avoid watering in the evening if there's any danger of frost.

Wobbler

During the growing season, a wobbler makes a topiary-like support for ivy, sweet pea, or beans, and during the winter it warms the garden with candles or miniature lights.

This is another project that makes ingenious use of copper plumbing materials. The construction is so simple that you can easily make several for your own garden—and maybe one or two to give as gifts. The spiral is shaped by forming flexible copper tubing into a coil and then elongating the coil into a tree-like shape. Flexible copper tubing is malleable and fairly forgiving as long as you don't crimp it, so the key is to work slowly, using a firm but gentle touch. The stand is merely a piece of copper pipe set in a paint can filled with quick-setting concrete, and the candle holders are copper end caps supported by reshaped pipe straps.

During the holiday season it should be easy to find miniature candles for the wobbler, but they're available year-round at specialty candle retailers, on the internet, or through catalogs. These small candles burn down quickly, so keep a supply on hand.

If you train plants to twine up your wobbler, be sure to tie the tendrils loosely with soft ties, such as strips cut from old cotton t-shirts (see page 307). And keep in mind that container-grown plants require more careful watering than plants in open ground (see page 253).

TOOLS & MATERIALS

- Tape measure
- Tubing cutter
- Level
- Jig saw
- Drill
- Hammer
- Screwdriver
- Channel-type pliers
- Pop rivet gun
- Locking pliers
- Aviation snips
- Propane torch
- Awl
- Pliers
- Empty 1-gallon paint can
- Quick-setting concrete mix
- ½" rigid copper pipe
  (at least 65")
- Duct tape
- Two scraps of plywood,
  (each at least 20" square)
- 1" deck screws (6)
- ¼" flexible copper tubing
  (25 ft.)
- #6 copper wire
- 2"-dia. tin can
- ¾" copper pipe or wood dowel
- ½" copper end caps (21)
- Flux and flux brush
- Solder
- ⅜" copper pipe straps (20)
- #3-32 × ⅜" self-tapping
  screws (20)
- ½ × 4" candles

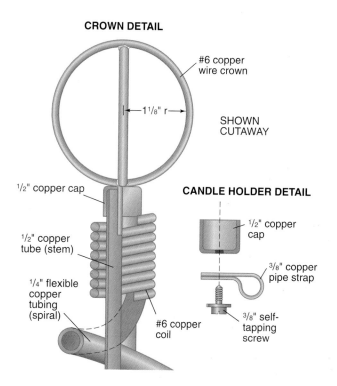

CROWN DETAIL

#6 copper wire crown

1⅛" r

SHOWN CUTAWAY

½" copper cap

½" copper tube (stem)

¼" flexible copper tubing (spiral)

#6 copper coil

CANDLE HOLDER DETAIL

½" copper cap

⅜" copper pipe strap

⅜" self-tapping screw

HOW TO BUILD A WOBBLER

Step A: Build the Stem Assembly

1. Cut a 65" length of ½" copper pipe, using a tubing cutter (see page 310).

2. Mix quick-setting concrete, following manufacturer's instructions; pour the concrete into a 1-gallon paint can.

3. Set the copper pipe in the center of the paint can. Use a level to make sure the pipe is plumb, then tape it in position, using duct tape. Set this assembly aside for several hours or until the concrete is thoroughly dry.

Step B: Build a Bending Jig & Form the Spiral

1. Cut two 20" squares from scrap plywood. Centered on one of the squares, mark a 16"-diameter circle, then use a jig saw to cut out the circle.

2. Use 1" deck screws to secure the frame of the cutout to the remaining plywood square, creating a jig that will contain the flexible tubing as you form it into a coil.

3. Cut a 25 ft. length of ¼" flexible copper tubing. Using channel-type pliers, flatten the first 2 to 3" of one end of the tubing. If necessary, use a hammer to smooth the flattened tubing.

4. Position the opposite (round) end of the tubing

A. *Plant a 65" piece of ½" copper pipe in a paint can filled with quick-setting concrete. Make sure the pipe is plumb, then tape it position and let the concrete dry.*

at the outer edge of the bending jig; form the tubing into a loose coil until you reach the flattened end. Leave about an inch between the loops in the outer edges, and gradually form the loops closer together as you near the center of the coil.

5. Grasp the flattened end and lift the coil from the bending jig. Pull up on the center of the coil and gently reshape the coil until it forms a tree-shaped spiral approximately 50" tall.

Step C: Attach the Spiral to the Stem Assembly

1. Position the stem assembly inside the spiral, with the flattened tubing near the top of the stem. Use channel-type pliers to bend the flattened tubing around the stem, continuing the general spiral shape up and around the stem; stop about ½" from the end of the stem. Clamp the spiral in place with locking pliers.

2. Drill two pilot holes through the tubing and stem, then secure the spiral to the stem, using a pop rivet gun and steel pop rivets.

3. Cut one 7½" and one 6⅜" length of #6 copper wire. Shape the 6⅜" length of wire around a 2"-dia. tin can, forming a circle. Shape the 7½" piece of wire around the tin can; at the end of the resulting circle, bend the wire at a 90° angle to form a stem approxi-

B. *Flatten 2 to 3" of one end of a 25 ft. length of ¼" flexible copper tubing, then push the tubing into a bending jig, forming a loose coil. Reshape the coil into a tree-shaped spiral.*

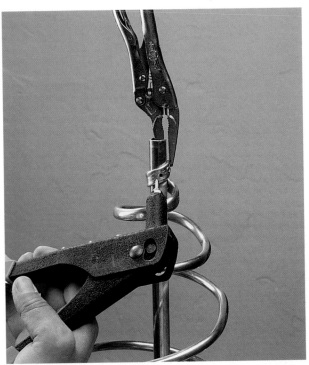

C. *Clamp the spiral into position on the stem assembly, then drill pilot holes and secure the spiral to the stem, using pop rivets.*

D. *To form candle holders, shape ⅜" copper pipe straps around the spiral. Secure one ½" copper end cap to each pipe strap, using ⅜" self-tapping screws.*

mately 1" long.

4. To form the crown, place the first circle inside and perpendicular to the second. Gently reshape the wire to form the circles into a crown. At the top of the crown, mark the intersection of the circles, then use aviation snips to cut a V-shaped notch in the wire on the inside face of the outer circle (see diagram on page 255).

5. Balance the circles in the open end of the tin can, with the inner circle resting in the notch on the outer circle. Flux and solder the intersection of the circles (see page 310). Let the joint cool completely.

6. Drill a pilot hole in the center of a ½" copper end cap. Insert the stem of the crown into the pilot hole in the end cap. Flux and solder the intersection of the wires to the end cap and let the joint cool.

7. Wrap #6 wire in 8 tight loops around a piece of ¾" copper pipe or wood dowel. Cut the wire, then slip the coil off of the pipe or dowel. Slide the coil down over the stem of the wobbler, then place the crown at the top of the stem.

Step D: Add the Candle Holders

1. Wrap each of the ⅜" pipe straps around the tubing so the flanges meet. Use an awl to center punch each of the remaining end caps, then secure a reshaped pipe strap to the bottom of each end cap with a ⅜" self-tapping screw.

2. Back the screws out enough to open the straps, then position these assemblies so they form candle holders at the outside edge of the spiral, roughly equidistant from one another. Use pliers to gently flex each candle holder until it's vertical.

4. Carefully screw one ½ × 4" candle onto the screw at the center of each candle holder.

VARIATIONS: WOBBLER WITH MINIATURE LIGHTS OR IVY

The glow of a garden by candlelight is appealing, but not always practical. If you prefer to use miniature lights on your wobbler, follow the same procedure, but omit Step D. Then string miniature lights along the tubing and secure them with fishing line or floral tape.

You may also want to omit the candle holders if you plan to train ivy to grow on your wobbler. Simply select a large pot or other planting container with adequate drainage, add a 2" layer of washed gravel, and position the wobbler in the center. Fill the planting container with potting soil and plant the ivy. As it grows, loosely tie the tendrils along the tubing, and prune as necessary to retain the spiral shape.

Right: Miniature lights bathe the wobbler in sparkling swirls that add a special glow to dinner on the deck, parties in the garden, or holiday lighting schemes.

Far Right: Training ivy to grow along a wobbler creates a topiary-like ornament that looks right at home on a deck or patio or beside a sidewalk or entry.

Garden Furnishings

Comfortable, attractive furnishings invite visitors into your garden and encourage them to linger. From a bench that provides a comfortable place for two or more people to sit and relax (page 274), to a mosaic table that's alluring on its own or as a place for refreshments (page 266), or recycled treasures (page 264) that evoke fond memories, furnishings add immeasurably to a garden's ambience. With a few simple tools and materials, you can build or reinvent pieces that reflect your interests and abilities and imbue your garden's atmosphere with your personal style.

Furnishings can also provide a source of entertainment, as in the case of the Tabletop Zen Garden (page 278). Zen gardens are intriguing, from the desktop versions in catalogs and gift stores, to the full-scale gardens pictured in magazines. But they're a little like the Three Bears—one's too small and one's just too big to be practical. With these instructions, you can build a version scaled to the proportions of your deck or patio. You can invite guests to sit around, sharing quiet conversation and perhaps a glass of wine, as you rake sand and compose the garden's shells, stones, and other elements.

Hypertufa Planter

Gardening magazines and catalogs often feature stone or concrete troughs brimming with flowers or planted as alpine gardens. Many of the pieces pictured in magazines are antiques, but others are reproductions that merely look weathered and worn. With all the interest in them, antique versions have become hard to find, and even reproductions are expensive.

With hypertufa, you can create inexpensive, long-lasting planters that resemble aged stone sinks or troughs. Or, if your taste runs more toward contemporary shapes, you can easily create more streamlined pieces. Hypertufa is a versatile material, and the simple construction methods (page 312) are fun to use.

You have to plan ahead for this project. It takes several weeks for hypertufa to cure and several more to wash out the alkaline residue enough to use the planter.

TOOLS & MATERIALS

- Tape measure
- Jig saw
- Straightedge
- Drill
- Hacksaw
- Wheelbarrow or mixing trough
- Hammer
- Chisel or paint scraper
- Wire brush
- Propane torch
- 12-quart bucket
- 2"-thick polystyrene insulation board

- 3½" deck screws (40)
- Gaffer's tape
- Scrap of 4"-dia. PVC pipe
- Dust mask
- Gloves
- Portland cement
- Peat moss
- Perlite
- Fiberglass fibers
- Concrete dye (optional)
- Plastic tarp
- Scrap 2 × 4

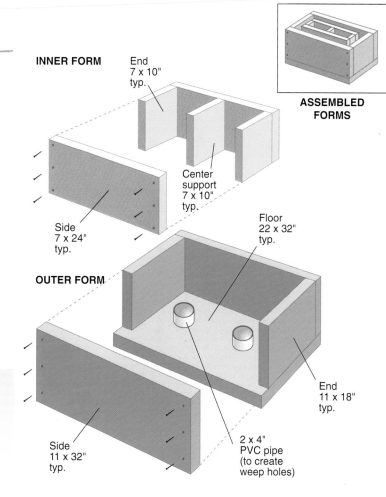

INNER FORM
End 7 x 10" typ.
Center support 7 x 10" typ.
Side 7 x 24" typ.

ASSEMBLED FORMS

OUTER FORM
Floor 22 x 32" typ.
End 11 x 18" typ.
Side 11 x 32" typ.
2 x 4" PVC pipe (to create weep holes)

CUTTING LIST

Outer Form	Inner Form
22" × 32" (1, for floor)	7" × 24" (2, for sides)
11" × 32" (2, for sides)	7" × 10" (3, for ends and
11" × 18" (2, for ends)	center support)

HOW TO BUILD A HYPERTUFA PLANTER
Step A: Build the Forms

1. Measure, mark, and cut pieces of 2"-thick polystyrene insulation board to the dimensions in the cutting list above, using a jig saw.

2. To construct the outer form, fit an end piece between the two side pieces and fasten each joint, using three 3½" deck screws. Repeat to fasten the other end. Wrap gaffer's tape entirely around the form. Place one loop of tape near the top and another near the bottom of the form. Set the bottom squarely on top of the resulting rectangle, and then screw and tape it securely in place.

3. Construct the inner form, following the same method.

4. Cut two 2" pieces of 4"-dia. PVC pipe, using a hacksaw, and set them aside.

A. *To construct the forms, fasten the joints with 3½" deck screws; then reinforce them with gaffer's tape.*

Step B: Form the Floor

1. Center the pieces of PVC pipe in the floor of the outer form and press them into the foam; these pipes establish the planter's weep holes.

2. Mix the hypertufa, following the directions on pages 312 to 313. Be sure to wear a dust mask and gloves when handling dry cement mix; also wear gloves when working with wet cement.

3. Pack hypertufa onto the floor of the form, pressing it down firmly and packing it tightly around the pieces of PVC. Continue to add hypertufa until you've created a solid, level, 2"-thick floor.

B. *Pack hypertufa onto the floor of the form; press it down firmly to create a level, 2"-thick floor.*

Step C: Build the Walls

Place the inner form within the outer form, centering it carefully. Add hypertufa between the outer and inner forms, using a scrap 2 × 4 to tamp it down as you go. Try to be consistent in the amount of pressure you use while tamping the hypertufa—the walls of the planter need to be strong enough to withstand the weight and pressure of soil, moisture, and growing plants. Continue adding and tamping the hypertufa until it reaches the top of the forms.

Step D: Allow to Dry & Remove the Forms

1. Cover the planter with a plastic tarp, and let it dry for at least 48 hours. If the weather is exceptionally warm, remove the tarp and mist the planter with water occasionally during the curing process.

2. Remove the tape and screws from the outer form, working carefully so the form can be reused, if desired. If the walls appear to be dry enough to handle without damaging the planter, remove the inner forms. If not, let the planter cure for another 24 hours, then remove the inner form.

You may notice that the planter's surface looks almost hairy, an effect created by the fiberglass in the hypertufa mixture. Don't be concerned about it at this point—the hairy fringe will be removed later.

Step E: Complete the Curing Process

1. Many of the stone planters on the market have a somewhat rustic appearance. If you like that look, this is the time to create it. Working slowly and carefully, use a hammer to round the corners and rough up the edges of the planter.

C. *Center the inner form within the outer form, and then tamp hypertufa between the two, forming the walls.*

D. *After the planter has dried for 48 hours, remove the screws and carefully disassemble the forms.*

2. To add texture, gouge grooves on the sides and ends of the planter, using a chisel or paint scraper. Complete the aging process by brushing the entire planter with a wire brush. Be bold with these aging techniques—the more texture you create, the more time-worn the planter will appear to be.

3. Cover the planter with plastic, and let it cure for about a month. Uncover it at least once a week, and mist it with water to slow down the curing process. Although it's natural to be impatient, don't rush this step. The more slowly the hypertufa cures, the stronger and more durable the planter will be.

4. Unwrap the planter and let it cure outside, uncovered, for several weeks. Periodically wash it down with water to remove some of the alkaline residue of the concrete (which would otherwise endanger the plants grown in the planter). Adding vinegar to the water speeds this process somewhat, but it still takes several weeks. Again, this step is important, so don't rush it.

After the planter has cured outside for several weeks, put it inside, away from any sources of moisture, to cure for several more weeks.

5. When the planter is completely dry, use a propane torch to burn off the hairy fringe on the surface. Move the torch quickly, holding it in each spot no more than a second or two. If pockets of moisture remain, they can get so hot that they explode, leaving pot holes in the planter. To avoid that problem, make sure the planter is dry before you begin, and work quickly with the torch so no significant amount of heat builds up.

E. *Round the edges and corners of the planter with a hammer, and gouge it with a chisel or paint scraper. Brush the entire planter with a wire brush, and then set it outside to cure.*

ENCOURAGING MOSS

Moss helps ornaments blend into a garden as though they've been there forever. If you don't want to wait for moss to form naturally, there are several ways to encourage its growth. These recipes work best if you place the ornaments in moist, shady locations.

• Pour buttermilk over the ornament, and then press patches of fresh moss onto it. Mist the surface occasionally while you wait for new patches of moss to form.

• Generously paint the surface with water from a fish pond or water garden, which generally contains mold spores. Repeat this procedure several times over 24 hours, and then brush on a solution of 2 tablespoons of white school glue dissolved in a quart of water.

• Dissolve 8 ounces of blue clay or porcelain clay in 3 cups of water. Add a cup of fish emulsion fertilizer and a cup of fresh moss. Blend the mixture thoroughly—an old, otherwise unused blender would be ideal—and paint it onto the ornament.

Recycled Treasures

According to Ralph Waldo Emerson, things may be pretty, graceful, rich, elegant, or handsome, but until they speak to the imagination, they're not yet beautiful. You may occasionally come across an odd or interesting piece that speaks to your imagination—sometimes a piece virtually shouts that it would be a beautiful garden ornament. You can use almost any piece if you find or create the right setting for it.

Before you decide to invest in an unusual piece, assess its condition. Make sure any wood is free of rot and pests. You don't have to rule out clay, ceramic, or masonry pieces that have chips or minor cracks, but avoid pieces with major structural damage. Rust adds character to metal pieces, but edges that are rusted through may be dangerous or unstable.

Not every unique item needs to become a planting container—consider using an unusual piece as sculpture, turning it into a furnishing piece, or adapting it to support other planting containers, such as hanging baskets.

The ironwork pictured below (and at far right) was rescued from a flea market. Part of its appeal comes from knowing that it stood sentry over the gateway to an Egyptian courtyard for nearly a century. With very little work, it became a beautiful backdrop for a cutting garden.

TOOLS & MATERIALS

- Stiff-bristled brush
- Utility knife
- Drill and carbide-tipped bit
- Hand maul
- Horticultural disinfectant
- Horticultural preservative
- Masking tape
- Zinc gauze or fine wire mesh
- Washed pea gravel
- #4 rebar
- Copper wire
- Pressure-treated 2 × 4
- Galvanized deck screws

HOW TO PREPARE PLANTING CONTAINERS

1. Soak the item in clean water for several hours or overnight to loosen any debris. Using a mild detergent and a stiff brush, scrub the entire piece, particularly the surface of the planting area. Rinse thoroughly, and then apply a disinfectant formulated to remove latent fungi or bacterial growth from planting containers. Thoroughly rinse the entire piece again, removing all residue, and then let it dry.

2. Check the piece to see if it needs repair. Look for cracking, chipping, flaking, or other signs of damage that might affect the health of plants in the container. If the piece is wood, prod all surfaces, especially the corners and the bottom, with a utility knife to evaluate it for rot. To protect wood from rot and pests, apply a horticultural preservative.

3. With most pieces, the simplest way to create drainage is to drill three or four holes in the bottom. If the piece is clay or ceramic, you can prevent cracking or chipping by placing a piece of masking tape over the area before you begin drilling, and by using a carbide-tipped bit.

Cover each drainage hole with a section of thin zinc gauze or fine wire mesh. To filter out debris and provide additional drainage, add a layer of washed pea gravel to the container before you add the potting soil and plants.

HOW TO SUPPORT DECORATIVE PIECES

Select a location for the piece; typically, a level site is preferable. Consider the support requirements of the piece and select an appropriate method of securing your treasure so it won't be disturbed by the wind or a playful pet.

- Drive 32" pieces of rebar about 18" into the ground, located at opposite corners of the piece or at other strategic points. Position the piece and use copper wire to secure it to the rebar.

- Cut a pressure-treated 2 × 4 to extend at least 6" beyond each end of the piece to be supported. Drill pilot holes through the bottom of the piece and corresponding ones into the 2 × 4. Align the pilot holes and secure the piece by driving deck screws through the brace and into the piece. Finally, drive spikes through the brace and into the ground, anchoring the piece securely.

Scrub and disinfect items to be used as planting containers. Drill drainage holes, and cover them with thin zinc gauze or fine wire mesh, and then add a 2" layer of washed pea gravel.

Stake or support decorative pieces by wiring them to lengths of rebar driven at least 18" into the ground.

Mosaic Table

Webster's defines composition as "...the arrangement into proper proportion or relation and esp. artistic form." Furnishing outdoor rooms requires an eye for composition, and certain elements are necessary to create the right proportions and form.

One element that gets used over and over is an end table. Whether placed beside a comfortable chair in a corner of the garden or nestled between a couple of love seats along the edge of a patio, an end table can add the touch that completes an arrangement.

This mosaic table combines two rewarding activities—recycling unused pieces and playing with color. The base shown here was removed from a table found at a garage sale. Once the base was given a quick coat of spray paint, it was ready to be transformed. This happens to be a small, square table, but you can adapt the plans to a base of any size or shape. And although the pattern shown is a simple arrangement of shades of one color, there's really no limit to the range of colors and designs that will work for mosaic projects. Once you've mastered the basic techniques of doing mosaics, design your own patterns. Anything goes—from simple, inexpensive tile patterns to more elaborate arrangements of seashells, tumbled glass, or decorative stones.

TOOLS & MATERIALS

- Tape measure
- Circular saw or jig saw
- Finishing sander
- Tile nippers
- Rubber mallet
- Masonry file
- Grout float
- Table base
- ½" exterior grade plywood
- Sandpaper
- Wood sealer
- ½" wood screws
- Transfer paper
- Permanent marker

- Safety goggles
- Gloves
- Tile
- Accent stones
- Craft sticks
- Silicone adhesive
- Tile mastic
- Grout
- Grout colorant (optional)
- Grout sponge
- Soft cloth
- Silicone grout sealer
- Paintbrush

A. *Measure the table base and cut a plywood base to match. Seal the plywood and securely attach it to the table base.*

HOW TO BUILD A MOSAIC TABLE

Step A: Prepare the Mosaic Base

1. Measure the table base and determine appropriate dimensions for the mosaic. Mark those dimensions onto exterior-grade plywood, and cut out the base for the mosaic, using a circular saw or jig saw. Lightly sand the plywood.

2. Apply two coats of wood sealer to one side of the plywood base; let it dry thoroughly between coats.

3. Make placement marks on the sealed side of the plywood; use them as guides to position the plywood on the base. Secure the plywood to the table base, using ½" wood screws.

Step B: Enlarge & Transfer the Pattern

1. Using the grid method or a photocopier, enlarge the pattern shown at right.

2. Transfer the pattern to the surface of the plywood base, using transfer paper and a pencil or stylus. To make the pattern easier to see, draw over the traced lines with a permanent marker.

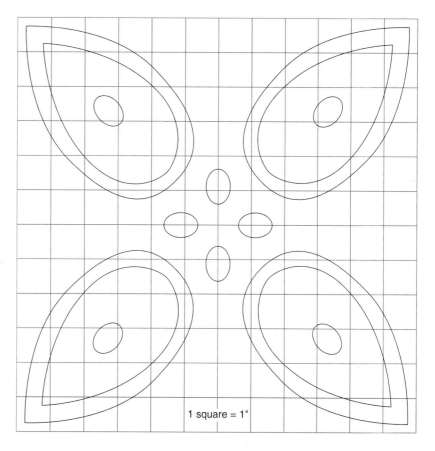

1 square = 1"

Step C: Apply the Mosaic

1. Place the items to be broken between heavy layers of newsprint or in a heavy paper bag. Wearing safety goggles and heavy gloves, tap the tile with a rubber mallet. It's best to break items of different colors separately to make it easier to select and place colors within the design.

B. *Enlarge the pattern using a grid system or a photocopier; transfer the enlarged pattern to the plywood base.*

2. Cut and shape tiles as necessary, using tile nippers, and use a masonry file to file off any sharp edges. Be sure to wear heavy gloves as you work, at least until you've filed the sharp edges off of the tile.

3. Use silicone adhesive to adhere the media to the plywood base. Wear rubber gloves and spread the adhesive with a craft stick. Glue on the accent stones at the center of the design. Fill in the center of the flower petals with medium-colored pottery shards. Fill the remaining area of the petals with dark-colored pottery shards. Place tile fragments in the background. Arrange the border tiles, alternating the direction of the triangle points. Let the adhesive dry thoroughly, according to manufacturer's directions.

Step D: Set Tile on the Edges

Use silicone adhesive to secure tile along the edges of the table, arranging them to create a uniform edge for the table.

Step E: Grout the Tile

1. Wearing rubber gloves, mix grout and water, according to manufacturer's instructions, usually about three parts grout to one part water. If the spaces between tiles in the mosaic are more than ¼", be sure to use sanded grout. Grout can't be saved from one project to the next after it's mixed, so unless you're adding grout colorant it's best to mix a little at a time. If you're coloring the grout, mix enough for the entire project at once because it's

C. *After breaking the tile, shape the pieces with tile nippers and file away any sharp edges. Use silicone adhesive to glue the pieces to the plywood base.*

D. *Set tile around the edges of the plywood base; position the tile to create a uniform edge around the table.*

very difficult to match colors from one batch to the next.

2. With a small grout float, spread grout over the mosaic design. Let the grout dry for 5 to 10 minutes.

3. Wipe the excess grout off the surface of the mosaic, using a damp sponge and rinsing it often. Keep rinsing and wiping until the grout is completely gone—if you let grout dry on the surface of the mosaic, it will be very difficult to remove. When you've removed all the grout, let the surface dry.

4. Polish away the haze from any grout residue, using a soft, dry cloth. Let the mosaic dry for 48 hours.

5. To seal the grout and protect it from the elements, apply one or two coats of silicone grout sealer. Follow manufacturer's instructions and let the sealer dry between coats.

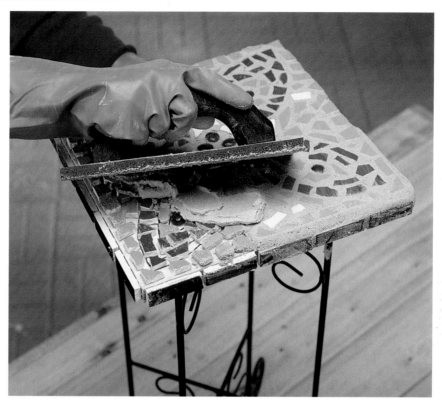

E. *Apply grout, filling cracks completely. Let dry for 5 to 10 minutes, and then rinse away excess grout. Let the mosaic dry for 48 hours; seal it with silicone grout sealer.*

ALTERNATIVE MATERIALS

A wide variety of materials for mosaics, such as the ¾" square ceramic tiles, faceted stones, and tumbled glass used in this mosaic, are available at craft and hobby stores. To successfully combine materials, establish a color scheme and select a variety of items that complement the scheme.

Many other materials work well for mosaics. To create unique decorative pieces, try using broken china or pottery, buttons, polished pebbles, glass marbles, or seashells.

You can use tile adhesive to secure small tile and other flat items, but you need silicone adhesive for uneven pieces, such as broken pottery or seashells.

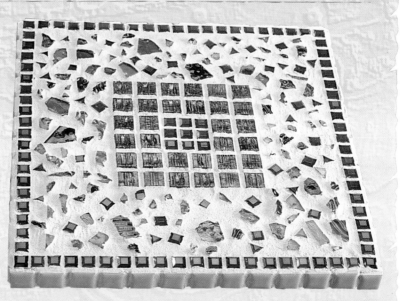

Planter Boxes

Decorating a garden is much like decorating a room in your home—it's nice to have pieces that are adaptable enough that you can move them around occasionally and create a completely new look. After all, most of us can't buy new furniture every time we get tired of the way our living rooms look. And we can't build or buy new garden furnishings every time we want

to rearrange the garden.

That's one of the reasons this trio of planter boxes works so well. In addition to being handsome — especially when flowers are bursting out of them— they're incredibly adaptable. You can follow these plans to build a terrific trio of planter boxes that will go well with each other and will complement most gardens, patios, and decks. Or you can tailor the plans to suit your needs. For instance, you may want three boxes that are exactly the same size. Or you might want to build several more and use them as a border that encloses a patio or frames a terraced area.

Whatever the dimensions of the boxes, the basic construction steps are the same. If you decide to alter the designs, take a little time to figure out the new dimensions and sketch plans. Then devise a new cutting list and do some planning so you can make efficient use of your wood. To save cutting time, clamp together parts that are the same size and shape, and cut them as a group (called *gang cutting*).

When your planter boxes have worn out their welcome in one spot, you can easily move them to another, perhaps with a fresh coat of stain and new plantings. You can even use the taller boxes to showcase outdoor relief sculptures—a kind of alfresco sculpture gallery.

TOOLS & MATERIALS

- Tape measure
- Circular saw
- Straightedge
- Drill
- Finishing sander
- Miter box and backsaw
- 8 ft. cedar 1 × 2s (3)
- 8 ft. cedar 1 × 4s (6)

- 4 × 8 ft. sheet of ⅝" fir siding
- 2 × 4 ft. piece ¾" CDX plywood
- 1¼" galvanized deck screws
- 1½" galvanized deck screws
- 6d galvanized finish nails
- Exterior wood stain
- Paintbrush

DIMENSIONS

Front Bin Overall Size
12" High
18" Wide
24" Long

Back Bin Overall Size
24" High
18" Wide
12" Long

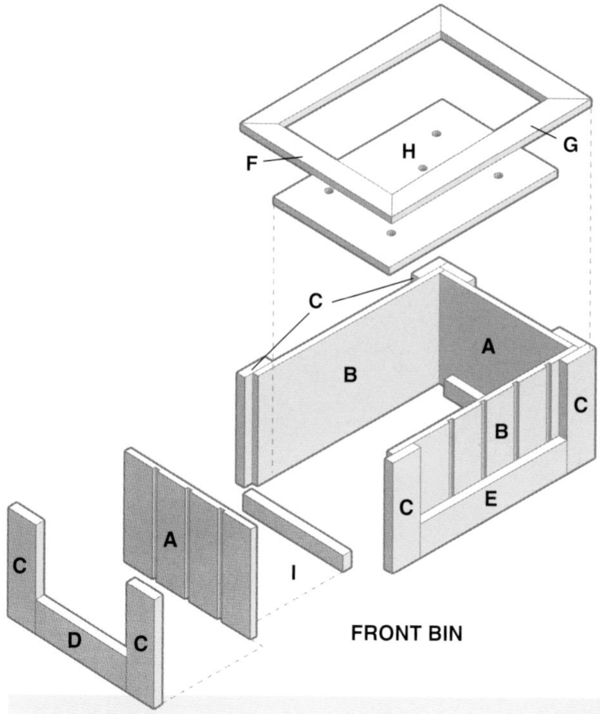

Middle Bin Overall Size
18" High
18" Wide
12" Long

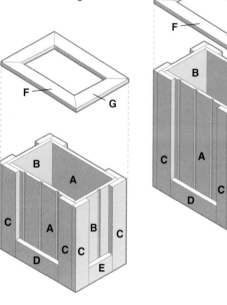

FRONT BIN   **MIDDLE BIN** 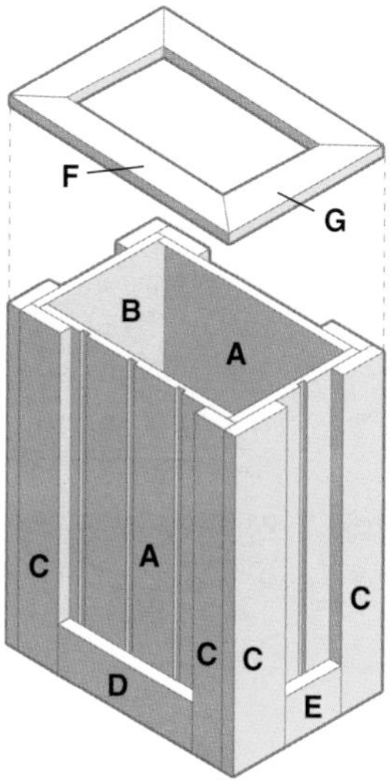   **BACK BIN**

CUTTING LIST

Key	Part	Front Bin Dimension	Pcs.	Middle Bin Dimension	Pcs.	Back Bin Dimension	Pcs.	Material
A	End panel	⅝ × 15 × 11⅛"	2	⅝ × 15 × 17⅛"	2	⅝ × 15 × 23⅛"	2	Siding
B	Side panel	⅝ × 22¼ × 11⅛"	2	⅝ × 10¼ × 17⅛"	2	⅝ × 10¼ × 23⅛"	2	Siding
C	Corner trim	⅞ × 3½ × 11⅛"	8	⅞ × 3½ × 17⅛"	8	⅞ × 3½ × 23⅛"	8	Cedar
D	Bottom trim	⅞ × 3½ × 9¼"	2	⅞ × 3½ × 9¼"	2	⅞ × 3½ × 9¼"	2	Cedar
E	Bottom trim	⅞ × 3½ × 17"	2	⅞ × 3½ × 5"	2	⅞ × 3½ × 5"	2	Cedar
F	Top cap	⅞ × 1½ × 18"	2	⅞ × 1½ × 18"	2	⅞ × 1½ × 18"	2	Cedar
G	Top cap	⅞ × 1½ × 24"	2	⅞ × 1½ × 12"	2	⅞ × 1½ × 12"	2	Cedar
H	Bottom panel	¾ × 14½ × 19½"	1	¾ × 14½ × 8½"	1	¾ × 14½ × 8½"	1	Plywood
I	Cleat	⅞ × 1½ × 12"	2	⅞ × 1½ × 12"	2	⅞ × 1½ × 12"	2	Cedar

Note: Measurements reflect the actual size of dimension lumber.

HOW TO BUILD PLANTER BOXES
Step A: Make & Assemble the Box Panels

1. Following the cutting list on page 271, cut the end panels (A) and side panels (B), using a circular saw and a straightedge cutting guide.

2. Put one end panel face-down on your work surface, butting it up against the side panel, face-side-out. Mark positions and drill several counterbored ³⁄₃₂" pilot holes in the side panel.

3. Fasten the side panel to the end panel with 1½" deck screws. Repeat this process to fasten a second side panel to the end panel.

4. Put the remaining end panel face-down on the work surface. Take the assembled pieces and place the open end over the second end panel, side panels flush with the end-panel edges. Drill counterbored pilot holes in the side panels, and attach the side panels to the end panel, using deck screws.

Step B: Attach the Trim

1. Cut the corner trim (C) to length. Overlap the edges of the corner trim pieces at the corner, forming a square butt joint. Fasten the corner trim pieces to the panels by driving 1¼" deck screws through the inside faces of the panels and into the corner pieces.

2. To provide extra support, drive screws or galvanized finish nails through the overlapping corner trim pieces and into the edges of the adjacent trim piece.

3. Cut the bottom trim pieces (D, E) to length. Fasten them to the end and side panels, between the corner trim pieces. Drive 1¼" deck screws through the side and end panels and into the bottom trim pieces.

4. Cut the top caps (F, G) to length. Cut 45° miters at both ends of one cap piece, using a miter box and back saw.

5. Tack the mitered cap piece to the top edge of the planter, with the outside edges flush with the outer edges of the corner trim pieces. For a proper fit, use this cap piece to guide the marking and cutting of the miters on the other cap pieces.

6. Miter both ends of each piece. Tack it to the box so it makes a square corner with the previously installed piece. If the corners don't fit just right, loosen the pieces, and adjust them until everything is square.

7. Permanently attach all the cap pieces to the box, using 6d galvanized finish nails.

A. *Cut the end panels and side panels to size.*

B. *Drive screws through the inside faces of the panels to fasten the corner trim pieces.*

Step C: Install the Box Bottom & Finish the Planter

1. Cut the cleats (I) to length, and screw them to the end panels with 1½" deck screws. On taller planters, it's best to mount the cleats higher on the panels so you won't need as much soil to fill the box—a savings in cost and weight. In that case, add cleats on the side panels for extra support.

2. Cut the bottom panel (H) to size from ¾"-thick CDX plywood. Drill several 1"-diameter weep holes in this panel. Set the panel onto the cleats—it does not need to be fastened in place.

3. Using a finishing sander, remove rough spots and splinters from all edges and surfaces. Apply two or three coats of exterior wood stain to all surfaces, and let the planter dry.

C. *Cut the cleats to length and screw them into the end panels.*

TIPS: SIMPLIFY PLANTING & MAINTENANCE

To help keep planter boxes from becoming discolored, line them with landscape fabric before adding soil. Simply cut a piece of fabric large enough to wrap the box as if you were gift-wrapping it, and then fold it to fit inside the box. Staple the fabric at the top of the box and trim off the excess. Add a 2" layer of gravel, and then add potting soil and plants.

If your yard or garden is partially shaded, you may want to add wheels or casters to your planter boxes so you can move them to follow the sun; casters also make it easier to bring the planters indoors during cold weather. Be sure to use locking wheels or casters with brass or plastic housings.

If you're not experienced at arranging color combinations, start with a simple approach. Stay within the basic hot (red, yellow, and orange) or cool (blue, purple, and green) color families to create

visual harmony. You can plant a collection of flowers and foliage in your favorite color or try combining a variety of hues of the same color. If you want to add contrast, add some plants in neutral tones.

Proportion, or the size and scale of plants in relationship to one another and the container, is another important component of successful plantings. In general, plant tall plants in large containers and low-lying plants in smaller ones. To achieve balance, use a dominant plant to establish a focal point, and then fill in around it with a combination of colors, textures, and shapes.

Before purchasing plants for any container, consider their preferred growing conditions. Grouping plants with similar soil, watering, and fertilization requirements simplifies your work during the growing season.

Garden Bench

In much the same way paths suggest that you wander, benches invite you to linger, to contemplate, to savor. For people who usually view their gardens from their knees or who mainly see them as works in progress, benches offer a different perspective, a change of view and attitude. Benches remind gardeners to relax and enjoy the beauty they are helping to create.

In *The Principles of Gardening*, Hugh Johnson says that garden benches should always look permanent; deliberately placed. One way to achieve that look is to start with a simple design such as this cedar bench. It has the sort of solid simplicity that suggests perma-

nence. And the color of the cedar blends effortlessly into surrounding trees, flowers, and foliage, adding to the impression that the bench is and always will be an essential part of the garden.

Placing a bench deliberately is important, but not complicated. Walk around the garden and think about where you stop to rest, to enjoy a special view, or to appreciate pleasant fragrances. Take note of where visitors pause, and consider what draws them to those spots. A bench can provide a place for the eyes to rest, as well as the body. As you wander, imagine how you might use a bench to draw the eye down a path or into a quiet corner.

With its subtle design, this easy-to-build bench lends itself to being used in combination with other ornaments or furnishings. Flank the ends with cedar planter boxes (page 270) or a copper trellis (page 298) to create a lovely focal point at the edge of a bed or border.

TOOLS & MATERIALS

- Circular saw
- Drill
- Tape measure
- Hammer
- Long metal ruler
- Jig saw
- Finishing sander
- 1½" deck screws
- 2½" deck screws
- Exterior wood glue
- Casing nails (3)
- Wood sealer/stain

- 1 × 4 × 12' cedar (1)
- 2 × 2 × 6' cedar (1)
- 2 × 2 × 10' cedar (4)
- 2 × 4 × 6' cedar (1)
- 2 × 6 × 10' cedar (1)
- 2 × 8 × 6' cedar (1)

HOW TO BUILD A GARDEN BENCH

Step A: Begin the Leg Assemblies & Attach the Trestle

1. Cut the leg halves (A), cleats (B), and trestle (D) to length. Sandwich one leg half between two cleats so the cleats are flush with the top and the outside edge of the leg half. Then join the parts by driving four 1½" deck screws through each cleat and into the leg half. Assemble two more cleats with a leg half in the same fashion.

2. Stand the two assemblies on their sides, with the open ends of the cleat pointing upward. Arrange the assemblies so they are roughly 4 ft. apart. Set the trestle onto the inner edges of the leg halves, pressed flush against the bottoms of the cleats.

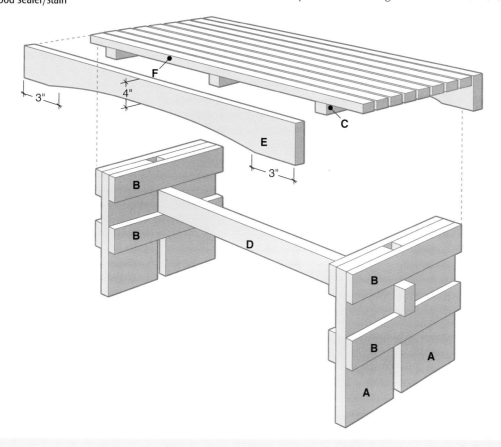

CUTTING LIST

Key	Part	Dimension	Pcs.	Material	Key	Part	Dimension	Pcs.	Material
A	Leg half	1½ × 7¼ × 14½"	4	Cedar	D	Trestle	1½ × 3½ × 60"	1	Cedar
B	Cleat	¾ × 3½ × 16"	8	Cedar	E	Apron	1½ × 5½ × 60"	2	Cedar
C	Brace	1½ × 1½ × 16"	3	Cedar	F	Slat	1½ × 1½ × 60"	8	Cedar

Note: Measurements reflect the actual size of dimension lumber.

A. *Position the trestle against the leg half and the cleats, overhanging the leg half by 1½". Attach the trestle with glue and 2½" screws.*

B. *Attach the remaining leg half to the cleats on both ends to complete the leg assembly.*

C. *Attach the outer brace for the seat slats directly to the inside faces of the cleats.*

Adjust the position of the assemblies so the trestle overhangs the leg half by 1½" at each end. Fasten the trestle to each leg half with glue and 2½" deck screws.

3. Attach another pair of cleats to each leg half directly below the first pair, positioned so each cleat is snug against the bottom of the trestle.

Step B: Complete the Leg Assemblies

Slide the other leg half between the cleats, keeping the top edge flush with the upper cleats. Join the leg halves with the cleats, using glue and 2½" deck screws.

Step C: Add the Braces

Cut the braces (C) to length. Fasten one brace to the inner top cleat on each leg assembly so the tops are flush.

Step D: Shape the Aprons

1. Cut the aprons (E) to length.

2. Lay out the arch onto one apron, starting 3" from each end. The peak of the arch, located over the midpoint of the apron, should be 1½" up from the bottom edge.

3. Draw a smooth, even arch by driving one casing nail at the peak of the arch and one at each of the starting points. Slip a long metal ruler behind the nails at the starting points and in front of the nail at the peak to create a smooth arch. Then trace along the inside of the ruler to mark a cutting line.

4. Cut along the line with a jig saw; then sand the cut smooth.

5. Trace the profile of the arch onto the other apron; make and sand the cut.

TIP: LEVELING LEGS

Sometimes our best efforts produce furniture that wobbles because it's not quite level. Here's a trick for leveling furniture:

Set a plastic wading pool on a flat plywood surface. Add shims under the plywood surface until the floor of the wading pool is exactly level.

Fill the pool with about ¼" of water. Set the piece of furniture in the pool, and then remove it quickly. Mark the top of the waterline on each leg. Use these marks as cutting lines to trim the legs to exactly level.

D. *Pin a long, flexible ruler between casing nails, and then trace a smooth arch onto the aprons.*

E. *Attach a 2 × 2 slat to the top, inside edge of each apron, using glue and 2½" deck screws.*

Step E: Add Slats to the Aprons

Cut the slats (F) to length. Attach a slat to the top, inside edge of each apron, using glue and deck screws.

Step F: Install the Aprons & Slats

1. Apply glue at each end, on the bottom sides, of the attached slats. Flip the leg and trestle assembly, and position it flush with the aprons so that it rests on the glue on the bottoms of the two slats. The aprons should extend 1½" beyond the legs at each end of the bench. Drive 2½" deck screws through the braces and into both slats.

2. Position the middle brace between aprons, centered end to end. Attach it to the two side slats with glue and deck screws.

3. Position the six remaining slats on the braces, using ½"-thick spacers to help you create equal gaps between them. Attach the slats with glue and drive 2½" deck screws up through the braces and into each slat.

4. Sand the slats smooth with progressively finer sandpaper. Wipe away the sanding residue with a rag dipped in mineral spirits. Let the bench dry. Apply a finish of your choice—a clear wood sealer to protect the cedar without altering the color, or stain to provide deeper color for the cedar.

F. *Attach the seat slats with glue and 2½" deck screws. Insert ½"-thick spacers to help set gaps between the slats.*

TIP: COUNTERSINKING SCREWS

Take extra care to completely countersink screw heads whenever you are building furnishings that will be used as seating. When sinking galvanized deck screws, use a combination countersink/piloting bit that drills a ³⁄₃₂"-dia. pilot hole.

Tabletop Zen Garden

Every culture has a different idea of what a garden ought to be—as characteristic as its national cuisine. Many people are familiar with the classic Japanese garden. In common with art and architecture in Japan, its finest gardens are breathtakingly subtle and understated—somewhat like haiku poems formed out of rocks, sand, wood, and plant material.

For most of us, building a full-scale Japanese garden isn't practical—our gardens often double as outdoor living spaces in ways that aren't suited to the structure of a Zen garden. But this tabletop version contains the same basic elements and offers opportunities for peace-

ful contemplation and reflection without requiring a huge investment of time or money. Besides that, it's just plain fun—you can design patterns, rake sand, and rearrange elements to your heart's content.

It's best to use redwood or cedar lumber for the table. You can seal the lumber to maintain its fresh color or let it weather to a rustic gray—either is well suited to the earth-tone color schemes typical of Zen gardens.

Visualize your tabletop garden as a larger landscape and set the stage with sand or fine gravel. Then fill it with rocks, driftwood, an oriental sculpture, and maybe a bonsai tree or a tiny palm. But take care not to overfill it—you need room to "draw" gently curving patterns in the sand.

TOOLS & MATERIALS

- Tape measure
- Circular saw
- Drill
- Finishing sander
- Staple gun
- Utility knife
- 8 ft. cedar or redwood 2 × 4s (5)
- 8 ft. cedar or redwood 1 × 4s (2)
- ¾" CDX plywood, at least 34" × 44"
- Exterior wood glue

- ¼ × 3½" carriage bolts (8)
- 1½" galvanized deck screws
- 2" galvanized deck screws
- 2½" galvanized deck screws
- Exterior wood sealer
- Landscape fabric
- Nylon window screen
- Fine sand or gravel
- Decorative objects

HOW TO BUILD A TABLETOP ZEN GARDEN
Step A: Assemble End Units

1. Cut legs (A), top supports (C), and braces (D) to length, following the cutting list below.

2. Attach a top support to the top, inner sides of each pair of legs, using exterior wood glue and 2½" deck screws. Let the glue dry.

3. Attach a brace across each leg pair, placing the

bottom of the brace 6" from the bottom of the legs. Make sure the end unit is square, and secure the brace with glue and 2½" deck screws. Let the glue dry.

Step B: Join End Units to Form Table Base

1. Cut rails (B) and stretcher (E), following the cutting list (below, left).

A. *Attach a brace to each pair of legs, placing the bottom of the brace 6" from the bottom of the leg.*

CUTTING LIST

A, C, D	29" 2 × 4 (4 for A, 3 for C, & 2 for D)	
E	32" 2 × 4 (1, for E)	
B	42" 2 × 4 (2, for B)	
F	44" 1 × 4 (2, for F)	
G	32" 1 × 4 (2, for G)	
H	33½" × 44" piece of ¾" CDX plywood (1, for H)	

½" weep holes typ.

1½" deck screw typ.

1½" deck screw typ.

2" deck screw typ.

2½" deck screw typ.

¼ x 3½" carriage bolt typ.

2" deck screw typ.

2. Apply glue to the outside top areas of the end units, where the rails will connect. Attach the rails to the top supports with 2½" deck screws. Let the glue dry.

3. Drill ¼" holes into the ends of the rails and through the tops of the legs. Put a ¼" × 3½" carriage bolt through each hole from the outside and fasten each with a washer and nut.

4. Apply glue to both ends of the stretcher, and center it between the two braces. Secure the stretcher to the braces, using 2½" deck screws.

5. Attach the third top support midway between

B. *Turn the base on its side, and attach rails to the top supports, using glue and 2" deck screws.*

the rails with glue and 2½" deck screws. The top of the support should be flush with the tops of the rails and other supports. This provides extra strength to support the weight of the sand.

Step C: Assemble the Tray Tabletop

1. Cut the frame sides (F) and frame ends (G) to size. Attach the frame ends to the frame sides with glue and 2" deck screws driven through the frame sides and into the frame ends.

2. Cut ¾" CDX plywood to size for the tray bottom (H). Apply two coats of exterior wood sealer, and let it dry.

3. With the finished frame resting on a flat surface, position the tray bottom over the frame with all outside edges flush. Drive 1½" deck screws through the tray bottom and into frame.

Step D: Attach the Tray to the Base

1. Center the tray on top of the base. Measure carefully, and mark where the tray bottom rests directly on top of the rails and three top supports.

2. Drive 1½" deck screws through the tray bottom and into the rails and top supports in at least two locations for each rail and support.

Step E: Finish the Tabletop

1. Drill ½" weep holes through the tray bottom in four spots. Cut small pieces of nylon screen, and glue or staple one piece over each drainage hole.

2. Using a finishing sander or sandpaper block, smooth all rough surfaces. If desired, apply an exterior wood sealer to all surfaces, and let it

C. *Set the tray bottom onto the table frame, and secure it, using 1½" deck screws.*

D. *Turn the tray over, and drive 1½" deck screws through the tray bottom and into the rails and top supports.*

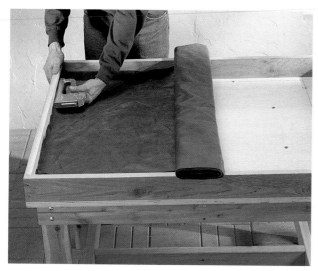

E. *Staple down the edges of the landscape fabric, extending it no more than 2½" above the tray bottom.*

F. *Arrange stones, driftwood, and other decorative objects in the garden. Rake the sand into a pleasing pattern.*

dry thoroughly.

3. Cut a piece of landscape fabric several inches larger in dimension than the tray tabletop. Tuck the fabric into the tray tabletop and tack down the corners with a staple gun. Then staple the edges no higher than 2½" above the tray bottom. Trim the landscape fabric just above the staples, using a utility knife.

Step F: Arrange the Elements

Put the table in place and fill the tabletop with clean, dry sand or gravel—covering the fabric. Experiment with placing stones, pieces of driftwood, or other decorative objects. Use a miniature rake or other appropriate tool to make curved patterns in the sand.

VARIATION: WATERSCAPE

Japanese gardens convey the idea of larger landscapes in confined spaces, often by using dwarf trees and shrubs. They sometimes create the illusion of a gentle waterscape by using raked patterns around "islands" of mounded sand, stones, or gravel. Or they may use an actual watercourse and miniature lake set amidst "mountains" and "forests." They frequently contain small buildings that can be used as places for rest and contemplation.

A fine Japanese garden is more the work of an artist than a gardener. Designing a good one requires both careful thought and spontaneity—very much a case of less being more.

Japanese gardens are miracles of subtlety and grace—full-sized landscapes translated into small, breathtaking spaces.

Weathervane

One of the great joys of building garden ornaments is creating something of value from very simple materials. This project shows you how to convert a tin can, some pieces of step flashing and a handful of hardware into a unique windmill.

Although it appears to be strictly ornamental, the windmill actually carries out several tasks in a garden. First, it adds motion to the scene, dancing in celebration of one of the fundamental forces of nature—the wind. It indicates wind velocity and direction as it contributes an interesting vertical element to a bed or border. And, finally, the post offers a support for twining plants such as morning glory, scarlet runner, or honeysuckle. Some of the items on the list may seem a little odd to you. We specify a can of chicken broth for the windmill hub simply because the broth drains easily from the can. Any 14½ oz. can containing liquid rather than solids will work just fine. The toilet flange is used simply as a form around which to bend wire; any 8"-dia. round object will do just as well.

Building the axle that enables the windmill to spin is a somewhat complex process, but it's not difficult. Use the drawings on page 283 to develop a clear picture of what you're trying to accomplish, and then go through the process one step at a time. Both this axle and the spindle are built on the same principle as the stem of the copper sprinkler pictured on page 223.

TOOLS & MATERIALS

- Razor knife
- Straightedge
- Tape measure
- Drill and bits
- Awl
- Tubing cutter
- Propane torch
- Bench grinder or rotary tool
- Workbench vise
- Hacksaw
- Aviation snips
- Pliers
- Flat file
- 14½ oz. can of chicken broth
- Permanent marker
- #6 copper wire
- 1½" wood dowel
- PVC toilet flange or other 8"-dia. form

- Flux and flux brush
- Solder
- ½" copper pipe straps (6)
- 5 × 7" flat step flashing (6)
- #3–32 × ¼" machine screws (12)
- ½" copper pipe (5 ft.)
- ⅜" (o.d.) brass tube
- ½" (o.d.) × ⅜" (i.d.) bronze bushings (3)
- $^{11}/_{32}$" round brass tubing
- $^{5}/_{16}$" round brass tubing
- Brass hinge pin bushings (GM #38375) (4)
- 12 × 18" piece of galvanized sheet metal
- #3-32 × ⅝" machine screws and nuts (5)
- Small cotter pin

HOW TO BUILD A WEATHERVANE
Step A: Construct the Hub

1. Use a razor knife and a straightedge to cut the label off the tin can, keeping the label in one piece. Lay it flat and mark six equal divisions onto the label, then tape it back in place, marked side out.

2. At each end of the can, use a fine-tip permanent marker to transfer the six divisions to the rim. With the marker and a straightedge, draw lines connecting the marks that lie directly opposite one another. The point where the marks intersect is the exact center of the can.

3. Punch the center point, using an awl, then drill a ½" hole in one end of the can. Drill slowly and carefully—the drill will jump when the drill bit breaks through the metal. Empty the contents of the can and wash it out, then drill a ½" hole in the other end of the can.

4. On each end of the can, use an awl to punch one hole at each division mark, as close to the rim as possible.

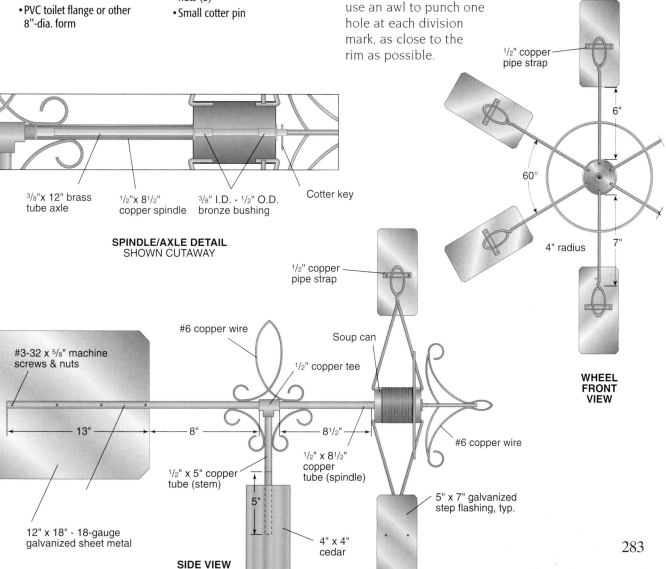

⅜"x 12" brass tube axle

½"x 8½" copper spindle

⅜" I.D. - ½" O.D. bronze bushing

Cotter key

SPINDLE/AXLE DETAIL
SHOWN CUTAWAY

½" copper pipe strap

½" copper pipe strap

Soup can

#6 copper wire

½" copper tee

#3-32 × ⅝" machine screws & nuts

13"

8"

8½"

½" x 5" copper tube (stem)

½" x 8½" copper tube (spindle)

#6 copper wire

5"

5" x 7" galvanized step flashing, typ.

12" x 18" - 18-gauge galvanized sheet metal

4" x 4" cedar

SIDE VIEW

6"

60°

4" radius

7"

WHEEL FRONT VIEW

Step B: Form the Spokes

1. Cut seven 24" lengths of #6 bare copper wire. Set one piece of wire aside—it will become the rim later in the process. On each of the remaining six pieces, mark the center point (12"), then make a

A. *Drill at ½" hole at the intersection of the division marks, and empty the can. Punch a hole at each division mark, as close to the rim as possible. Repeat on the other end of the can.*

mark 1" from each end. Lightly crimp the wires on these end marks and bend the 1" segments back toward each other, slightly more than 90°.

2. Hold a length of wire with the mark centered on a 1½" dowel. Wrap the wire tightly around the dowel and twist it twice. Try to keep the twists even. Remove the wire from the dowel and repeat with five more wires; make sure all six spokes are identical—adjust if necessary.

3. Adjust the pitch of the spokes by slipping each spoke back onto the dowel and twisting until the plane of the spoke lies at a 45° angle to the dowel.

Step C: Assemble the Hub & Spokes

1. To form the rim of the wheel, wrap the remaining 24"-length of #6 wire around a PVC toilet flange or other round, 8"-dia. form. Snip the ends of the wire to form a perfect circle. (When the wire is released, don't worry if it springs to a slightly larger diameter.)

2. Insert the bent segments of each spoke into the tin-can hub—one in a hole at the top and one in the corresponding hole at the bottom of the can.

3. Place the assembly on a soft, thick surface, such as a pillow. Position the spokes opposite one another, using the marks on the can as reference points. Place the rim over the spokes, with the open ends of the circle positioned between two sets of spokes. Mark each point where the rim meets a spoke.

4. Move the assembly to a level soldering surface,

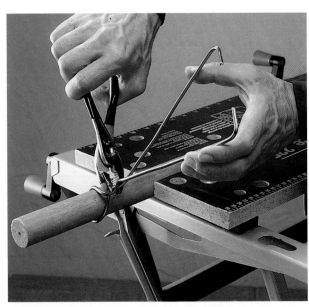

B. *To make a spoke, cut a 24" length of #6 copper wire. Bend the ends of the wire back toward one another, slightly more than 90°. Next, wrap the wire around a 1½" dowel and twist it to create two tight, even twists.*

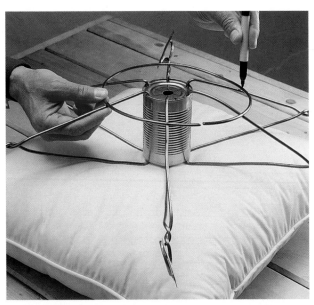

C. *Insert the spokes into the hub, then set the rim in position and mark the points where the spokes meet the rim. Move the assembly to a soldering surface and solder the spokes in place.*

then flux and solder the marked contact points (see page 310).

5. Flatten six ½" copper pipe straps. On each spoke, clamp a flattened strap to the face of the loop, positioned so that the strap is centered across the loop and the holes in the strap overhang evenly. Flux and solder the straps to the wire loops.

Step D: Add the Blades

1. For the blades, trim ½" off of each corner of each piece of step flashing, using aviation snips.

2. Position each blade on a spoke with the outer edge of the pipe strap 3" from one end of the blade and centered from side to side. Mark reference points through the strap holes, then remove the blades and drill a ³⁄₃₂" hole at each marked point.

3. Reposition the blades and fasten each one with a pair of #3-32 × ¼" machine screws.

Step E: Construct the Spindle

1. Cut a 8½" length of ½" copper pipe for the spindle and a 12" length of ⅜" o.d. brass tube for the axle. Test-fit a ½" × ⅜" bushing inside each end of the ½" copper pipe. If necessary, use a rotary tool or a bench grinder to slightly shape the flange of each bushing so it fits snugly within the pipe. Note: *Using a scrap of the ⅜" tubing as a handle helps you get a uniform edge when you grind the bushings.*

2. On the 12" length of ⅜" brass tube, mark a point 4½" (the length of the hub plus ½") from one end. Apply flux to the tube at this index mark and at the opposite end. Slide two of the bushings onto the brass tube, both with their raised flanges pointing toward the fluxed end of the tube. Position one bushing with its flange at the index mark and the other flush with the fluxed end of the tube. Solder these bushings in place and allow them to cool.

3. To complete the spindle assembly, slide this axle assembly inside the copper pipe until the flange of the bushing at the index mark is flush with the end of the copper pipe. Flux this joint and solder it in place.

4. Slide the tin-can hub onto the axle, followed by another bushing with its barrel inside the hub and its flange snug against the end of the hub. Mark this position on the brass tube and remove the hub and bushing. Measure an additional ¹⁄₃₂" beyond the mark and drill a ³⁄₃₂" hole all the way through the brass tube. Set this spindle assembly aside.

Step F: Make the Stem

NOTE: For photos of this step, refer to the Copper Sprinkler project, pages 223 and 224.

1. Cut one 5" piece and one 6" piece of ½" copper

pipe, using a tubing cutter. Also cut one 2" and one 4" piece of ¹¹⁄₃₂" brass tubing, and one 6" piece of ⁵⁄₁₆" brass tubing. Deburr the pieces, being careful not to flare the ends; use a wire brush or emery cloth to polish the ends.

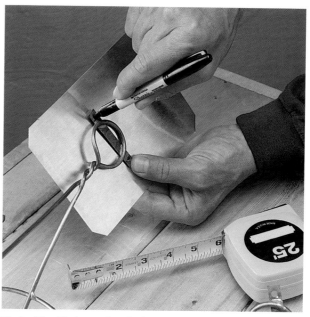

D. *Position blades so that the lower edge of the strap is 3" from the lower edge of the blade. Mark reference points through the strap holes, drill pilot holes, then fasten the blades to the spokes, using machine screws.*

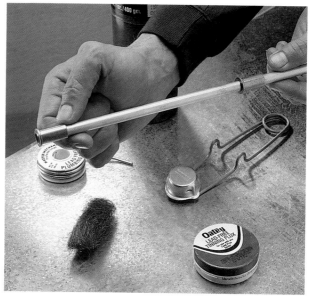

E. *On a 12" length of ⅜" brass tube, position one bushing 4½" from the end of the tube and another at the opposite end, with the flanges facing forward.*

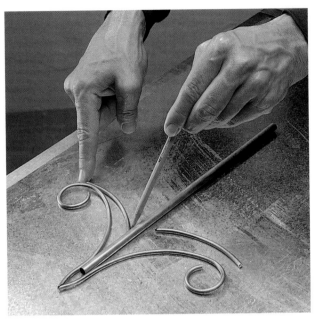

G. *On a 21" length of ½" copper pipe, mark and cut a centerline, 13" long, then slit the pipe along this line. Drill holes in the pipe, then mark and drill corresponding holes in the tail. Secure the tail to the pipe with machine screws.*

H. *Form arcs of #6 copper wire, then place them around an 8" length of brass tube to form an arrow. Flux the joints and solder the pieces in place.*

2. Test-fit the bushings inside the 5" piece of copper. If necessary, use a rotary tool or a bench grinder to slightly shape the flanges of the bushings so they fit snugly within the pipe.

3. To form the upper assembly, slide a bushing onto each end of the 2" length of ¹¹⁄₃₂" brass tubing, with the flanges facing the ends of the tube. Set the flange of one bushing back ⅛" from the end of the tube; position the other bushing flush with the opposite end. Slide the 6" length of ⁵⁄₁₆" brass tubing inside the ¹¹⁄₃₂" tube, positioning the inner tube to protrude ⅜" beyond the top (setback) bushing.

4. To form the lower assembly, slide a bushing onto each end of the 4" piece of ¹¹⁄₃₂" brass tubing, flanges facing outward, flush with the ends of the tube.

5. Begin soldering at the top of the upper assembly. Heat all three pieces—the ⁵⁄₁₆" tube, the ¹¹⁄₃₂" tube, and the bushing. These pieces heat up quickly: be careful not to overheat them. Feed solder into the joint between the two brass tubes first, then feed solder into the bushing joint, approaching that joint from the side opposite the flange.

6. Solder the three remaining bushing joints, each time feeding the solder into the joint from the side opposite the flange.

7. Flux the inside of the 5" piece of ½" copper and the flange of the bushing on the upper assembly.

Slide the assembly inside the copper pipe, positioning the lower bushing to be flush with the end of the copper pipe.

8. Flux the inside of the 6" piece of copper and the shoulder of one bushing on the lower assembly. Slide the assembly inside the pipe, positioning the bushing flange to be flush with the top of the pipe.

9. Place the assembled pieces at the edge of a protected work surface, and solder each one, being careful not to displace the bushings. Concentrate the flame on the copper pipe as you heat the joints, and feed the solder from the bottom; don't let the solder run into the brass tube.

Step G: Construct the Tail

1. Cut a 21" length of ½" copper pipe. To slit this pipe to accommodate the tail's sail, mark a 13"-long centerline on both sides of the pipe. Clamp the pipe in a workbench vise or comparable pipe vise, then cut down the centerline, using a hacksaw with its blade positioned at 90°. (This cut can be a workout. Try cutting 4" at a time, then letting 4" more out of the vise. Use full strokes of the saw for an accurate, efficient cut.)

2. Turn the pipe 90° in the vise. Starting ½" from the cut end, make four marks—one every 4". Center punch these positions, then drill ³⁄₃₂" holes, perpendicular to the cut line.

I. *Assemble the spindle, tail, and upper assembly of the stem, and a ½" copper tee, then use a straightedge to make sure they're aligned properly. Flux and solder the pieces in place.*

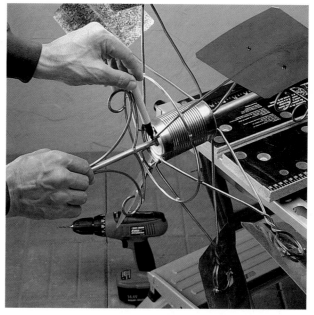

J. *Insert the shaft of the arrow into the axle, with the back of the arrow positioned about 1" from the spokes of the wheel. Mark and drill a hole through the shaft. Pin the shaft in place with a cotter pin.*

3. Trim ¾" off the corners of a 12 × 18" piece of galvanized sheet metal and then mark a centerline from end to end. Slide the sheet metal into the slot in the copper pipe, aligning it so the centerline is visible through the screw holes in the pipe. Mark the sheet metal through these screw holes, then remove it and drill one ³⁄₃₂" hole at each mark. Assemble the tail, using #3-32 × ⅝" machine screws and nuts.

Step H: Make the Arrow

1. Cut a 27" piece of #6 bare copper wire. Mark off positions at 3½", 7", and 17". Wrap the wire around a 8-dia. form, such as a PVC toilet flange. Once the ring is formed, cut it at the marks. This process yields two 3½" arcs and two 10" arcs.

2. At one end of each of the 10" arcs, slightly bend the wire in the opposite direction of the arc to form a slight curve for the point of the arrow. Bend the opposite end of the wire around a 1" dowel to form the decorative accent at the back of the arrow.

3. Cut an 8" length of ¹¹⁄₃₂" o.d. brass tubing for the shaft of the arrow. On a level soldering surface, arrange the 10" pieces around the shaft, forming the tip of the arrow, then place one of the 3½" pieces behind each of the 10" pieces to form the arrow shape. Use a flat file to bevel the ends of the wires at the intersections, then flux and solder the joints.

Step I: Connect the Spindle, Tail & Stem

1. Flux the spindle, tail, and upper assembly of the stem and join them (see diagram, page 285) with a ½" copper tee. Lay out the assembly on a level soldering surface and use a straightedge along the top to check for alignment. Adjust if necessary, then solder each joint and let the assembly cool.

2. On one end of a 12 ft. 4 × 4, mark the diagonals to find the center. Use a ½" spade bit to bore a 5¾" hole straight down the center of the 4 × 4. Gently tap the lower assembly of the stem into this hole.

Step J: Assemble the Windmill

1. Slide the hub and its bushing onto the spindle, then slide the shaft of the arrow into the axle of the hub. Position the back of the arrow approximately 1" from the spokes of the wheel. Mark the shaft of the arrow through the hole in the axle, then remove the shaft and drill a ³⁄₃₂" hole all the way through the tubing at that mark. Slide the shaft of the arrow back into the axle and align all four holes. Pin the shaft in place with a cotter pin.

2. Set the post in the desired location (see the Post and Wire trellis, pages 295 and 296).

3. Insert the upper assembly of the stem into the lower assembly (lodged in the 4 × 4).

Trellises & Arbors

As with people, the most interesting gardens are multi-dimensional. Uninterrupted expanses, even beautiful ones, just don't have the allure of spaces punctuated with vertical elements.

Trellises, arbors, and gates add interest to a garden no matter what the season. In springtime they provide backdrops for bright bursts of low-growing color; in summer they showcase the lush growth of vines and climbers; in autumn they frame dramatic views; and in winter they lend shape to the sleeping landscape, particularly in climates where snow transforms their basic forms into fanciful sculpture.

Different styles of trellises and arbors lend themselves to different types of climbing plants. For example, a rustic arbor (page 304) looks wonderful when supporting the luxuriant growth of an annual vine such as a morning glory, or crowned with a potato vine. On the other hand, the lattice pattern of a post and wire trellis would be overwhelmed by such abundance—it's better suited to the more refined growth of a twining vine such as a winter creeper. The weathered patina of a copper trellis (page 298) is spectacular when offset by a riotous pink climbing rose such as Bubble Bath or a clematis in full bloom.

Many of these projects are similar to trellises and arbors that cost hundreds of dollars in catalogs or retail stores. The cost of materials for them, however, ranges from virtually nothing for the rustic arbor to under $75 for the largest copper trellis. Each uses simple construction techniques and inexpensive, readily-available materials. What could be better?

IN THIS CHAPTER

Lath Trellis

When you want to showcase a climbing plant with spectacular blossoms or foliage, the trellis shouldn't fight for attention. In those situations, these simple lath trellises are perfect.

They're also easy to build, using parting stop for the vertical legs and wide lath (sometimes called lattice) for the horizontal supports. Just secure a horizontal lath piece to both the front and back of the trellis for all but the bottom horizontal support. Then trim the trellis with motifs, such as squares, diamonds, and arrows, cut from screen molding. Parting stop, lath, and screen molding are readily available at home centers.

Although this project gives directions for a specific trellis, the basic plan can be adapted in many ways. When designing a trellis, be sure to take into consideration the space where it will be displayed and the anticipated height of the climbing plants. To make your design more interesting, stagger the lengths of the vertical legs. An odd number of legs is usually more attractive than an even number. It's important to support tall trellises with three horizontal pieces of lath.

Experiment with ideas and sketch possible designs until you find a pleasing arrangement. You can even customize trellis motifs to repeat a theme or design found in surrounding elements, such as furniture or fences.

For a subtle look, you can paint a trellis to match the background surface. Or, to make a design statement year-round, paint the trellis in a color that contrasts with the background.

TOOLS & MATERIALS

- Drill
- Miter saw
- Aviation snips
- $\frac{1}{2}" \times \frac{3}{4}"$ pine parting stop
- $\frac{1}{4}" \times 1\frac{3}{8}"$ pine lath
- $\frac{1}{4}" \times \frac{3}{4}"$ pine or oak screen moldings
- Exterior wood glue
- #19 × ½" wire brads
- Exterior primer
- Exterior paint
- Wire clothes hanger or #3 rebar (2 pieces)

HOW TO BUILD A LATH TRELLIS
Step A: Create a Plan

Sketch the trellis to scale. Allow 4" to 8" between each pair of vertical legs. The finished width of the trellis will equal the sum of the distance between the vertical legs plus ¾" for each vertical leg. Plan to position one horizontal support at the bottom, one about two-thirds of the way up, and another about

2" from the top. Include additional supports if necessary.

Step B: Cut & Arrange the Pieces

1. Draw a full-size pattern of the basic trellis. Cut ¾" strips of paper and experiment with screen molding motifs. To help keep the brads from splitting the wood when you secure the screen molding, make sure the ends of the design motifs extend beyond the legs of the trellis .

2. Make paper patterns for the motifs, marking the lines for miter cuts on both the upper and lower pattern pieces.

3. Mark and cut the parting stop to the desired length for each vertical leg. For the horizontal supports on the back of the trellis, cut pieces of lath equal to the finished width of the trellis. (You'll cut the remaining horizontal supports for the front of the trellis later.)

4. Working on a smooth, flat surface, arrange the vertical legs with the bottom of all the legs aligned. Place the horizontal supports over the legs, as determined by your design.

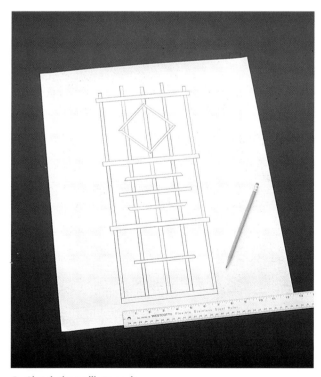

A. *Sketch the trellis to scale.*

B. *Create a full-size pattern of the trellis. Take measurements and create pattern pieces.*

C. *Position lath over the horizontal supports, extending 1" beyond the legs on each side. Glue and nail these pieces in place.*

D. *Apply exterior primer to both sides of the trellis, then paint it as desired. When the trellis is dry, mount it securely.*

Step C: Construct the Trellis

1. Glue and nail the bottom horizontal support to the legs, securing it with two brads at each joint. Start at one side and work toward the opposite side, staggering the placement of the nails to keep the wood from splitting. Secure the remaining horizontal supports in the same fashion.

2. Cut pieces of lath 2" longer than the width of the trellis. Turn the trellis over and position this lath over the top and middle horizontal supports, extending 1" beyond the legs on each side. Secure each piece of lath with exterior wood glue and a brad driven at each vertical leg.

3. Transfer the markings from the motif patterns (created in Step A) to the screen moldings and cut the pieces necessary for your design. To save time and ensure uniform lengths, clamp together sets of molding strips and cut them in tandem.

4. Glue the screen molding to the trellis. When the glue is tacky, drive brads wherever the screen molding overlaps a leg; place a scrap of lath under the trellis to support it while you drive the brads.

Step D: Finish & Mount the Trellis

1. Apply exterior primer to both sides of the trellis and let it dry. Paint as desired.

2. Mount the trellis, using one of the following methods.

Surface mount: Cut a clothes hanger, using aviation snips; form two loops. Position the trellis against a wall or fence. Use the wire loops to stake the bottom of the trellis, placing one wire loop over each end of the bottom horizontal support. Drill pilot holes in the wall or fence, one hole at each side of the trellis, near the top. Install shoulder hooks to secure the trellis in position.

Freestanding mount: Drive two pieces of #3 rebar into the ground, one at each edge of the trellis. Secure the trellis to the stakes at several points on each side, using plastic-coated wire. The stakes should be buried at least 12" inches beneath the soil and extend above ground to at least half the height of the trellis.

CLIMBING PLANTS

ANNUALS	PERENNIALS
Asarina (Climbing Snapdragon)	Clematis
Morning Glory	Climbing Hydrangea
Nasturtium	Climbing Rose
Scarlet Runner Bean	Dutchman's Pipe
Sweet Pea	Porcelainberry
	Silver Lace Vine

VARIATIONS: WINDOW TRELLIS

To surround a window with foliage without completely obscuring the view, you can build a window trellis (as shown at right). First, measure the window, decide on the dimensions of the trellis and draw a sketch. Make the trellis at least 2" wider than the window and plan to place the upper edge of the top horizontal support just below the bottom of the window. Extend the outer legs of the trellis to support the string portion of the trellis.

Cut the pieces and assemble the trellis as in Step B (page 291). Mark the outer legs at the upper edge of the top horizontal support.

Mark holes on the inside face of the outer legs, indicating 3" to 4" intervals from the horizontal support to the top of the trellis. Drill a hole at each of these marks, using a ¹⁄₁₆" drill bit.

Put the outer legs in position and assemble the trellis as in Steps B and C (page 291). Mount the trellis (Step D, page 292).

Lace monofilament fishing line through the drilled holes, starting at the top of the legs and carrying the line from side to side of the trellis in the same way you would lace a shoe. Cut the line, leaving excess at the ends. Wrap the fishing line around the outer leg of the trellis and tie it in a knot; pull the line taut and tie off the remaining end.

Combine lath and string or nylon fishing line to create a trellis. Train vines to surround the window with foliage.

Discarded wrought iron pieces, such as this window guard (above), old gates, or pieces of fence, are almost instant trellises. Simply mount the piece to some support (page 265) and add plants.

You can make a rustic trellis (left), using both straight and curved branches. Secure the branches with nails or wrap joints with wire. If you plan to shape areas of the trellis, select green branches and construct the trellis as soon as possible after cutting the branches—green, freshly-cut branches are much easier to bend and shape than older, drier branches.

Post & Wire Trellis

Successful gardens often seem to be studies in contrast. Great gardeners blend and contrast plant forms, colors, and textures, using each to its greatest advantage. Texture is an important element of this design equation and one of the main features of a post and wire trellis.

To create the illusion of depth in a shallow planting bed, designers recommend using a vertical display of fine-textured foliage as a backdrop for several plants with large, coarse leaves.

Although many trellises are designed to support a riot of flowers or a rambunctious layer of foliage, there are very few available to provide an adequate showcase for the type of delicate texture required in this situation.

It may sound like a big challenge to build a trellis that accomplishes this mission, matches the average person's construction abilities, and falls within a reasonable budget, but this project is remarkably simple. By topping cedar posts with decorative finials and stringing a lattice of plastic-coated wire between them, you can create a trellis that would be ideal for many garden settings. The construction is simple, the materials are inexpensive, and the finished effect is stunning.

The best plants for this trellis are twining climbers with small leaves. Among annual vines you can try sweet pea or cardinal climber. Good perennial vines include trumpet creeper, English ivy, and winter creeper. You can put your climbers in the ground or select a variety that thrives in planters or pots. Be sure, however, that the plants you choose are well-suited to the light exposure they'll receive.

TOOLS & MATERIALS

- Tape measure
- Posthole digger
- Level
- Drill
- Mason's string
- Reciprocating saw
- Wheelbarrow
- Trowel
- Hammer
- Wood sealer
- Compactible gravel
- Quick-setting concrete mix

- 8 ft. cedar 4 × 4s (2)
- Scrap 2 × 4s
- Deck post finials (2)
- 2 × 3 fence brackets (4)
- 8 ft. cedar 2 × 4s (2)
- 1", 1½" pan-head sheet metal screws
- 1½" screw eyes
- Plastic-coated wire
- Galvanized finish nails

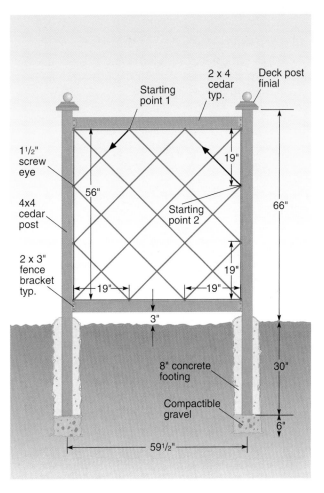

HOW TO BUILD A POST & WIRE TRELLIS
Step A: Prepare & Set the Posts

1. Apply a wood sealer to the bottom 2½" ft. of each post and let dry. For extra protection, let the bottom of the post soak in wood sealer overnight.

2. At the chosen site, mark the posthole locations by setting two wooden stakes in the ground, 59½" apart.

3. Dig the postholes 36" deep. Doing this job properly requires a posthole digger or power auger. Put a 6" layer of compactible gravel in the bottom of each posthole.

4. Set the first post into a hole. Take a carpenter's level and make sure the post is plumb on two

A. *Dig two 36"-deep postholes, and then add a 6" layer of gravel to each. Set a post into each hole, and align it. When it's plumb, use 2 × 4s to brace the post in position.*

B. *Pour quick-setting concrete into the postholes, adding concrete until it's slightly above ground level. Form the wet concrete into a gentle mound around the base of the post.*

adjacent sides.

5. When the post is plumb, use stakes and scrap pieces of 2 × 4 to brace it in position. Repeat the process for the other post.

6. When both posts are plumb and braced, use a mason's string to make certain the tops and sides are aligned. Adjust as necessary.

C. *On top of each post, set a decorative deck finial. Drill pilot holes and secure the finials with small galvanized finish nails.*

Step B: Pour the Footings

1. Following the manufacturer's instructions, mix quick-setting concrete in a wheelbarrow. Mix only enough for one post—quick-setting concrete sets in about 15 minutes.

2. Pour the concrete into one posthole, until the concrete is slightly above ground level.

3. Check the post one more time to make sure it's plumb and properly aligned.

4. With a trowel, form the wet concrete into a gentle mound around the base of the post.

5. Repeat the process for the other post, taking care that it's plumb and aligned with the first post.

6. Let the concrete set for one to two hours.

Step C: Install the Finials

1. Check the tops of the posts to make sure they're level. If not, use a reciprocating saw to trim one post until it's level with the other.

2. Set a decorative deckpost finial on top of each post. Drill two pilot holes on each side and secure the finials with galvanized nails.

Step D: Install the Stringers

1. Attach the bottom 2 × 3 fence brackets with 1½" pan-head sheet metal screws, 3" above the bottom of each post.

2. To make the stringers, measure the distance between brackets and cut two cedar 2 × 4s to length. Insert one 2 × 4 in the bottom set of brackets and attach it with 1" pan-head sheet metal screws.

D. *Attach the fence brackets 3" from the bottoms of the posts, using sheet metal screws.*

E. *Run wire diagonally between the screw eyes on the posts and stringers.*

3. Measure 56" up from the top of the first stringer. Install top brackets and fasten the second 2 × 4 to the top set of brackets.

Step E: Install the Screw Eyes & String the Wire

1. Starting in one corner where a stringer meets a post, make a mark on the inside edge of the stringer, 19" from the corner. Next, mark the inside face of the post, 19" from the corner. Repeat the process for the remaining three corners.

2. Drill pilot holes and attach screw eyes at each of the marked points. At the corners, angle the pilot holes at 45° toward the center of the trellis frame.

3. Using plastic-coated wire or clothesline, begin putting the trellis together by knotting the wire on the screw eye at the marked starting point. Feed it through the closest screw eye on the post and down through the screw eye below that. Following the diagram on page 295, continue stringing the wire in a diagonal, back and forth pattern, finishing at the lower screw eye on the opposite post.

4. Beginning at the second starting point (as indicated on the diagram on page 295), string a second wire. Thread it as described above to complete the opposing diagonal runs.

VARIATION: SIMPLE TRELLIS PLAN

1. You can build an easier, less decorative version of the Post & Wire Trellis without the stringers and the crosshatch wire layout. Start by following the directions for Steps A through C.

2. Measuring 1" from the inside tops of the posts, mark the location of the first screw eye. Then continue marking screw eye locations every 8" down the post, putting the last mark a few inches off the ground. Repeat the process for the other post.

3. Drill pilot holes and install the screw eyes, twisting them so that the "eyes" are parallel to the ground, not at right angles to it.

4. Attach the plastic-coated wire with a secure knot to one of the top screw eyes. Then feed the wire through the screw eye on the opposite side, then down through the screw eye directly below.

5. Pull the wire across to the second screw eye down on the opposite side, feeding it through and down to the screw eye directly below. Keep the wire as taut as possible at every run.

6. Continue this process until you reach the final screw eye, and then knot the wire securely.

HANGING BASKETS ADDITION

1. To make use of the outside or front edge of the posts, install decorative brackets for hanging plants. Position brackets along the side or front of the post as desired, centered along the post. Mark the screw holes and drill pilot holes. Each post should accommodate at least two brackets.

2. Attach brackets with the screws supplied, and hang planter baskets.

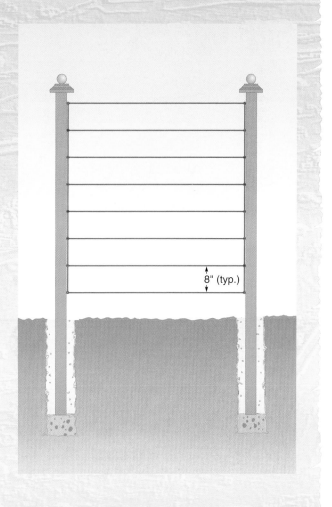

8" (typ.)

Copper Trellises

Building garden ornaments from copper plumbing materials is just plain fun. And the results are impressive, despite the fact that the pieces are as easy to put together as children's construction toys. Even mastering the technique of soldering (see pages 310 to 311) is simple, especially since the joints don't have to be watertight.

Plumbing materials are meant to be exposed to water, heat, and cold, so copper ornaments are naturally weather-resistant. Their appearance gradually changes as the bright glow of new copper gives way to the rich patina of older pieces. If you prefer the look of bright copper, spray the finished piece with a clear acrylic sealer to help maintain its color.

As building materials go, copper is quite reasonably priced.

Amazingly enough, you can build either of these trellises for well under $100, a fraction of the price of similar pieces featured in many catalogs and stores.

Copper plumbing materials are available at many hardware stores and virtually every home center. However, the arch project on page 302 employs two brass cross fittings that aren't as widely available. You may have to order them through a plumbing supply house, but it should take only a phone call or two to locate a source. The model shown is a #735 ½" sweat cross manufactured by NIBCO.

If you haven't worked with copper before, you'll probably want to start by following these directions exactly. Once you're comfortable with the basic techniques, you can tailor the design to the style of your garden and the location you have in mind. Remember that if an idea doesn't work, the materials aren't wasted: Just reheat the solder, pop off the fittings, and start again.

TOOLS & MATERIALS

- Drill
- Tape measure
- Tubing cutter
- Propane torch
- Jig saw
- Hand maul
- Plywood scraps
- 6" to 8" pieces of ³⁄₈" dowel (4)
- Wood glue
- ¹⁄₂" copper pipe (25 ft.)
- ¹⁄₂"copper tees (16)

- ¹⁄₂" copper 90° elbows (4)
- ¹⁄₂" flexible copper tubing
- Solder
- Flux
- Flux brush
- Nylon scouring pad
- Wire brush
- 3 ft. sections of #3 rebar (2)

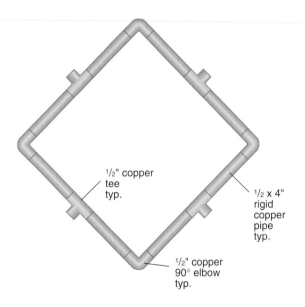

¹⁄₂" copper tee typ.

¹⁄₂ x 4" rigid copper pipe typ.

¹⁄₂" copper 90° elbow typ.

CROWN DETAIL

HOW TO BUILD A SQUARE COPPER TRELLIS

Step A: Build a Support Jig

It can be difficult to balance the growing structure of a trellis while it's being dry-fitted, and during the soldering process the pipe gets too hot to handle. The simple solution is to build a jig to support the trellis as you're building it.

Mark a 20" square on a scrap of plywood. Drill a ³⁄₈" hole at each corner, and glue a 6"- to 8"-long dowel into each hole. As you build the trellis, slide the pipes over the dowels.

Step B: Cut the Pipe

1. Measure and mark the copper pipe, following the cutting list shown below.

2. Cut the copper pipe to length. The best way to cut either rigid or flexible copper pipe is with a tubing cutter (page 310). You can cut copper pipe with a hacksaw, but it's more difficult to make straight cuts, and straight cuts make it much easier to solder the joints.

Step C: Assemble the Base

1. Clean and flux the pipes for the base (see page

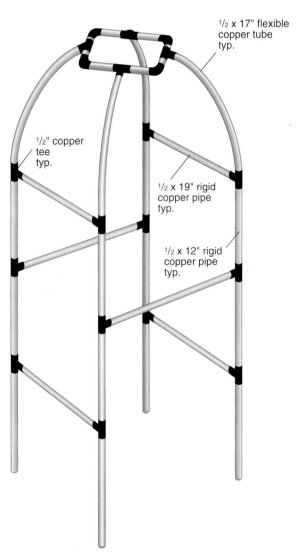

¹⁄₂ x 17" flexible copper tube typ.

¹⁄₂" copper tee typ.

¹⁄₂ x 19" rigid copper pipe typ.

¹⁄₂ x 12" rigid copper pipe typ.

CUTTING LIST
¹⁄₂" Rigid Copper Pipe

Quantity	Length
12	12"
6	19"
8	4"

¹⁄₂" Flexible Copper Tubing

4	17"

310 for directions on cleaning and fluxing copper pipe). Work in a well-ventilated area.

2. Slide one 12" section of pipe (see drawing on page 299) over each dowel of the support jig. Add a tee to each piece, as indicated.

3. Fit 19" sections of pipe between pairs of tees,

creating horizontal supports between sets of legs opposite one another.

4. Add a second 12" vertical piece and a tee to each leg of the base. Fit another 19" section between a pair of these tees, forming a horizontal support perpendicular to one of the horizontal supports already installed. Add a second horizontal support on the opposite side.

5. Add another 12" vertical piece and a tee to each leg of the base. Fit 19" sections between pairs of tees to form horizontal supports parallel to the first pair of supports.

6. When you're sure the pieces fit correctly and the base is square and sturdy, take it apart and solder the joints (see pages 310 to 311), working from the ground up once again.

Step D: Create the Crown

1. Clean and flux the pipes for the crown. Dry-fit the pieces, following the diagram on page 299.

2. To form one side of the crown, connect a 4" length of copper pipe to each side of a $1/2$" copper tee, and then add a 90° elbow at each end. Repeat this process to form the opposite side of the crown.

3. Connect a 4" piece of copper pipe to each end of a $1/2$" copper tee. Add this run to one side of the crown. Repeat this process to complete the crown. For the dome to be symmetrical, the crown must be perfectly square, so measure and assemble these

A. *Make a jig to hold the base as you build it: Mark a 20" square on a piece of plywood, and then drill a hole at each corner. Glue a $3/8$" dowel into each hole.*

B. *Cut the copper pipe to length, using a tubing cutter or hacksaw. Remove any metal burrs inside the pipe with the reaming tool.*

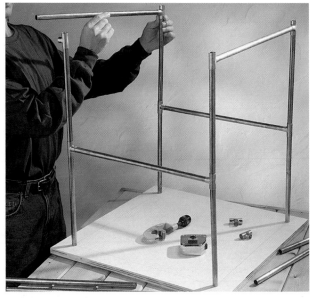

C. *Slide pieces of copper pipe over the dowels of the support jig, dry-fitting the entire base. Solder the joints of the base, working from the ground up.*

pieces carefully.

Step E: Build the Crown & Assemble the Trellis

1. Dry-fit one 17" length of ½" flexible copper tubing between the base and the crown. Bend the copper so that the crown will sit level and square at the top of the trellis. Use this piece as a template to

D. *Combine 4" lengths of copper pipe, tees, and 90° elbows to form a square piece for the crown.*

E. *Dry-fit one arch of the dome, and then use that piece to create a bending jig for the remaining pieces of the dome.*

draw the curve of the arch on a piece of plywood. Cut along the marked line, using a jig saw, and then screw that arched piece of plywood to a larger piece of plywood to form a bending jig.

2. Bend the three remaining pieces of flexible copper tubing by simply shaping each one around the bending jig.

3. Assemble the arched pieces of the dome and the crown, and then fit this assembly on the base. Make sure the arches are equally curved and positioned symmetrically, and that the crown is level and square within the trellis. Adjust as necessary.

4. Solder the joints of the crown and dome, then the joints attaching the dome to the base.

5. When the solder on the joints has lost its shiny color, clean excess solder and flux from each joint, using a nylon pad.

Step F: Install the Trellis

1. Select a site for your trellis, and mark a 20" square on the ground, tracing it on the soil or making the lines with a trail of flour.

2. At two opposite corners of the marked square, drive a 3 ft. piece of rebar about 18" into the ground. (Caution: buried utility lines are dangerous. Always call your utility providers before digging any holes or driving anything deep into the soil.)

3. Fit two legs of the trellis over the buried rebar, firmly anchoring it in place.

F. *Mark a 20" square on the ground, and drive pieces of rebar at two of the corners, 18" deep. Position the trellis over the rebar.*

VARIATION: COPPER ARCH

TOOLS & MATERIALS

- Drill
- Tape measure
- Tubing cutter or hacksaw
- Round file (optional)
- Propane torch
- Plywood scraps, at least 10 × 60" (2)
- 6" to 8" pieces of $\frac{3}{8}$" dowel (6)
- 1 × 2s, at least 46" long (3)
- 1" deck screws (12)
- Wood glue
- $\frac{1}{2}$" copper pipe (80 ft.)

- $\frac{1}{2}$" copper tees (24)
- $\frac{1}{2}$" copper 45° elbows (6)
- $\frac{1}{2}$" copper 90° elbows (3)
- $\frac{1}{2}$" sweat crosses (2)
- Solder
- Flux
- Flux brush
- Emery cloth or nylon scouring pad
- Wire brush
- 30" sections of #3 rebar (6)
- Hand maul

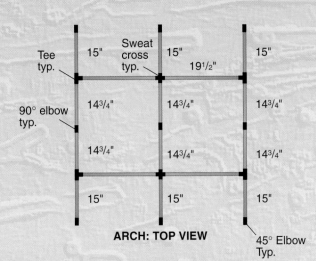

ARCH: TOP VIEW

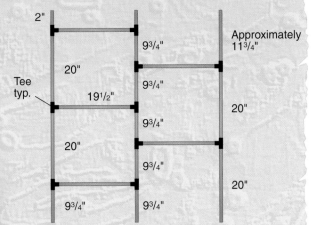

LEG ASSEMBLY: SIDE VIEW

HOW TO BUILD A COPPER ARCH

Step A: Cut the Pipe & Build a Support Jig

1. Measure, mark, and cut the copper pipe, following the cutting list shown at right below. Clean and flux the pipes (page 310).

2. To build a support jig, start with two scraps of plywood at least 10" wide and 60" long. Down the center of each piece, draw a 40" line, and then drill three $\frac{3}{8}$" holes, placed at 20" intervals along the line. Glue a 6" to 8" piece of dowel in each hole. On each of three 1 × 2s, draw a pair of marks 42½" apart. Lay the 1 × 2s across the pieces of plywood, aligning the marks on the 1 × 2s with the lines on the plywood to set the exact spacing for the sides of the arch. Secure the

A. *Make two supports by gluing dowels at 20" intervals to scraps of plywood. On three 1 × 2s, make marks 42½" apart. Align the marks and screw the 1 × 2s to the plywood supports.*

CUTTING LIST

$\frac{1}{2}$" Copper Pipe

Quantity	Length
8	20"
14	19½"
12	9¾"
6	15"
6	14¾"
2	14"
4	2"

B. *Dry-fit the entire leg assembly, alternating pipe and tees to form the legs, and adding horizontal supports in between.*

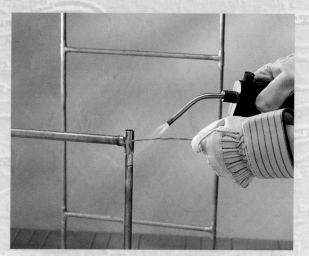

C. *Disassemble the pieces and solder each joint, working from the ground up.*

1 × 2s to the plywood, using 1" screws.

Step B: Construct the Leg Assemblies

1. Slide a 9¾" length of pipe over the first dowel, add a tee; then alternate pipe and tees as indicated on the drawing on page 86.

2. Slide a 9¾" length of pipe over the second dowel, and then alternate tees and pipe as indicated.

3. Fit 19½" lengths of pipe between pairs of tees to form horizontal supports.

4. Slide a 20" length of pipe over the third dowel, and then alternate tees and 20" lengths as indicated. To make sure the arch remains square, cut the final piece in place: Add a 14" piece of pipe, and then use a level to mark and cut it to match the first two legs (it should measure approximately 11¾").

5. Fit 19½" pieces of pipe between the remaining pairs of tees, creating horizontal supports.

6. Repeat numbers 1 through 5 to construct a leg assembly for the other side.

Step C: Solder the Leg Assemblies

Disassemble the pieces and solder the joints in each leg assembly, working from the ground up. When the joints are cool, set the assemblies aside.

Step D: Construct the Arch

1. Working on a flat surface, connect two 14¾" lengths of pipe, using a 90° elbow. Add a tee, then a 15" length of pipe to each side. Repeat to form a second, identical arch.

2. To form the center arch, connect two 14¾" lengths of pipe, using a 90° elbow. Add a sweat cross and a 15" piece of pipe to each side.

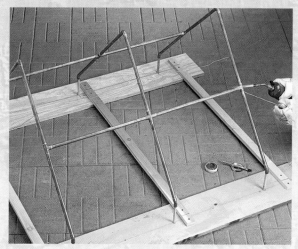

D. *Using 90° elbows, pipe, and tees, build three arch assemblies. Connect the arches with horizontal braces, tees, and crosses.*

3. Slide a 45° elbow onto each dowel of the support jig, and then slide the legs of the arches into those elbows.

4. Add 19½" lengths of pipe between sets of tees and crosses, forming horizontal supports as indicated on page 86.

5. Disassemble the pieces, and rebuild the arch assembly, soldering as you go. When the joints are cool, set the assembly aside.

6. Put the leg assemblies back onto the support jig, and fit the arch assembly in place and solder the joints.

7. Follow Step F (page 301) to install the arch in the garden.

Rustic Arbor

Truly successful gardens reflect the architectural style of the surrounding buildings as well as the shape of the terrain and the personality of the gardener. Some settings call for formal accessories and manicured plantings; others call for contemporary forms, while still others require informal arrangements and accessories. A large piece, such as this rustic arbor, can set the tone for a garden or help reinforce an established theme.

This arbor would harmonize beautifully with any landscape that calls for a natural, unstructured form. In a woodland setting, you can take advantage of the fact that most of the materials are free for the cutting. Even in a city, it shouldn't be hard to come by the branches you need. The ones shown here were cut from a suburban construction site—with permission, of course. Although we gathered vines for the decorative accents from the woods, it might be easier to buy grapevines, which are available at most craft and hobby stores.

Cut the straightest branches you can find, but don't worry if some of them are slightly bent or misshapen. Position the branches to maintain the basic dimensions, and consider any variations to be artistic character.

Although a rustic arbor is simple to construct, it's much easier with two people. Lashing pieces in place simplifies the process of securing the braces, but maneuvering the crosspieces into position is definitely a job for two.

TOOLS & MATERIALS

- Tape measure
- Loppers
- Jig saw
- Scrub brush
- Drill
- Aviation snips
- Hammer
- Stapler
- Shovel
- Whiskey barrel halves (2)
- Horticultural disinfectant
- Exterior wood sealer

- Washed pea gravel
- Zinc gauze or tight wire mesh, at least 1 ft. × 1 ft.
- Freshly cut 1½"-dia. branches
- Flexible vines, such as grapevines
- 2½" galvanized deck screws
- 1½" galvanized brads
- Raffia or natural twine
- Large rocks (4 to 6)
- Potting soil
- Climbing vines

HOW TO BUILD A RUSTIC ARBOR

Step A: Gather & Prepare the Branches

1. Cut a supply of branches 1½" in diameter, lopping them off at approximately the following lengths: four branches 9 ft. long (for the uprights); two branches 7 to 8 ft. long (for the crosspieces); an assortment that produces four 4½ ft. pieces (for the diagonal supports); and an assortment that produces ten 2 ft. pieces (for the braces). Also, cut the vines into eight 46" pieces.

2. Remove any twigs and small branches, using loppers. Cut the pieces to size, using a jig saw to

A. *Gather branches for the framework of the arbor. Cut the branches to size and seal the ends with exterior wood sealer.*

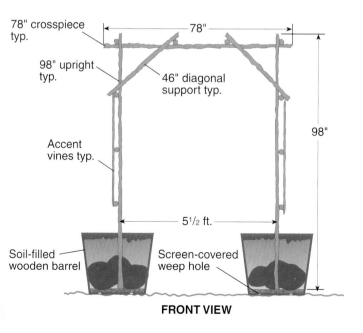

78" crosspiece typ.

78"

98" upright typ.

46" diagonal support typ.

Accent vines typ.

98"

5½ ft.

Soil-filled wooden barrel

Screen-covered weep hole

FRONT VIEW

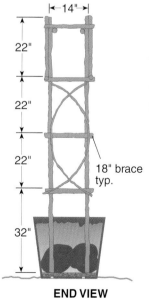
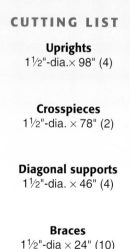

14"

22"

22"

22"

32"

18" brace typ.

END VIEW

CUTTING LIST

Uprights
1½"-dia.× 98" (4)

Crosspieces
1½"-dia. × 78" (2)

Diagonal supports
1½"-dia. × 46" (4)

Braces
1½"-dia × 24" (10)

make each cut as square as possible.

3. Apply exterior wood sealer to each branch, particularly the cut ends. Allow the branches to dry.

Step B: Prepare the Barrels

1. Select two half-size whiskey barrels to anchor the arbor. Prod the surfaces of the barrels, especially the corners and bottoms, with a knife to make sure they're sound and free of rot.

2. Fill the barrels with water and let them soak for several hours. Scrub each barrel inside and out with

B. *Scrub and disinfect two whiskey barrels, and then drill weep holes in the bottom of each. Seal the interiors, staple mesh over the weep holes, and add a 2" layer of gravel.*

C. *Arrange uprights parallel to one another and 14" apart on center. Position 18" branches as braces, placing one every 22". Drill pilot holes and secure the joints with 2½" deck screws.*

a stiff brush and a mild detergent; then rinse thoroughly. Apply a disinfectant that's been specially formulated to remove latent fungi or bacterial growth from garden containers. Rinse the barrels and let them dry overnight.

3. Drill three or four ⅜" weep holes in the bottom of each barrel.

4. Apply a coat of exterior wood sealer to the interior of each barrel, making sure the raw edges of the drainage holes are coated. Let the sealer dry.

5. Using aviation snips, cut small squares of zinc gauze and then staple one over each drainage hole. Add a 2" layer of washed pea gravel to the bottom of each barrel.

Step C: Build the Framework

1. Lay out two uprights on a work surface, positioning them parallel to one another and 14" apart. Measure the distance between the uprights and adjust them until they are roughly parallel, given the natural shape of the branches.

2. Position an 18" branch across a pair of uprights, 32" from the bottom ends and centered horizontally. Holding this brace firmly in place, drill pilot holes through each end and into the uprights. Secure each joint with a 2½" deck screw. Add another brace every 22" along the uprights, ending with one 2" from the top ends. Repeat this process to construct the other pair of uprights.

3. Follow the general procedures in numbers 1 and 2 to form the crosspiece. Beginning and ending 6"

D. *Position one pair of uprights in each barrel and add soil, tamping the soil around the uprights to hold them in place.*

E. *Lash a diagonal support across each corner of the arbor. Drill pilot holes and secure the diagonal supports to the uprights, using 2½" deck screws.*

F. *Test-fit, mark, and cut vines for the decorative accents. Drill pilot holes and secure the branches to the uprights, using 1½" galvanized brads.*

from the ends, position one brace every 22" along the crosspiece.

Step D: Assemble the Framework

1. Put the barrels in place, positioning them 5½ ft. on center from one another. Set a pair of uprights into one of the barrels and have a helper support them while you prop them in place with several large rocks. Add potting soil, tamping it firmly around the uprights to hold them in place. Continue adding soil to within 2" of the top of the barrel. Repeat the process to install the other pair of uprights.

2. Lift the crosspiece into place, centering it between the uprights. Holding the crosspiece firmly in place, drill pilot holes through each end and into the uprights. Secure each joint with a 2½" deck screw.

Step E: Add Diagonal Supports

1. Lash a diagonal support in place on each side of each corner of the arbor, using raffia or twine. Position these supports to reach from the third brace of the uprights to the first brace of the cross-piece (see diagram, page 305).

2. Drill pilot holes and drive 2½" deck screws through the supports and into the uprights and crosspieces.

Step F: Add the Accents

1. Test-fit a vine for the decorative accents, curving it from the inside edge of the first brace, across the

upright to the opposite side of the next brace and then up to the third brace on the original side (see diagram, page 305). Mark and cut the vine to length, then lash it in place.

2. Drill pilot holes and secure the vine in place, using 1½" galvanized brads. Add a vine in the opposite direction, and then repeat the process on the other set of uprights.

3. Secure the vines at the intersections by tying them with raffia or twine.

4. Plant vines in the barrels, placing one plant on each side of each pair of uprights. As they grow, train the vines to grow up and over the arbor.

TIP: EASY TIES

Tying vines requires a material that's both strong and gentle—strong enough to support the vine and gentle enough not to damage the tendrils.

Old 100 percent cotton t-shirts make terrific, inexpensive ties that can go into the compost bin for further recycling after the growing season is over.

Starting at the bottom, cut around the shirt in a continuous spiral about 1½" wide. When you reach the armholes, begin making straight cuts from the edge of one sleeve to the other. One shirt usually produces 15 to 20 yards of tying material.

Basic Techniques

Stop worrying; help is on the way! If any of the projects on the previous pages fill you with dread, you can now relax. The projects designed for this book are simple enough that just about anyone can complete them.

Still, if a project uses materials or techniques that are new to you, you may need an introduction to some basic skills, whether its cutting copper pipe (page 310), mixing hypertufa (page 312), or working with bricks (page 314). Allow yourself extra time to become familiar with the techniques and materials used in the project you're building, perhaps practicing with scrap materials before you begin. For example, even if you've soldered copper pipe, you may find it reassuring to review the techniques for working with a torch before starting a new pipe-fitting project. And working with hypertufa—that strange mud with the odd name—may be a new experience altogether. In that case, this chapter will give you some useful background information for building the projects in the book.

This chapter is intended as a reference, so don't feel you need to read it from start to finish. You probably have your eye on a project you're planning to build. Select the information you need and start having fun. Later, as you build your third, fourth, or fourteenth project, you can return to these pages to pick up new skills.

IN THIS CHAPTER

Cutting & Soldering Copper

A soldered pipe joint, also called a sweated joint, is made by heating a copper or brass fitting with a propane torch until the fitting is just hot enough to melt solder. The heat then draws the solder into the gap between the fitting and the copper pipe, forming a strong seal.

Using too much heat is the most common mistake made by beginners. To avoid this error, remember that the tip of the torch's inner flame produces the most heat. Direct the flame carefully—solder will flow in the direction the heat has traveled. Heat the pipe just until the flux sizzles; remove the flame and touch the solder to the pipe. The heated pipe will quickly melt the solder.

Soldering copper pipe and fittings isn't difficult, but it requires some patience and skill. It's a good idea to practice soldering pieces of scrap pipe before taking on a large project.

HOW TO SOLDER COPPER PIPE

Step A: Cut the Pipe

1. Measure and mark the pipe. Place a tubing cutter over the pipe with the cutting wheel centered over the marked line. Tighten the handle until the pipe rests on both rollers.

2. Turn the tubing cutter one rotation to score a continuous line around the pipe. Then rotate the cutter in the other direction. After every two rotations, tighten the handle.

3. Remove metal burrs from the inside edge of the cut pipe, using the reaming point on the tubing cutter or a round file.

Step B: Clean the Pipe & Fittings

To form a good seal with solder, the ends of all pipes and the insides of all fittings must be free of dirt and grease. Sand the ends of pipes with emery cloth, and scour the insides of the fittings with a wire brush.

Step C: Flux & Dry-fit the the Pipes

1. Apply a thin layer of water-soluble paste flux to the end of each pipe, using a flux brush. The flux should cover about 1" of the end of the pipe.

2. Insert the pipe into the fitting until the pipe is tight against the fitting socket, and twist the fitting slightly to spread the flux. If a series of pipes and fittings (a run) is involved, flux and dry-fit the entire run without soldering any of the joints. When you're sure the run is correctly assembled and everything fits, take it apart and prepare to solder the joints.

Step D: Heat the Fittings

1. Shield flammable work surfaces from the heat of the torch. Although heat-absorbent pads are avail-

A. *Position the tubing cutter, and score a line around the pipe. Rotate the cutter until the pipe separates.*

B. *Clean inside the fittings with a wire brush, and deburr the pipes with the reaming point on the tubing cutter.*

C. *Brush a thin layer of flux onto the end of each pipe. Assemble the joint, twisting the fitting to spread the flux.*

able for this purpose, you can use a double layer of 26-gauge sheet metal. The reflective quality of the sheet metal helps joints heat evenly.

2. Unwind 8" to 10" of solder from the spool. To make it easier to maneuver the solder all the way around a joint, bend the first 2" of the wire solder to a 90° angle.

3. Open the gas valve and light the propane torch. Adjust the valve until the inner portion of the flame is 1" to 2" long.

4. Hold the flame tip against the middle of the fitting for 4 to 5 seconds or until the flux begins to sizzle. Heat the other side of the joint, distributing the heat evenly. Move the flame around the joint in the direction the solder should flow. Touch the solder to the pipe, just below the fitting. If it melts, the joint is hot enough.

Step E: Apply the Solder

Quickly apply solder along both seams of the fitting, allowing capillary action to draw the liquefied solder into the fitting. When the joint is filled, solder begins to form droplets on the bottom. A correctly soldered joint shows a thin bead of silver-colored solder around the lip of the fitting. It typically takes about ½" of solder wire to fill a joint in ½" pipe.

If the solder pools around the fitting rather than filling the joint as it cools, reheat the area until the solder liquifies and is drawn in slightly.

Note: *Always turn off the propane torch immediately after you've finished soldering; make sure the gas valve is completely closed.*

Step F: Wipe Away Excess Solder & Check the Joint

1. Let the joint sit undisturbed until the solder loses its shiny color, then wipe away any excess solder with a wet cloth.

2. When the joint is cool enough to touch, wipe away excess flux, using a clean, dry rag. Check for gaps (which indicate weakness) in the soldered joint. If you find gaps, follow the procedure below to disassemble the joint, then carefully resolder it.

3. If, for some reason, you need to take apart a soldered joint, you can reverse the process. First, light the torch and heat the fitting until the solder becomes shiny and begins to melt. Then use channel-type pliers to separate the pipe from the fitting. To remove the old solder, heat the ends of the pipe, and then use a dry rag to carefully wipe away the melted solder. When the pipe is cool, polish the ends down to bare metal, using emery cloth. Discard the old fittings—they can't be reused.

D. *Heat the fitting until the flux begins to sizzle. Concentrate the tip of the torch's flame on the middle of the fitting.*

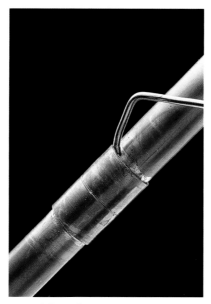

E. *Push ½" to ¾" of solder into each joint, allowing capillary action to draw liquefied solder into the joint.*

F. *When the joint has cooled, wipe away excess solder with a dry rag. Be careful: pipes will be hot.*

Working with Hypertufa

Hypertufa is wonderfully suited to building garden ornaments. There are many recipes available, and some are more reliable than others. Experience leads me to prefer these two recipes. Recipe #1, which contains fiberglass fibers, is ideal for producing lightweight, durable, medium-to-large planting containers. Recipe #2, which contains sand, is especially appropriate for smaller items and those that must hold water.

The ingredients for both recipes are widely available at home and garden centers. Use portland cement rather than a prepared cement mix that contains gravel (which contributes unnecessary weight and gives the finished container a coarse texture). In Recipe #1, perlite, a soil lightener, takes the place of the aggregate typically found in concrete. For Recipe #2, use fine-textured mason's sand—it produces a stronger container than coarser grades of sand.

Peat moss naturally includes a range of textures, some of which are too coarse for hypertufa. Sifting

HYPERTUFA RECIPES

Recipe #1

2 buckets portland cement
3 buckets sifted peat moss
3 buckets perlite
1 handful of fiberglass fibers
    powdered cement dye (optional)

Recipe #2

3 buckets portland cement
3 buckets sand
3 buckets sifted peat moss

the peat moss through hardware cloth takes care of that problem. If you plan to make several hypertufa pieces, it's most efficient to buy a large bale of peat moss, sift the entire bale, then store the sifted material for use over time.

The fiberglass fibers in Recipe #1 contribute strength to the mixture. This product is available at most building centers, but if you have trouble locating it, try a concrete or masonry supply center.

Hypertufa dries to the color of concrete. If you prefer another color, simply add a powdered concrete dye during the mixing process. Tinting products are very effective, so start with a small amount and add more if necessary.

HOW TO MAKE HYPERTUFA
Step A: Sift the Peat Moss

Place the hardware cloth across a large bucket or wheelbarrow. Rub the peat moss across the hardware cloth, sifting it through the mesh. Discard any debris or large particles.

The materials for making hypertufa are inexpensive and widely available. They include portland cement, perlite, peat moss, fiberglass fibers, mason's sand, concrete dye, hardware cloth, a plastic tarp, a dust mask, and gloves.

A. Sift the peat moss through hardware cloth to remove any debris or large particles and break up clumps.

Step B: Mix the Ingredients

1. Measure the cement, peat moss, and perlite or sand, and add them to a mixing trough or wheelbarrow. Using a hoe or small shovel, blend these ingredients thoroughly. If you're using Recipe #1, add the fiberglass fibers and mix again. Add concrete dye, if desired, and mix until the fiberglass fibers and the dye powder are evenly distributed throughout.

2. Add water and blend thoroughly. The amount of water required varies, so add a little at a time. It's easy to add more, but very difficult to correct the situation after you've added too much. The hypertufa is ready to be molded when you can squeeze a few drops of water from a handful.

Step C: Form the Hypertufa

1. Build forms from 2" polystyrene insulation (see individual projects). Secure joints with 2½" deck screws, and reinforce them with gaffer's tape. If the piece is a planting container, be sure to provide adequate drainage holes.

2. Pack the hypertufa into the form and firmly tamp it down. Continue adding and tamping until hypertufa reaches the recommended depth or fills the form (see individual projects).

3. Cover the project with plastic, and let it dry for 48 hours.

4. Disassemble the forms and remove the piece.

Step D: Shape & Cure the Piece

1. Sculpt the appearance of the piece by knocking off the corners and sharp edges. Add texture to the sides of the piece by using a paint scraper or screwdriver to scrape grooves into them. Finally, brush the surface with a wire brush.

2. Wrap the piece in plastic, and put it in a cool place to cure for about a month. Remember, the longer the hypertufa cures, the stronger it will be.

3. Unwrap the piece and let it cure outside, uncovered. If you're building a planter, let it cure for several weeks, periodically rinsing it with water to remove some of the alkalinity, which could harm plants that are grown in the container. Adding vinegar to the rinse water speeds this process, .

After the planter has cured outside for several weeks, move it inside, away from any sources of moisture, to cure for another week or so.

4. The fiberglass fibers in Recipe #1 produce a hairy fringe. Make sure pieces made from this recipe are dry, and then use a propane torch to burn off the fringe. Move the torch quickly, holding it in each spot no more than a second or two. If pockets of moisture remain, they may get hot enough to explode, leaving pot holes in the piece.

5. Apply a coat of masonry sealer to basins or other pieces that must hold water.

B. *Measure the ingredients into a mixing container and blend thoroughly. Add water, a little at a time, and mix.*

C. *Pack the hypertufa into the forms, and tamp it firmly. Cover the project with plastic, and let it cure for 48 hours.*

D. *Let the piece cure. Rinse it repeatedly; let it dry completely. Use a propane torch to burn off any fiberglass fibers.*

Building with Bricks

Bricks are easy to work with if you use the right tools and techniques. Before starting a brick project, plan carefully, evaluate the bricks you're using, and practice handling them. When working with bricks, wear gloves whenever possible. And always wear eye protection when cutting or splitting bricks, or any other masonry units.

Remember that you need to build a frost footing if the proposed brick structure is more than 3 ft. tall or if it will be tied to another permanent structure. Frost footings should extend about 12" past the frost line in your area.

Don't add mortar joint thickness to the total dimensions when you're planning a brick project. The actual size of a brick is ⅜" smaller than the nominal size, which allows for ⅜"-wide mortar joints. For example, a 9" (nominal) brick actually measures 8⅝", so four 9" bricks set with ⅜" mortar joints will measure 36" in length. To make sure planned dimensions work, test project layouts using ⅜" spacers between bricks. Whenever possible, make plans that use whole bricks, eliminating extensive cutting.

You'll need to learn a few brick-handling skills before you begin building projects. Always buy extra bricks—you'll need to make practice cuts on a sample and test the water absorption rate to determine their density before you begin any project.

To test the absorption rate of a brick, use an eye-dropper to drop 20 drops of water onto one spot and check it after 60 seconds. If the surface is completely dry, dampen the bricks with water before you lay them. Otherwise, they'll wick the moisture out of the mortar before it has a chance to set properly.

HOW TO MARK & CUT BRICKS

Step A: Mark Straight Cutting Lines

When you can't avoid cutting bricks, the first thing you have to do is mark the cuts. If you're making many identical cuts, use a T-square and pencil to mark groups of bricks at the same time. Align the ends and hold the bricks in place as you mark.

Step B: Score Straight Cuts

1. To avoid cracking them, set the bricks on a bed of sand as you work. If the cutting line falls over the core, score the brick on two sides; if it falls over the web area, score all four sides.

2. For small jobs, use a mason's chisel and hammer both to score and to cut the bricks. To score a brick, use a hammer to tap on the mason's chisel, leaving cut marks ⅛" to ¼" deep. For large jobs, you can speed up the process by scoring the bricks with a circular saw and a masonry-cutting blade. Set the

A. *Use a T-square and pencil to mark several bricks for cutting. Make sure the ends of the bricks are all aligned.*

B. *Use a circular saw with a masonry-cutting blade to score a group of bricks. Clamp the bricks together, ends aligned.*

C. *To split a brick, align a mason's chisel with the scored line. Tap on the chisel with a hammer until the brick splits.*

saw's blade depth between $1/8$" and $1/4$". Carefully align the ends of the bricks, and clamp them securely at each end, using pipe clamps or bar clamps.

Step C: Make Straight Cuts

Use a mason's chisel and a hammer to split the bricks. Hold the chisel at a slight angle and tap it firmly with the hammer.

HOW TO MIX AND THROW MORTAR

Mixing the mortar properly is critical to the success of a brick project. If the mortar's too thick, it falls off the trowel in a heap. If it's too watery, it's impossible to control. Finding the perfect water ratio calls for experimentation. Mix only as much mortar as you can use within about 30 minutes—once mortar begins to set up, it's difficult to work with and yields poor results.

Step A: Mix the Mortar

1. Empty the mortar mix into a mortar box or wheelbarrow and form a depression in the center. Pour about three-fourths of the recommended amount of water into the depression, and then mix it in with a masonry hoe. Be careful not to overwork the mix. Continue mixing in small amounts of water until the mortar clings to a trowel just long enough for you to deliver it in a controlled, even line that holds its shape after settling. Take careful notes on how much water you add to each batch, and record the ratios for the best mixture.

2. Set a piece of plywood on blocks at a convenient height, and place a shovelful of mortar on the surface. Slice off a strip of mortar from the pile, using the edge of a mason's trowel. Slip the trowel, point-first, under the section of mortar and lift up. Snap the trowel gently downward to dislodge any excess mortar clinging to the edges. A good load of mortar is enough to set three bricks. Don't get too far ahead of yourself—if you throw too much at one time, it will set up before you're ready.

Step B: Throw the Mortar

Position the trowel at your starting point. In one motion, begin turning your wrist over, and quickly move the trowel across the surface to spread the mortar consistently along the bricks. Don't worry if you don't get this right the first time. Throwing mortar is a quick, smooth technique that takes time to perfect, but even a beginning bricklayer can successfully use the basic technique in pretty short order. Keep practicing until you can consistently throw a rounded line about $2\frac{1}{2}$" wide and about 2 ft. long.

Step C: Furrow the Mortar Line

Drag the point of the trowel through the center of the mortar line in a slight back-and-forth motion.

A. *Mix mortar to the proper consistency. Place a shovelful on a plywood work surface, and slice off a strip of mortar.*

B. *Throw the mortar in a rounded line about $2\frac{1}{2}$" wide and about 2 ft. long.*

C. *"Furrow" the mortar line by dragging the point of the trowel through its center, using a slight back-and-forth motion.*

TIP: BUTTER YOUR BRICKS

"Buttering" is a term used to describe the process of applying mortar to a brick before adding it to the structure being built. To butter a brick, apply a heavy layer of mortar to one end, then cut off the excess with a trowel.

This action, called "furrowing," helps distribute the mortar evenly.

HOW TO LAY BRICKS

Step A: Mark Reference Lines & Lay the First Course

1. Before you can lay any bricks, you have to create a sturdy, level building surface. So, first pour a footing or slab, as required for your project (see page 177), and let that concrete cure.

2. Dry-lay the first course of bricks, centered on the footing or slab, using a ⅜"-diameter dowel for spacing. Mark reference lines around the bricks.

3. Dampen the footing or slab with water, and dampen the bricks if necessary (see page 314).

4. Mix mortar and throw a bed of mortar inside the reference lines. Butter the inside end of the first brick. Press this brick into the mortar, creating a ⅜" mortar bed. Cut away the excess mortar.

5. Plumb the face of the end brick, using a level. Tap lightly with the handle of the trowel to adjust the brick if it's not plumb. Level the brick end to end.

6. Butter the end of a second brick, and then set it into the mortar bed, pushing it toward the first brick to create a joint of ⅜". Continue to butter and place bricks, using the reference lines as a guide and following the plans for the specific project.

Step B: Check Your Work with a Level

Add courses, frequently checking your work with a level to make sure it's both level and plumb. Adjust any bricks that are misaligned by tapping them lightly with the handle of the trowel.

Step C: Tool the Joints & Complete the Project

Every 30 minutes, stop laying bricks and tool all joints that have hardened enough to resist minimal finger pressure. Tooling joints involves drawing a jointing tool across each joint in a fluid motion to smooth away excess mortar. Tool the horizontal joints first, then the vertical ones. Use a trowel to cut away any excess mortar you pressed from the joints. When the mortar is set, but not completely hardened, brush any excess off the faces of the bricks.

A. *Dry-lay the first course and mark reference lines. Then lay a bed of mortar, butter the bricks, and begin laying them.*

B. *Frequently check your work with a level; adjust bricks as necessary.*

C. *Every 30 minutes, smooth the joints, using a jointing tool.*

Index

Appendix

Contributing Photographers:

© Walter Chandoha: pp. 32 both, 35b, 67 both, 74

© Crandall & Crandall: pp. 15b, 81a, 134a
  for Nick Williams & Associates: p. 13b
  for Michael Glassman & Associates: p. 62b
  for Greg Grisamore & Associates: p. 66a
  for Rogers Gardens: p. 159d

© R. Todd Davis: p. 65a

© Derek Fell: pp. 16, 25a, 75b, 83c, 99

© Sue Hartley Photography: main cover photo, p. 30a

© Saxon Holt: pp. 11b, 22, 65b, 75a, 159a, 167c,

© Mark A. Madsen: p. 9, 110-111

© Charles Mann: pp. 11a, 34c, 39b, 66b, 68, 72 both, 77, 167d

© Karen Melvin: pp. 79 all, 81c, 83b
  for Judy Onofrio: p. 21a
  for Sylvestre Construction: p. 37b
  for Mike McGuire, Architect: p. 83a

© Jerry Pavia: pp. 21b, 34a, 64, 69c, 73b, 135c, 135e, 189a

© Robert Perron: p. 81b

© Michael S. Thompson: p. 135a

Contributing Manufacturers:

Tad Anderson Landscape Design: pp. 30b, 54, 57, 71 both, 73a, 195a
  P. O. Box 5264
  Minnetonka, MN 55343-2264
  tel: 612-473-8387
  www.land-design.com

Bachman's Landscape Services: pp. 17b, 30a, 33b, 33d, 39a, 158
  6010 Lyndale Avenue So.
  Minneapolis, MN 55419-9986
  tel: 612-861-7653

By the Yard, Inc.: p. 49a
  P. O. Box 154
  Jordan, MN 55352
  tel: 612-492-2777

California Redwood Association: pp. 13a, 43a, 62a
  405 Enfrente Drive, Suite 200
  Novato, CA 94949
  tel: 415-382-0662
  fax: 415-382-8531
  www.calredwood.org

Featherock, Inc.: p. 37c
  20219 Bahama Street
  Chatsworth, CA 91311
  tel: 800-423-3037
  fax: 818-882-9643

Hunter Industries Incorporated: p. 36b
  1940 Diamond Street
  San Marcos, CA 92069
  fax: 760-471-9626
  www.hunterirrig.com

Idaho Wood: Cover, 36a
  P. O. Box 488
  Sandpoint, ID 83864
  tel: 800-635-1100
  fax: 208-263-3102

Interlock Concrete Products, Inc.: p. 31a
  3535 Bluff Drive
  Jordan, MN 55352-8302
  tel: 612-492-3636
  fax: 612-492-3668

Intermatic Incorporated: pp. 37d, 159b, 159c
  Intermatic Plaza
  Spring Grove, IL 60081-9698
  tel: 815-675-6565
  fax: 815-675-7055

Lloyd/Flanders All-Weather Wicker: p. 38a
  P. O. Box 550
  Menominee, WI 49858
  tel: 1-888-CASUAL 2
  www.lloydflanders.com

Milt Charno & Associates, Inc.: p. 31c
  611 North May Fair Road
  Wauwatosa, WI 53226
  tel: 414-475-1965
  fax: 414-475-0881

T.C.T. Landscaping: p. 23a
  P. O. Box 1218
  Solvang, CA 93464
  tel: 805-688-3741

Weatherend Estate Furniture: p. 25b
  6 Gordon Drive
  Rockland, ME 04841
  tel: 800-456-6483
  fax: 207-594-4968

Weber-Stephen Products Co.: p. 37a
  200 East Daniels Road
  Palatine, IL 60067-6266
  tel: 1-800-446-1071
  fax: 1-847-705-7971
  www.weberbbq.com

Materials Sources:

Mist maker (page 221)
  Fountains of Tranquility
  1-800-229-3376

Hinge pin bushing (page 223)
  Motormite Mfg. Div. of R&B, Inc.
  P.O. Box 1800
  Colmar, PA 18915-1800
  1-800-382-1322

½ sweat cross (page 302)
  NIBCO
  1-800-234-0227